I Never
Had It Made

I Never Had It Made

AN AUTOBIOGRAPHY

Jackie Robinson

AS TOLD TO ALFRED DUCKETT

Foreword by **Cornel West**
Introduction by **Hank Aaron**

THE ECCO PRESS

Copyright © 1995 Rachel Robinson

The Ecco Press
100 West Broad Street
Hopewell, New Jersey 08525

Printed in the United States of America

Library of Congress Cataloging-in-Publication Data

Robinson, Jackie, 1919–1972.
  I never had it made / by Jackie Robinson as told to Alfred Duckett.
    p. cm.
  Originally published: New York : Putnam, 1972.
  ISBN 0-88001-419-9 (cloth) : $24.00
  1. Robinson, Jackie, 1919–1972. 2. Baseball players—United States—
Bibliography. I. Duckett, Alfred. II. Title.
GV865.R6A3   1995
796.357'092—dc20   94-45279

The text of this book is set in Times Roman
Photograph on page iii from The Bettmann Archive.

To my wife, Rachel,
to my children Sharon and David,
and to the memory of Jackie, Jr.

Contents

Foreword

CORNEL WEST

Three fundamental events between March and June of 1947 in America changed the course of world history in the twentieth century. On March 12, 1947, President Harry Truman proclaimed in a historic speech before a special joint session of Congress the intention of the U.S. government "to support free peoples who are resisting subjugation by armed minorities or by outside pressures." This, the famous Truman Doctrine was declared in response to both the beginning of the collapse of the most powerful empire the world has ever seen (the British Empire) and the emergence of one of the most repressive, the Soviet Empire. In short, Truman announced the aim of the American Empire to police the world in the light of its democratic ideals and imperial interests.

On April 15, 1947, before 26,623 Americans (more than half of them black) at Ebbets Field in Brooklyn, Jackie Robinson became the first African-American to play professional, major league baseball. In this historic opening game against the Boston Braves, a dignified and heroic descendant of American slaves and sharecroppers who wore number 42 on his Dodger uniform played first base in one of the sacred spaces of American culture. More even than either Abraham Lincoln and the Civil War, or Martin Luther

King, Jr. and the Civil Rights movement, Jackie Robinson graphically symbolized and personified the challenge to the vicious legacy and ideology of white supremacy in American history.

Soon afterward, on June 5, 1947, Secretary of State George C. Marshall delivered an address at Harvard University's graduation ceremonies, in which he put forward an American plan for European economic recovery with huge U.S. assistance in order to combat Soviet domination. The basic requirements of the Marshall Plan were U.S. influence over the internal budgets of the European recipient states and the disproportionate purchase of American exports for European recovery.

These three events represent the most fundamental processes of this century—the end of the Age of Europe (and the preeminence of its last great empire), the acceleration of the challenge to white supremacy (a pillar of European imperialism and American history), and the move of the American Empire to the center of the world-historical stage (in opposition to the Soviet Empire). In this way, a historic presidential speech, an unforgettable baseball game, and an influential commencement address take us to the very heart of the agony and anguish, the achievements and accomplishments, of our time.

With the surprising collapse of the Soviet Empire in 1989, the Truman Doctrine has run its course. And with the economic recovery of Europe—alongside the phenomenal growth of the U.S. economy—between 1947 and 1973, the Marshall Plan did what it set out to do. Despite the significant gains of the Civil Rights movement in the 1960s, the challenge to white supremacy in America remains incomplete, unfinished. That is why, today, the life and work, the achievements and suffering, of Jackie Robinson continue to speak to us with such power and poignancy.

In 1947, Jackie Robinson not only symbolized all of black America on trial in the eyes of white America and the expansion of the ideals of democracy, he also represented the best of a traditional black quest for dignity, excellence, and integrity. This quest was primarily a moral effort to preserve black sanity and spirituality in the face of white-supremacist barbarity and bestiality; it was a human attempt to hold on to dreams deferred and hopes dashed, owing mainly to slavery and Jim Crow in America. The deep and devastating effects of psychic scars, physical abuse, and material deprivation could not suffocate the black tradition of moral struggle and political resistance. When Jackie Robinson states that he "never had it made," he means, in part, that he had to fight in a variety of ways and on a number of fronts to preserve both his sense of dignity and his integrity; and in part that he was able to fight primarily because of the love and support of those fighters who came before him and those who now stood by his side.

The most striking features of this marvelous book are its honesty, its courage, and its wisdom. Here is a great American hero who refuses to be a mythical hero. Instead, he tells the painful truth about himself as a human being—someone who, like all of us, needs love, struggles with insecurity, makes mistakes, revels in achievements, and weeps in sorrow. Here is a transracial figure beloved by blacks and whites who rails against the absurdities of white racism and the seductive security of black xenophobia. Here is a celebrity who takes us on a journey through the valleys and over the mountaintops of intimate relations with his family, friends, and mentors. Here is one of the greatest athletes of our century disclosing his developing sense of political engagement and community empowerment as a liberal Republican in a right-wing Republican party. Here is a black man and father—with a strong sense of his masculinity—who talks about his maturity in terms of lessons painfully learned from his loving mother, his brilliant and self-confident wife, his adventurous children, and his supportive father figures. I revelled in his exchanges—critical and respectful—with Malcolm X, Martin Luther King, Jr., Richard Nixon, William Buckley, Black Panther leaders, and Lewis Micheaux.

Jackie Robinson's life and book constitute an antiphonal "song of a great composite democratic individual." This grand phrase of Walt Whitman captures the *jazz-like* character of Jackie Robinson—his noble experiment in which restraint and performance, improvisation, and discipline under severe pressure are exercised with excellence; his openness to others; his generosity to others, and his relentless self-criticism without recourse to self-pity and self-indulgence. And yet, his disillusionment with America is real. Robinson cannot stand and sing the national anthem or salute the flag. His deep patriotism and his hatred of white supremacy will not allow him to engage in such empty gestures of country-worship. He knows that "money is America's God" and that he is "a black man in a white world."

Jackie Robinson's historic challenge to white supremacy in America was not an attempt to "prove" himself and his humanity to white America. Rather, it was to *be* himself, to allow his God-given humanity to be seen, acknowledged, and recognized by those who questioned it. He gained respect because he so deeply respected himself, because he respected black people and others. He willingly took on the awesome burden of symbolizing black humanity in the one arena of fairness in a country predicated, in part, on unfairness to black people. And he bore this burden with great dignity—not because he wanted to *be* somebody but, rather, because he was already a great *somebody* to be in a land where all black folk were nobody to most white people. This is why his grand example is, in the moving and wise words of George Will (with whom I rarely agree!), "One of the great achievements not only in the annals of sports, but of the human drama anywhere, anytime." This book reveals why and how Jackie Robinson's life was an exemplary testimony of the black and human "Love Supreme"—the same moral and spiritual ideal toward which Martin Luther King, Jr., Fannie Lou Hamer, and John Coltrane asked us to aspire.

Harvard University
1995

Introduction

HANK AARON

The first time I saw Jackie Robinson, he was playing baseball in Mobile, Alabama. He was touring at that time with the Brooklyn Dodgers. They had a farm team in Mobile, and they used to pass through. I just happened to be in the crowd; I was fourteen, maybe fifteen. I had had a vision, a vision that if things worked out, I probably would get to the big leagues before Jackie retired. As it turned out, I did get there. I played against him for three or four years before he retired.

I've always looked at Jackie as some kind of icon. He was a pillar of strength, and he gave me a lot of inner strength. I knew some of the things he had gone through; so, when I looked at him, I thought—not only is this man a great athlete, but he's a great man off the field for people like myself. When I think of my background, where I came from and what I had to go through, I think of those who gave me strength—my mother and father and a few outsiders. The outsiders were Jackie Robinson and people like Dr. King; those are the people who gave me the strength I needed to go forward.

Jackie Robinson gave all of us—not only black athletes, but every black person in this country—a sense of our own strength.

However, because I was an athlete, I looked at Jackie a little differently. I followed every trail he had made. I wanted to emulate him in some way, which is one of the reasons why I speak so directly now about the injustice in baseball today: because Jackie Robinson gave me the strength to continue to do what he had done.

When Jackie got to the big leagues, he was told that he couldn't do certain things, that he couldn't be aggressive, that he couldn't respond to what was going on around him, that he had to keep his mouth shut. But, once he proved to everybody that he was a great baseball player and was allowed to talk—having earned the right to do whatever he wanted to do—many people saw a very different Jackie Robinson. Some now saw him as aggressive, demanding his own rights. They saw him as a kind of Dr. Jekyll and Mr. Hyde. But he wasn't; he was one person. He was quiet during those first years because he was told it had to be that way. If he had come into the majors and been aggressive when people were sliding into him and saying things most men would have responded to, had he been aggressive in that way, he would have delayed breaking the color barrier another ten or fifteen years. I think my style in the early days was similar to Jackie's. When I first got to the major leagues, I had nothing to say. The reason I didn't have anything to say is simply that I hadn't done anything. In order for people to listen to you, you have to have done something. I've been asked, "Now you've gotten to be a big mouth, talking about the injustice in baseball, but why didn't you speak out when you first got to the big leagues?" If I'd said the same thing when I first got to the majors, who would have reported it in the papers? Now that I've hit 755 home runs, people probably notice what I say a little bit more. That's what Jackie had to do; but he had to do it alone. He had to be patient while he proved himself. You have to marvel at a person like that, because he handled an awful lot inside himself all those years. I think this was a factor in his passing away at so young an age.

When I reached the big leagues, I didn't meet a single player who was sympathetic to what we were going through as black players. It's true that some of the players were aware of our situation, but I played with a lot of players who didn't give a damn. Things were going well for them, and they didn't want to shake the apple tree. But it wasn't just the players; the owners were not at all sympathetic to the black players. They were making a lot of money off the black players—we were drawing cards—and they took advantage of us. For example, they barnstormed us all through the South; the ballparks would fill with black people who didn't get a chance to see us on television. The owners did very well on those tours.

On the playing field, Jackie Robinson was a tremendous athlete. He was a big man, but gifted in his running. You would think a person his size couldn't move, but he ran very well. And he was a very good second baseman. He had a great deal of enthusiasm, which was communicated to the other players on his team. He didn't like to lose! He wanted to win at any cost, and he instilled this in his teammates. He knew what it took to get those guys geared up to play a championship season—152 games. He could bring out the enthusiasm in a crowd just by taking infield practice. He knew exactly what it would take to excite the fans—his presence alone on the field would do it.

Who knows what Robinson's stats would have been if he hadn't been the first black player in the major leagues. This man was under tremendous pressure, pressure most people didn't know about or couldn't understand, if they did. People say, don't ever criticize another person until you walk a mile in their shoes. I haven't walked that mile, but I've walked half a mile in those shoes, and in just that half mile I understood exactly what kind of pressure Jackie Robinson had to deal with. He probably would have hit a lot more home runs, stolen more bases, been an even better ballplayer if it hadn't been his fate to have to endure that pressure, not only on the field, but off the field as well. In fact, he was often under more pressure off the field than he was on. If he had gone into a bar, the morning papers would have reported that he had gotten drunk—although Jackie didn't drink at all. If he happened to speak to a woman, sportswriters claimed he was dating her.

I'll never forget the first time I was in Jackie's presence off the field. It was in a room in Nashville, Tennessee, with Jackie, Don Newcombe, Roy Campanella, and a few other Dodgers; they were playing cards. I was only about nineteen at the time, and I was standing by the wall looking at these guys seated at the table. I was in awe of all of them. After a while I went to get something to eat. I returned three hours later. They were still in the room, playing cards. "Don't you ever go out?" I asked. They said, no, because Jackie would immediately be the center of attention, and people were always trying to make something out of nothing. It wasn't until much later that I understood that fully.

What Jackie Robinson represents today is a complicated issue. I'm sure many of the black players know what he did, but it's possible that some of the younger players don't know that he was the man responsible for their being in the major leagues. I don't know this to be true, but it would really disturb me if I went into a locker room and found a black player who didn't know what players like Jackie Robinson, Larry Doby, and Don Newcombe did forty or fifty years ago. Things were very tough back in those days—and it was Jackie Robinson who paved the way. Many of these young black athletes are making all kinds of money, much more money than they're ever going to spend. But I wonder how many of them would take it upon themselves to contribute to The Jackie Robinson Foundation, which provides fellowships to send black kids to school. It goes a little further than just baseball. This man paved the way for a lot of athletes to be where they are today. I'm not aware of such contributions being made, but this would be a way for today's athletes to show their appreciation for a man who stood tall when he had to stand up.

As I've said many times (and I'll say it again) Jackie Robinson was a pillar of strength to me. It meant an awful lot to know that there was somebody before me who paved the way, who gave me an opportunity to play the big leagues. When I was going through the things I had to go through—doubting myself—I knew this was only the tip of the iceberg of what Jackie Robinson had gone through. I said to myself I would be doing him an injustice if I quit. And this gave me the strength to continue.

When I think about Jackie Robinson, there is something that bothers me a great deal, which shows what baseball is all about. At the end of his career, Jackie was traded to the Giants. At the last moment, after all the things he'd done for the Dodgers, after everything he had suffered, they found it necessary to trade a man of his stature, a man who *was* the Dodgers. I thought at the time: Stan Musial was never traded; Ted Williams was never traded. We're talking about someone who was very special, who should have always had a place with the Dodgers. It should have been understood that this man started with the Dodgers and that he would end up with the Dodgers. Certain people you never trade, and Jackie Robinson should never have been traded.

Even before he retired, Jackie Robinson was involved in politics. He was always concerned about what was going to happen to blacks in this country. His involvement with the NAACP and other civil rights organizations merely demonstrated that his skills and concerns went further than the baseball diamond. I will never forget Jackie's last speech, especially the end of it. He said baseball will always have its head buried in the sand until it can find the strength and the vision to have a black man coaching at third base. This was in Cincinnati and he was half blind by then; it was the last time I heard him speak.

It's as clear now as it was then that Jackie Robinson was the right man for the right job—intelligent, educated—I think that's what we needed. There were so many temptations put before him. He was a man on trial—not only on the field. But off the field as well, and he had the skills to survive and transcend this ordeal.

I'm often asked if I miss the game. But I don't miss anything at all about baseball. I had a very good career. I did just about everything I wanted to do in baseball, and I am satisfied with my accomplishments. Now my life has changed, it's a new life for me. I played baseball for twenty-three years, and I owe it in part to

Jackie Robinson, who gave me the strength I needed and the opportunity to play—the chance to do everything I could do.

Atlanta, Georgia
1995

Preface: Today

JACKIE ROBINSON

I guess if I could choose one of the most important moments in my life, I would go back to 1947, in the Yankee Stadium in New York City. It was the opening day of the world series and I was for the first time playing in the series as a member of the Brooklyn Dodgers team. It was a history-making day. It would be the first time that a black man would be allowed to participate in a world series. I had become the first black player in the major leagues.

I was proud of that and yet I was uneasy. I was proud to be in the hurricane eye of a significant breakthrough and to be used to prove that a sport can't be called national if blacks are barred from it. Branch Rickey, the president of the Brooklyn Dodgers, had rudely awakened America. He was a man with high ideals, and he was also a shrewd businessman. Mr. Rickey had shocked some of his fellow baseball tycoons and angered others by deciding to smash the unwritten law that kept blacks out of the big leagues. He had chosen me as the person to lead the way.

It hadn't been easy. Some of my own teammates refused to accept me because I was black. I had been forced to live with snubs and rebuffs and rejections. Within the club, Mr. Rickey had put down rebellion by letting my teammates know that anyone who didn't want to accept me could leave. But the problems within the Dodgers club had been minor compared to the opposition outside. It hadn't been that easy to fight the resentment expressed by players on other teams, by the team owners, or by bigoted fans screaming "nigger." The hate mail piled up. There were threats against me and my family and even out-and-out attempts at physical harm to me.

Some things counterbalanced this ugliness. Black people supported me with total loyalty. They supported me morally; they came to sit in a hostile audience in unprecedented numbers to make the turnstiles hum as they never had before at ball parks all over the nation. Money is America's God, and business people can dig black power if it coincides with green power, so these fans were important to the success of Mr. Rickey's "Noble Experiment."

Some of the Dodgers who swore they would never play with a black man had a change of mind, when they realized I was a good ballplayer who could be helpful in their earning a few thousand more dollars in world series money. After the initial resistance to me had been crushed, my teammates started to give me tips on how to improve my game. They hadn't changed because they liked me any better; they had changed because I could help fill their wallets.

My fellow Dodgers were not decent out of self-interest alone. There were heartwarming experiences with some teammates; there was Southern-born Pee Wee Reese who turned into a staunch friend. And there were others.

Mr. Rickey stands out as the man who inspired me the most. He will always have my admiration and respect. Critics had said, "Don't you know that your precious Mr. Rickey didn't bring you up out of the black leagues because he loved you? Are you stupid enough not to understand that the Brooklyn club profited hugely because of what your Mr. Rickey did?"

Yes, I know that. But I also know what a big gamble he took. A bond developed between us that lasted long after I had left the game. In a way I feel I was the son he had lost and he was the father I had lost.

There was more than just making money at stake in Mr. Rickey's decision. I learned that his family was afraid that his health was being undermined by the resulting pressures and that they pleaded with him to abandon the plan. His peers and fellow baseball moguls exerted all kinds of influence to get him to change his mind. Some of the press condemned him as a fool and a demagogue. But he didn't give in.

In a very real sense, black people helped make the experiment succeed. Many who came to the ball park had not been baseball fans before I began to play in the big leagues. Suppressed and repressed for so many years, they needed a victorious black man as a symbol. It would help them believe in themselves. But black support of the first black man in the majors was a complicated matter. The breakthrough created as much danger as it did hope. It was one thing for me out there on the playing field to be able to keep my cool in the face of insults. But it was another for all those black people sitting in the stands to keep from overreacting when they sensed a racial slur or an unjust decision. They could have blown the whole bit to hell by acting belligerently and touching off a race riot. That would have been all the bigots needed to set back the cause of progress of black men in sports another hundred years. I knew this. Mr. Rickey knew this. But this never happened. I learned from Rachel who had spent hours in the stands that clergymen and laymen had held meetings in the black community to spread the word. We all knew about the help of the black press. Mr. Rickey and I owed them a great deal.

Children from all races came to the stands. The very young seemed to have no hangup at all about my being black. They just wanted me to be good, to deliver, to win. The inspiration of their innocence is amazing. I don't think I'll ever forget the small, shrill voice of a tiny white kid who, in the midst of a racially tense atmosphere during an early game in a Dixie town, cried out, "Attaboy, Jackie." It broke the tension and it made me feel I had to succeed.

The black and the young were my cheering squads. But also there were people—neither black nor young—people of all races and faiths and in all parts of this country, people who couldn't care less about my race.

Rachel was even more important to my success. I know that every successful man is supposed to say that without his wife he could never have accomplished success. It is gospel in my case. Rachel shared those difficult years that led to this moment and helped me through all the days thereafter. She has been strong, loving, gentle, and brave, never afraid to either criticize or comfort me.

There I was the black grandson of a slave, the son of a black sharecropper, part of a historic occasion, a symbolic hero to my people. The air was sparkling. The sunlight was warm. The band struck up the national anthem. The flag billowed in the wind. it should have been a glorious moment for me as the stirring words of the national anthem poured from the stands. Perhaps it was, but then again perhaps the anthem could be called the theme song for a drama called *The Noble Experiment*. Today as I look back on that opening game of my first world series, I must tell you that it was Mr. Rickey's drama and that I was only a principal actor. As I write this twenty years later, I cannot stand and sing the anthem. I cannot salute the flag; I know that I am a black man in a white world. In 1972, in 1947, at my birth in 1919, I know that I never had it made.

Stamford, Connecticut
1972

The Noble
Experiment

Chapter I

A Dream Deferred

My grandfather was born into slavery, and although my mother and my father, Mallie and Jerry Robinson, lived during an era when physical slavery had been abolished, they also lived in a newer, more sophisticated kind of slavery than the kind Mr. Lincoln struck down. My parents were married in 1909, and my father worked on a plantation for twelve dollars a month. My mother encouraged him to confront his boss and ask for a better deal. Since he didn't want to lose him, the boss agreed to let my father become a "half-cropper." That means that, instead of working for a flat sum, he would get half the profits from whatever he produced from the earth. My father began to make more money and to provide a better living for his family—my mother and five children. Six months after I was born in 1919, my father told my mother he was going to visit his brother in Texas. I learned as a grown man he had been complaining that he was tired of farming and he had been spending an increasing amount of time in Cairo, the city closest to the plantation. My mother was afraid that my father would not come back, and her fears were justified. Later she learned that he had left home and gone away with a neighbor's wife.

To this day I have no idea what became of my father. Later, when I became aware of how much my mother had to endure alone, I could only think of him with bitterness. He, too, may have been a victim of oppression, but he had no right to desert my mother and five children.

After my father left, my mother had the choice of going home to live with her people or trying to pacify the irate plantation owner. He had never forgiven her for forcing my father to ask for more money, and he felt that she had somehow had a hand in my father's leaving the plantation. When she refused to admit this, he ordered her off the land. She decided then that she would sell what little she had and take her family out of the South. She had a brother, Burton, in California, and she planned to take us there.

My mother was thirty when we started out for California. I remember nothing about it, since I was only sixteen months old at the time. I was the youngest child and had three brothers—Edgar, eleven; Frank, nine; Mack, seven—and one sister, Willa Mae, five.

As I grew older, I often thought about the courage it took for my mother to break away from the South. Even though there appeared to be little future for us in the West, my mother knew that there she could be assured of the basic necessities. When she left the South, she also left most of her relatives and friends. She knew that her brother in California would help all he could, but he, too, had heavy responsibilities.

After a long, tedious train ride across the country, we were generously received by Uncle Burton. He took us in, but my mother made arrangements to move soon after we arrived because we were too crowded. Almost immediately, she found a job washing and ironing. She didn't make enough, however, to support herself and five children and she went to welfare for relief. Her salary, plus the help from welfare, barely enabled her to make ends meet. Sometimes there were only two meals a day, and some days we wouldn't have eaten at all if it hadn't been for the leftovers my mother was able to bring home from her job. There was other times when we subsisted on bread and sweet water. My mother got up before daylight to go to her job, and although she came home tired, she managed to give us the extra attention we needed. She indoctrinated us with the importance of family unity, religion, and kindness toward others. Her great dream for us was that we go to school.

While my mother was at work, my sister Willa Mae took care of me. I went to school with Willa Mae, but I was too young to be enrolled in the school and my mother asked the teacher to allow Willa Mae to leave me in the sandbox in the yard while classes were going on. Every morning Willa Mae put me into the sandbox, where I played until lunchtime, when school was dismissed. If it rained, I was taken into the kindergarten rooms. Everyone was very nice to me; however, I certainly was happy when, after a year of living in the sand-box, I became old enough to go to school.

I have few early school memories after graduating from the sandbox, but I do remember being aware of the constant protective attitude of my sister. She was dedicated on my behalf.

We lived in a house on Pepper Street in Pasadena. I must have been about eight years old the first time I ran into racial trouble. I was sweeping our sidewalk when a little neighbor girl shouted at me, "Nigger, nigger, nigger." I was old enough to know how to answer that. I had learned from my older brother that, in the South, the most insulting name you can call a white person is "cracker." That is what I called her, and her father stormed out of the house to confront me. I don't remember who threw the first stone, but the father and I had a pretty good stone-throwing fight going until the girl's mother came out and made him go back into the house. That incident was part of a pattern. Our white neighbors had done un-friendly things before, such as summoning the police and complaining that my brother Edgar made too much noise on

5

their sidewalks with his skates. They had signed petitions to try to get rid of us. My mother never lost her composure. She didn't allow us to go out of our way to antagonize the whites, and she still made it perfectly clear to us and to them that she was not at all afraid of them and that she had no intention of allowing them to mistreat us.

I remember, even as a small boy, having a lot of pride in my mother. I thought she must have some kind of magic to be able to do all the things she did, to work so hard and never complain and to make us all feel happy. We had our family squabbles and spats, but we were a well-knit unit. My pride in my mother was tempered with a sense of sadness that she had to bear most of our burdens. At a very early age I began to want to relieve her in any small way I could. I was happy whenever I had money to give her.

Along with a number of other children in the neighborhood, I had a lot of free time, and a lot of freedom. Some of it I put to good use—I had a paper route, I cut grass and ran errands when I could. The rest of the time, I stole—all sorts of small things from stores, particularly food—and I was a member in good standing of the Pepper Street gang. Our gang was made up of blacks, Japanese, and Mexican kids; all of us came from poor families and had extra time on our hands. We never got into vicious or violent crime, but hardly a week went by when we didn't have to report to Captain Morgan, the policeman who was head of the Youth Division. We threw dirt clods at cars; we hid out on the local golf course and snatched any balls that came our way and often sold them back to their recent owners; we swiped fruit from stands and ran off in a pack; we snitched what we could from the local stores; and all the time we were aware of a growing resentment at being deprived of some of the advantages the white kids had. We were allowed to swim in the local municipal pool only on Tuesdays, and once we were escorted to jail at gunpoint by the sheriff because we had gone for a swim in the reservoir.

I suppose I might have become a full-fledged juvenile

delinquent if it had not been for the influence of two men who shared my mother's thinking. Carl Anderson was a mechanic who worked on automobiles in a shop close to where a lot of Pepper Street gang activities took place. After he had watched us for a while, he took me aside and talked to me about the gang. He didn't scold me, and he approached the subject from a point of view I couldn't ignore. He made me see that if I continued with the gang it would hurt my mother as well as myself. He told me I ought to admit to myself that I didn't belong in a gang, that I was simply following the crowd because I was afraid of being thought different, of being "chicken." He said it didn't take guts to follow the crowd, that courage and intelligence lay in being willing to be different. I was too ashamed to tell Carl how right he was, but what he said got to me.

The other man who influenced me powerfully and helped me disassociate myself from the gang was the Reverend Karl Downs. He was a young minister who came to Pasadena to pastor the church where our family worshiped. My mother had made it a point to see that we got to church and Sunday School, and when Reverend Downs came along, participation in church life became a pleasure instead of a duty. Reverend Downs was both stubborn and courageous. He believed in setting up programs and sticking to them, regardless of criticism. After he had been pastor for a short time, he concluded that our church needed some radical changes. The young people were part of the church life only because their parents insisted that they participate, and their relationship with the church was not a strong one. Reverend Downs set out to win the young members of the congregation who had become church dropouts and reached out to recruit some who had never attended our church or perhaps any church. Those of us who had been indifferent church members began to feel an excitement in belonging. We started planning dances at the church and playing on the new badminton court that the new minister had installed. Many of the youngsters who began

7

coming were finding the church an alternative to hanging out on street corners.

Despite the good it did, elder members objected to Reverend Downs' program. They felt tradition should be maintained. But their disapproval carried little weight because the new focus of the church was so obviously good for the youngsters, and since it attracted new parents and families, finances began to improve. It wasn't long before the new income started to make it possible for the church to operate on a sound basis. Finally, a majority of the congregation began to have a sense of pride in their pastor.

Karl Downs had the ability to communicate with you spiritually, and at the same time he was fun to be with. He participated with us in our sports. Most important he knew how to listen. Often when I was deeply concerned about personal crises, I went to him. One of the frustrations of my teens was watching Mother work so hard. I wanted to help more, but I knew how much my college education meant to her. It seemed impossible to earn enough part-time for college expenses and still be able to provide money to relieve her of her daily grind. When I talked with Karl about this and other problems, he helped ease some of my tensions. It wasn't so much what he did to help as the fact that he was interested and concerned enough to offer the best advice he could.

Inspired by Karl's dedication, I volunteered to become a Sunday School teacher. At that time I had a heavy athletic schedule at ULCA. On Sunday mornings, when I woke up sore and aching because of a football game the day before, I yearned to just stay in bed. But no matter how terrible I felt, I had to get up. It was impossible to shirk duty when Karl Downs was involved. My friendship with Karl continued for more than ten years. There was a healthy sense of competition in our relationship. Karl was both stubborn and good-natured about wanting to beat me at sports. "Jack," he would say, as we were about to play golf, "you know I'm a minister. So I can't bet you, but I've got to bond you ten cents." Even though Karl was a great friend, he never forgot he was a minister. Often he would find a way of applying a story in the Bible to something that happened in real life. He didn't preach and he didn't talk down like so many adults or view you from some holy distance. He was in there with you.

Sports had been a big thing with me ever since I was a little boy. In grammar school some of my classmates would share their lunches with me if I played on their team. When I went to John Muir Technical High I earned letters in football, basketball, baseball, and track. I enjoy competition and I was aggressive in my determination to win. Often I found myself being singled out by the other players. They decided that I was the best man to beat. I enjoyed having that kind of reputation, but I was also very much aware of the importance of being a team man, not jeopardizing my team's chances simply to get the spotlight. In my junior high school days and later, at Pasadena Junior College, my brother Frank was my greatest fan. He constantly encouraged and advised me. I wanted to win, not only for myself but also because I didn't want to see Frank disappointed. At Pasadena my football career was interrupted by a broken ankle acquired during a practice session. It took weeks to heal, but I made up for lost time when I got back into action playing first-string quarterback.

After my return we won the remaining five games, and the following year Pasadena won all eleven games. While at Pasadena Junior College, I had beaten the record of my older brother Mack in broad-jumping. I had the greatest respect for Mack because of his achievements in track. Even though doctors warned him that his participation in sports could be fatal because he had a heart ailment, he wouldn't give up. He earned a big name on the West Coast as a sprinter, and in 1936 he thrilled our family and neighborhood by finishing second to Jesse Owens in the Berlin Olympics. The heart condition never defeated Mack.

Frank, whose support was unceasing, was particularly proud in 1938 when I made local history in two different events, in two different cities on the same day. In the morning, in Pomona, I set a new running broad jump record of 25 feet 6 1/2 inches. In the afternoon, in Glendale, I played shortstop with the Pasadena team and we won the championship.

My athletic career had received a great deal of publicity, and there were a number of colleges putting out feelers, offering athletic scholarships. The college that offered me the most attractive scholarship was very far away from Pasadena, but I wanted to stay close to home. One of my major reasons was to be able to continue to benefit from Frank's encouragement. As a result I agreed to go to UCLA. Very shortly afterward Frank was killed in a motorcycle accident. I was very shaken up by his death. It was hard to believe he was gone, hard to believe I would no longer have his support.

At UCLA I became the university's first four-letter man. I participated in basketball, baseball, football, and track, and received honorable mention in football and basketball.

I didn't think anything could come into my life that would be more vital to me than my sports career. I believed that until Ray Bartlett, my best friend at UCLA, introduced me to Rachel Isum. Ray brought her into the student lounge where I was working part-time. I was immediately attracted to Rachel's looks and charm, but as in many love stories, I didn't have the slightest idea I was meeting a young lady who would become the most important person in my life.

When she left, I walked to the parking lot with her. She made me feel at ease, and I thoroughly enjoyed talking with her. Later, to my dismay, I learned that when Rachel had seen me play ball at Pasadena Junior College she felt that I was cocky, conceited, and self-centered. Part of this was because I was considered one of the most important athletes on campus, and she assumed it had gone to my head. Additionally, Pasadena Junior College and Los Angeles, where Rachel lived, were serious rivals. Rachel admits she had an unshakable adolescent belief in her team. When we met, she was a freshman and I was a senior. She was shy and wary of the campus hero. Rae told me later, after we knew each other well, that at football games she had watched the way I had stood in the backfield with my hands on my hips, and this stance reinforced her impression that I was stuck on myself.

Rachel quickly overcame her Jackie Robinson prejudices. There are few people it is easy for me to confide in, but when I was with Rae I was delighted to find that I could tell her anything. She was always understanding and, beyond that, very direct and honest with me. I respected the fact that she never hesitated to disagree with my point of view. From the beginning I realized there was something very special about Rae, but it wasn't until her father died in 1940 that I realized I was deeply in love with her. Rae's deep grief had a profound effect on me. In this time of sorrow we found each other and I knew then that our relationship was to be one of the most important things in my life no matter what happened to me. Rachel's mother, Zellee Isum, who was warm and kind to me from the beginning, approved.

After two years at UCLA I decided to leave. I was convinced that no amount of education would help a black man get a job. I felt I was living in an academic and athletic dream world. It seemed very necessary for me to relieve some of my mother's financial burdens even though I knew it had always been her dream to have me finish college. I had used up my athletic eligibility in the major sports at UCLA, but the university begged me to stay on and graduate; they even offered me extra financial support. Rae, too, felt strongly about the importance of a degree. Despite all this, I could see no future in staying at college, no real future in athletics, and I wanted to do the next best thing—become an athletic director. The thought of working with youngsters in the field of sports excited me.

To my surprise Rae reluctantly accepted my decision. She felt that if this was really what I wanted, then I should look for a job. Through Pat Ahearn, athletic director for National Youth Administration, I was offered a job as assistant athletic director at their work camp in Atascadero, California. It meant a great deal to me, and it was rewarding to be involved with the youngsters, most of whom had come from poor or broken homes. However, it was a short-lived experience because World War II broke out in Europe within a few months, and the government closed down all the NYA projects, even though America, at the time, wasn't involved in the war.

In those days no major football or basketball clubs hired black players. The only job offered me was with the Honolulu Bears, and when I reported there I got a job with a construction company headquartered near Pearl Harbor. I worked for them during the week and played football on Sundays with my first pro team, the Bears. They were not major league but they were integrated. The football season ended in November and I wanted to get back to California. I arranged for ship passage and left Honolulu on December 5, 1941, two days before the Japanese bombed Pearl Harbor.

The day of the bombing we were on the ship playing poker, and we saw the members of the crew painting all the ship windows black. The captain summoned everyone on deck. He told us that Pearl Harbor had been bombed and that our country had declared war on Japan. When we arrived home, I knew realistically that I wouldn't be there long. Being drafted was an immediate possibility, and like all men in those days I was willing to do my part.

In May, 1942, the Army sent me to Fort Riley, Kansas, for basic training and I found myself in a cavalry outfit. After that I applied for Officers' Candidate School. It was then that I received my first lesson about the fate of a black man in a Jim Crow Army. The men in our unit had passed all the tests for OCS. But we were not allowed to start school; we were kept sitting around waiting for at least three months, and we could get no answers to our questions about the delay. It seemed to be a case of buck passing all along the line. Joe Louis was transferred to Fort Riley, and when we told him about the delay, he immediately contacted some powerful people in the government. The Fort Riley command began to get some heat from Washington and we suddenly found ourselves being welcomed into OCS. I became a second lieutenant in January, 1943.

I gave Rachel a special bracelet and a ring, and we formally announced our engagement and agreed to get married when Rachel finished school. Everything seemed fine to me, though we were far apart. Since Rae didn't complain, I didn't know how tough things were for her. We had been together for three years, and Rachel, because we were engaged, felt she shouldn't date anyone else. The school of nursing in San Francisco she had transferred to in September, 1943, had rigid rules, and Rae lived under strict house rules in a town flooded with servicemen. Rae was in a dormitory with other girls who were having the time of their lives. I had been the first man in Rachel's life, and she was still quite young. She began to wonder if she had sufficient experience to make a choice that would last for life. One day she wrote me that she was thinking of becoming a Cadet. I shook with rage and youthful jealousy as I read the letter far away in Kansas. I did not want her to become a Cadet. In fact I was adamant, and I made the bad mistake of issuing an ultimatum. I wrote her to forget about our relationship if she went into the Armed Forces.

She mailed the bracelet and the ring back to me. We both had a lot of pride, and now I realize it was my fierce possessiveness that had forced her to act. But then I was stunned by Rae's reaction, and stubbornly I vowed to forget about her. It was the last thing I wanted to do, and I didn't know that she felt as badly as I did. Several miserable months went by. I tried dating another girl. I even gave her the bracelet Rae had sent back to me. I knew, deep inside, that it wouldn't work and it didn't.

After OCS some of us were assigned to the provisional truck battalion at another section of Fort Riley, and I was made morale officer. Several of my men had come to me about the seating in the post exchange. The post exchange at Fort Riley was huge, and after the theater or other activities, many men would go to it for a snack. There were only six or seven seats assigned to blacks, and my men would be kept waiting despite the many empty seats available. I told them I would try to do something about this.

My statement was met with scorn. I realized that not only did these soldiers feel nothing could be done, but they did not believe any black officer would have the guts to protest. Their pessimism only served to challenge me more. The following day I telephoned the provost marshal, a Major Hafner; I made the call from my desk in our company headquarters. After identifying myself as the morale officer of my outfit, I told him about the lack of seats for blacks at the post exchange. I tried to appeal to the major by saying that we were all in this war together and it seemed to me that everyone should have the same basic rights. The major said that there was nothing to be done. I insisted that the men's protest ought to be given consideration. The major said it was hopeless. Finally, taking it for granted that I was white, he said, "Lieutenant, let me put it to you this way. How would you like to have your wife sitting next to a nigger?"

Pure rage took over; I was so angry that I asked him if he knew how close his wife had ever been to a nigger. I was shouting at the top of my voice. Every typewriter in headquarters stopped. The clerks were frozen in disbelief at the way I ripped into the major. Colonel Longley's office was in the same headquarters, and it was impossible for him not to hear me. The major couldn't get a word in edgewise, and finally he hung up. I was sitting there, still fuming, when Warrant Officer Chambers advised me to go to Colonel Longley immediately and tell him what had happened.

"I know that the colonel heard every word you said," Chambers said. "But you ought to tell him how you were provoked into blowing your top." I agreed and reported to the colonel. The colonel listened to me sympathetically and said that he would write a letter to the commanding general asking that conditions at the post exchange be corrected. A couple of weeks went by and I began to think the colonel had done nothing, but the master sergeant advised me that Colonel Longley had indeed written a sizzling letter to the commanding general. He had put in a strong request to change the seating situation and recommended that the provost marshal be disciplined for his racist attitude. I have always been grateful to Colonel Longley. He proved to me that when people in authority take a stand, good can come out of it.

Apparently, someone high up did rebuke the provost marshal. A few weeks after this incident I had another telephone confrontation with this same Major Hafner, and this time he was very respectful. One of my men had a girlfriend who worked for a colonel on the post. One night he visited the colonel's living quarters to see her. The GI got into an argument with his girl and beat her up. The girl's boss, the colonel, had the man arrested. I wasn't in favor of guys going around beating up women, but as morale officer, it was my duty to be informed about any problems involving my men. I called Major Hafner, not to seek a break for the enlisted man but just to learn the details of the incident. To my surprise, the major was very polite when I identified myself.

"Oh, yes," he said. "What can I do for you?" When I told him why I was calling, he promised to check the matter out immediately. He did, and within a matter of hours he had released the man back to my company. Ironically, this almost got me into trouble with the colonel who had ordered the man arrested. He phoned me, angrily accusing me of bypassing him to get the man released, but he understood when I explained.

My protest about the post exchange seating bore some results. More seats were allocated for blacks, but there were still separate sections for blacks and for whites. At least, I had made my men realize that something could be accomplished by speaking out, and I hoped they would be less resigned to unjust conditions.

When I had first arrived at Fort Riley, I had been invited to play on the football team. I'm sure it was because one of the colonels was determined to have a winning team. I had practiced with the team, and the first scheduled game was with the University of Missouri. They made it quite clear to the Army that they would not play a team with a black player on it. Instead of telling me the truth, the Army gave me leave to go home. Naturally I was delighted to leave, but I knew I would never play on that team.

Home in Pasadena, I was determined not to call Rachel. I moped around for several days, feeling terrible. My mother, who liked Rae a lot, sensed this and helped me face reality by telling me to bury my false pride. "You know you want to call Rachel, so call her," she said. I did know it and I called. After the first few words, I knew she was happy to hear from me. I got into my car, an old jalopy, and set some kind of a speed record getting to San Francisco. Making up was wonderful. I spent every possible minute of my leave with her. I had no money for a hotel and slept in my car every night, walking around the beautiful city, frittering away my time during the day, waiting for Rae to return from work. I was so happy to be reunited with her, and when my leave was over, I knew we'd be together forever once the war was over.

When I returned to Fort Riley, I was notified to come and pick up my football uniform. I reported but not to get a uniform. I said that I had no intention of playing football for a team which, because I was black, would not allow me to play in all the games. The colonel, whose son was on the team, reminded me that he could order me to play. I replied that, of course, he could. However, I pointed out that ordering me to play would not make me do my best.

"You wouldn't want me playing on your team, knowing that my heart wasn't in it," I said. They dropped the matter

16

but I had no illusions. I would never win a popularity contest with the ranking hierarchy of that post.

Soon after I was transferred to Fort Hood, Texas, where I was to take over a platoon of the 761st Tank Battalion. I had no knowledge, background, or experience in whatever it was a tank battalion did. I didn't worry about it because I was in a positive state of mind and was feeling so good about Rachel. But still I wasn't that sure about how I was going to do running a platoon in a tank outfit. I decided there was only one way to solve my problem and that was to be very honest about it. I was in charge of men who were training to go overseas. They had been together for quite a while, and they knew better than I how a tank battalion operated. If they needed any further preparation for overseas duty, they'd never be able to gain that knowledge from me. I went to the top sergeant of my platoon and told him that I knew nothing about tanks and would have to depend on him for guidance. I called all the men together and leveled with them. I said that I wasn't going to try to kid them. It would be up to their topkick and them to get the job done and let me know whatever it was I could do to help. I never regretted telling them the truth. The first sergeant and the men knocked themselves out to get the job done. They gave that little extra which cannot be forced from men. They worked harder than any outfit on the post, and our unit received the highest rating.

Colonel Bates, who was in charge of the battalion, was proud of the showing made by my platoon. He called me in to praise me and to ask if I would go overseas with the organization as morale officer. I told the colonel two facts of life: that it had been my men who got the job done—not me—and that while I would be willing to go overseas, I would probably be unacceptable since I was on limited service because of a bad ankle. The colonel replied that he didn't care how my men had got the job done. He was happy that it had been accomplished. He said that, obviously, no matter how much or how little I knew technically, I was able to get the best out of people I worked with. The business about my ankle could be resolved, he said, if I were willing to go to a nearby Army hospital and sign a waiver relieving the Army of any responsibility if anything happened to me during overseas duty because of my inability. I said I'd be willing to do that.

The hospital to which I was assigned for examination was a long bus ride away from the post. One evening, while I was there, I found myself with time on my hands and decided to come back to the post and talk with some of my friends at the officer's club. When I arrived, I found the whole outfit had gone off on maneuvers. I started back toward the bus to return to the hospital and met the wife of one of my fellow lieutenants. She was returning to her home, which was halfway between the hospital and the Army post. We sat down together in the bus, neither of us conscious of the fact that it made any difference where we were sitting. The driver glanced into his rear-view mirror and saw what he thought was a white woman talking with a black second lieutenant. He became visibly upset, stopped the bus, and came back to order me to move to the rear. I didn't even stop talking, didn't even look at him; I was aware of the fact that recently Joe Louis and Ray Robinson had refused to move to the backs of buses in the South. The resulting publicity had caused the Army to put out regulations barring racial discrimination on any vehicle operating on an Army post. Knowing about these regulations, I had no intention of being intimidated into moving to the back of the bus.

The driver had returned to his seat, assuming, I suppose, that I would obey his order. When he noted that I was not moving, he returned, even more angry. He shouted that if I didn't move to the rear of the bus he would cause me plenty of trouble. I told him hotly that I couldn't care less about his causing me trouble. I'd been in trouble all my life, but I knew what my rights were. When we reached the last stop on the post, where we were to get off and transfer to a city bus, the driver jumped out of the bus and rushed off somewhere, returning quickly with his dispatcher and some other drivers. Pointing me out, he cried, "There's the nigger that's been causing me trouble." I put my finger right in his face and warned him that he'd better get off my back, although I didn't say it exactly in those words. I turned away from him, with my lady companion, to go toward the city bus. We heard the screeching of tires and a military police jeep pulled up. The two military policemen asked a few questions, then, with great politeness, asked if I would be willing to go along with them to talk to their captain. They were enlisted men and they called me "sir" and seemed only interested in doing their duty under the circumstances. I agreed to go see their duty officer. My friend's wife volunteered to come with me. She was afraid someone was going to try to frame me. I told her that it wouldn't be necessary for her to get further involved. I was confident that it would be easily established that I had acted well within my rights.

I was naïve about the elaborate lengths to which racists in the Armed Forces would go to put a vocal black man in his place. My first indication that I might be up against a tougher situation than I thought came when I was interviewed by the duty officer, a Captain Gerald M. Bear. There was a civilian woman with him. I don't know whether she was his secretary or aide or what. But she was doing all the talking, asking all the questions. They were real, nice, objective questions like, "Don't you know you've got no right sitting up there in the white part of the bus?" It wasn't bad enough that she was asking that type of question. She wasn't even pausing long enough to hear my answer. At one point she snapped that one of my replies made no sense. I became very annoyed. In the back of my mind was a serious question as to whether she was the proper person, legally, to question me anyhow. So I replied sharply that if she would let me finish my sentences and quit interrupting, maybe my answers would make sense. At this point, traditional Southern chivalry for wounded white womanhood took over; Captain Bear came out of hibernation to growl that I was apparently an uppity nigger and that I had no right to speak to that lady in that manner. I objected. "She's asking the questions," I said. "I feel I have as much right to tell my story as she has to ask questions." The captain was very annoyed because I wouldn't back down. He began to rave. I interrupted him, asking, "Captain, tell me, where are you from anyway?" He stormed that that had nothing to do with it, that he wasn't prejudiced, that back home he owned a laundry, and that he employed a number of blacks—and all the rest of that stuff that bigots talk when confronted with the charge of being bigots.

As serious as the situation was, I had to laugh. It was so obvious what was happening. I was up against one of those white supremacy characters. Everything would have been all right if I had been a "yassuh boss" type. When the interview was over, the captain ordered an escort to take me back to the hospital. When we arrived there, we were met by a colonel and several military police. There was talk of a court-martial. The colonel advised me that he had been alerted to expect a black officer who had been drunk and disorderly and had been trying to start a riot. It must have been obvious to the colonel that I wasn't drunk, and when I told him calmly that I had never had a drink in my life, he said that for my own protection I must immediately have a blood test to prove that there was no alcoholic content in my blood. After I did that, I was advised to report to Colonel Bates. The news was not good. He told me there was rumor of a court-martial and recommended giving me leave. He wanted to ease the pressure while we waited to learn if the "limited service" issue had been resolved at the hospital so I could go overseas. Also he felt it would be better if I was not on the scene while the court-martial issue was being settled. He advised me to forget about my problems at Fort Hood, Texas, and suggested a trip to San Francisco.

In San Francisco after a joyous reunion I found Rae facing

herself honestly. She had begun to wonder if she had made her choice to someday marry me without sufficient background of experience and contact with other people. She had a stack of letters from me and almost every week a box of chocolates, but she began to doubt whether we should be tied to each other. Her loneliness and her frustration when all her companions around her were having fun began to work on her. To aggravate matters, Rae's family received news that her brother, a pilot, had been shot down over Germany. She began to feel that perhaps she owed it to him to become personally involved in the war effort. There was another compelling reason. Money. For the first two years of her college career, Rae had been on a scholarship. Now she was responsible for paying her own tuition. She learned that if she joined the Cadet Corps, a student organization, the government would pay her tuition and give her a small monthly allowance. She would remain in school and in her chosen field of nursing. She would also be helping to make up for the sacrifice of the brother she presumed to be dead. When Rae told me that she was thinking of becoming a Cadet, this aroused unreasonable but definite thoughts in my mind. I'd been around so often when guys in the service were discussing women soldiers. It really wasn't fair, but GI's had those conceptions about women in the Armed Forces—and particularly nurses—as being very loose morally. I can honestly say that I never thought of Rae except on the highest level. However my pride in her being my fiancée and my need for her as the most important person in my life made me stubborn, even adamant. But in my heart I knew we would resolve our problems. I told her of the problems and decision I faced on my return. When Rae got home from work every evening, I was right there waiting. Then things began looking up for her; one day she heard that her brother had been found alive. Rae was happy to forget about going into service.

There were still clouds on my horizon. I had to report back to duty and face the court-martial. My leave was over. Anyone who knows about the Army court-martial system can tell you that it's loaded mostly in favor of those bringing the charges. I was really fortunate. In spite of the obvious smell of frame-up in my case, it would have been an easy matter for me to be railroaded into some kind of punishment for simply insisting on my rights. My first break was that the legal officer assigned to defend me was a Southerner who had the decency to admit to me that he didn't think he could be objective. He recommended a young Michigan officer who did a great job on my behalf. He had a way of rephrasing the same question in so many clever ways that anyone who was lying would have a hard time not betraying himself. It became obvious during the proceedings that the prosecution had rehearsed and schooled witnesses—and had done a bad job of indoctrinating them. My lawyer tricked several of the witnesses into confusing testimony, and luckily there were some members of that court-martial board who had the honesty to realize what was going on. I was acquitted on all charges. There had been another factor which worked in my favor. Some of my black brother officers were determined to help me beat the attempted injustice in my case. They wrote letters to the black press. The Pittsburgh *Courier*, then one of the country's most powerful weeklies, gave the matter important publicity. The Army, sensitive to this kind of spotlight, knew that if I was unfairly treated, it would not be a secret.

The court-martial had caused me to miss going overseas with my outfit. I knew that I would be transferred into some new and strange organization. I was pretty much fed up with the service. So I did something which is very much frowned upon in GI procedure. I sent an airmail special delivery letter to The Adjutant General's office in Washington, D.C. This was in violation of the standard procedure of going through channels, forwarding any correspondence up through your own company, battalion, regiment, and division headquarters. On the way up, such correspondence, if it ever reaches its intended destination, can get marked up with disapproving notations from your superior officers. The disapproving endorsements have great weight with the top brass which is very likely to turn down any request you make which is not favorable in the eyes of your superiors. I bypassed all that. My letter was timed to reach The Adjutant General's desk about the same time my court-martial papers got to his desk. I was gambling that he would notice that I had been acquitted in an obvious attempt to frame me, that perhaps the top brass would view me as a potential troublemaker who would be better off in civilian life. I guess someone was really anxious to get rid of me fast. In November, 1944, I was transferred to Camp Breckinridge and received my honorable discharge.

While waiting for discharge, I ran into a brother named Alexander who, before going into uniform, had been a member of the Kansas City Monarchs. The Monarchs were one of the teams of the professional black baseball world. I saw him one day, throwing ball. The ball got away and I threw it back. I watched him for a while. He was throwing curve balls. I saw the way they broke off. I asked another guy who was catching if I could play with him and catch some of his pitches. Alexander and I got into a conversation, and he told me there was good money in black baseball. He said the Monarchs were looking for players. I was looking for a decent postwar job. So I wrote the Monarchs. After checking me out, they responded rather quickly and accepted me on a tryout basis for spring training. I was ordered to report to Houston. The pay of $400 a month was a financial bonanza for me. My pitcher friend had told the truth about the pay. He had also said that I would enjoy the life of a baseball pro. Well, maybe he enjoyed it. For me, it turned out to be a pretty miserable way to make a buck.

When I look back at what I had to go through in black baseball, I can only marvel at the many black players who stuck it out for years in the Jim Crow leagues because they had nowhere else to go. When you look at television today or scan the sports pages, and see how many blacks and Latins are starring in the game, it is almost impossible to conceive of those days, less than twenty-five years ago, when world series champs literally meant white champs. That was the way it was, and although there were spirited campaigns to break down the racial barriers in 1944, it appeared that it would be years before segregation in baseball was eliminated.

Blacks who wanted to play baseball could sign up on black teams only. These teams were poorly financed, and their management and promotion left much to be desired. Travel schedules were unbelievably hectic. Our team played in Kansas City, moved throughout the entire Midwest and sometimes went south and east. On one occasion, we left Kansas City on a bus on a Sunday night, traveled to Philadelphia, reaching there Tuesday morning. We played a doubleheader that night and the next day we were on the road again. This fatiguing travel wouldn't have been so bad if we could have had decent meals. Finding satisfactory or even passable eating places was almost a daily problem. There was no hotel in many of the places we played. Sometimes there was a hotel for blacks which had no eating facilities. No one even thought of trying to get accommodations in white hotels. Some of the crummy eating joints would not serve us at all. You could never sit down to a relaxed hot meal. You were lucky if they magnanimously permitted you to carry out some greasy hamburgers in a paper bag with a container of coffee. You were really living when you were able to get a plate of cold cuts. You ate on board the team bus or on the road.

In those days a white ballplayer could look forward to some streak of luck or some reward for hard work to carry him into prominence or even stardom. What had the black player to hope for? What was his future? The black press, some liberal sportswriters, and even a few politicians were banging away at those Jim Crow barriers in baseball. I never expected the walls to come tumbling down in my lifetime. I began to wonder why I should dedicate my life to a career where the boundaries for progress were set by racial discrimination. Even more serious was my growing fear that I might lose Rae again. I began to sense in her letters that her patience was thinning. She had been hoping I'd settle down in California to work out our future. The way I was traveling we saw each other rarely. I felt unhappy and trapped. If I left baseball, where could I go, what could I do to earn enough money to help my mother and to marry Rachel?

The solution to my problem was only days away in the hands of a tough, shrewd, courageous man called Branch Rickey, the president of the Brooklyn Dodgers.

I had never seen Branch Rickey. I had read about him, of course, and realized he was one of the big shots of the game. If I ever thought about him, even vaguely, I probably would have assessed him as one of the powerful clique which was keeping baseball lily-white. If anyone had told me that there was a ghost of a memory in this man's life which had haunted him for years and that this memory would be a prime cause in Mr. Rickey's deciding to challenge Jim Crow baseball, I would have thought it all a fantasy. Further, if someone had predicted that Mr. Rickey's momentous decision would involve me and change the whole course of my life and the course of sports in America, I would have called the predictor insane. Yet all this was to happen.

Chapter II

The Noble Experiment

In 1910 Branch Rickey was a coach for Ohio Wesleyan. The team went to South Bend, Indiana, for a game. The hotel management registered the coach and team but refused to assign a room to a black player named Charley Thomas. In those days college ball had a few black players. Mr. Rickey took the manager aside and said he would move the entire team to another hotel unless the black athlete was accepted. The threat was a bluff because he knew the other hotels also would have refused accommodations to a black man. While the hotel manager was thinking about the threat, Mr. Rickey came up with a compromise. He suggested a cot be put in his own room, which he would share with the unwanted guest. The hotel manager wasn't happy about the idea, but he gave in.

Years later Branch Rickey told the story of the misery of that black player to whom he had given a place to sleep. He remembered that Thomas couldn't sleep.

"He sat on that cot," Mr. Rickey said, "and was silent for a long time. Then he began to cry, tears he couldn't hold back. His whole body shook with emotion. I sat and watched him, not knowing what to do until he began tearing at one hand with the other—just as if he were trying to scratch the skin off his hands with his fingernails. I was alarmed. I asked him what he was trying to do to himself.

" 'It's my hands,' he sobbed, 'They're black. If only they were white, I'd be as good as anybody then, wouldn't I, Mr. Rickey? If only they were white.' "

"Charley," Mr. Rickey said, "the day will come when they won't have to be white."

Thirty-five years later, while I was lying awake nights, frustrated, unable to see a future, Mr. Rickey by now the president of the Dodgers was also lying awake at night, trying to make up his mind about a new experiment.

He had never forgotten the agony of that black athlete. When he became a front office executive in St. Louis, he had fought, behind the scenes, against the custom that consigned black spectators to the Jim Crow section of the Sportsmen's Park, later to become Busch Memorial Stadium. His pleas to change the rules were in vain. Those in power argued that if blacks were allowed a free choice of seating, white business would suffer.

Branch Rickey lost that fight, but when he became the boss of the Brooklyn Dodgers in 1943, he felt the time for equality in baseball had come. He knew that achieving it would be terribly difficult. There would be deep resentment, determined opposition, and perhaps even racial violence. He was convinced he was morally right, and he shrewdly sensed that making the game a truly national one would have healthy financial results. He took his case before the startled directors of the club, and using persuasive eloquence, he won the first battle in what would be a long and bitter campaign. He was voted permission to make the Brooklyn club the pioneer in bringing blacks into baseball.

Winning his directors' approval was almost insignificant in contrast to the task which now lay ahead of the Dodger president. He made certain that word of his plans did not leak out, particularly to the press. Next, he had to find the ideal player for his project, which came to be called "Rickey's noble experiment." This player had to be one who could take abuse, name-calling, rejection by fans and sportswriters and by fellow players not only on opposing teams but on his own. He had to be able to stand up in the face of merciless persecution and not retaliate. On the other hand, he had to be a contradiction in human terms; he still had to have spirit. He could not be an "Uncle Tom." His ability to turn the other cheek had to be predicated on his determination to gain acceptance. Once having proven his ability as player, teammate, and man, he had to be able to cast off humbleness and stand up as a full-fledged participant whose triumph did not carry the poison of bitterness.

Unknown to most people and certainly to me, after launching a major scouting program, Branch Rickey had picked me as that player. The Rickey talent hunt went beyond national borders. Cuba, Mexico, Puerto Rico, Venezuela, and other countries where dark-skinned people lived had been checked out. Mr. Rickey had learned that there were a number of black players, war veterans mainly, who had gone to these countries, despairing of finding an opportunity in their own country. The manhunt had to be camouflaged. If it became known he was looking for a black recruit for the Dodgers, all hell would have broken loose. The gimmick he used as a cover-up was to make the world believe that he was about to establish a new Negro league. In the spring of 1945 he called a press conference and announced that the Dodgers were organizing the United States League, composed of all black teams. This, of course, made blacks and prointegration whites indignant. He was accused of trying to uphold the existing segregation and, at the same time, capitalize on black players. Cleverly, Mr. Rickey replied that his league would be better organized than the current ones. He said its main purpose, eventually, was to be absorbed into the majors. It is ironic that by coming very close to telling the truth, he was able to conceal that truth from the enemies of integrated baseball. Most people assumed that when he spoke of some distant goal of integration, Mr. Rickey was being a hypocrite on this issue as so many of baseball's leaders had been.

Black players were familiar with this kind of hypocrisy. When I was with the Monarchs, shortly before I met Mr. Rickey, Wendell Smith, then sports editor of the black, weekly Pittsburgh *Courier*, had arranged for me and two other players from the Negro league to go to a tryout with the Boston Red Sox. The tryout had been brought about because a Boston city councilman had frightened the Red Sox management. Councilman Isadore Muchneck threatened to push a bill through banning Sunday baseball unless the Red Sox hired black players. Sam Jethroe of the Cleveland Buckeyes, Marvin Williams of the Philadelphia Stars, and I had been grateful to Wendell for getting us a chance in the Red Sox tryout, and we put our best efforts into it. However, not for one minute did we believe the tryout was sincere. The Boston club officials praised our performance, let us fill out application cards, and said "so long." We were fairly certain they wouldn't call us, and we had no intention of calling them.

Incidents like this made Wendell Smith as cynical as we were. He didn't accept Branch Rickey's new league as a genuine project and he frankly told him so. During this conversation, the Dodger boss asked Wendell whether any of the three of us who had gone to Boston was really good major league material. Wendell said I was. I will be forever indebted to Wendell because, without his even knowing it, his recommendation was in the end partly responsible for my career. At the time it started a thorough investigation of my background.

In August, 1945, at Comiskey Park in Chicago, I was approached by Clyde Sukeforth, the Dodger scout. Blacks have had to learn to protect themselves by being cynical but not cynical enough to slam the door on potential opportunities. We go through life walking a tightrope to prevent too much disillusionment. I was out on the field when Sukeforth called my name and beckoned. He told me the Brown Dodgers were looking for top ballplayers, that Branch Rickey had heard about me and sent him to watch me throw from the hole. He had come at an unfortunate time. I had hurt my shoulder a couple of days before that, and I wouldn't be doing any throwing for at least a week.

Sukeforth said he'd like to talk with me anyhow. He asked me to come to see him after the game at the Stevens Hotel.

Here we go again, I thought. Another time-wasting experience. But Sukeforth looked like a sincere person and I thought I might as well listen. I agreed to meet him that night. When we met, Sukeforth got right to the point. Mr. Rickey wanted to talk to me about the possibility of becoming a Brown Dodger. If I could get a few days off and go to Brooklyn, my fare and expenses would be paid. At first I said that I couldn't leave my team and go to Brooklyn just like that. Sukeforth wouldn't take no for an answer. He pointed out that I couldn't play for a few days anyhow because of my bum arm. Why should my team object?

I continued to hold out and demanded to know what would happen if the Monarchs fired me. The Dodger scout replied quietly that he didn't believe that would happen.

I shrugged and said I'd make the trip. I figured I had nothing to lose.

Branch Rickey was an impressive-looking man. He had a classic face, an air of command, a deep, booming voice, and a way of cutting through red tape and getting down to basics. He shook my hand vigorously and, after a brief conversation, sprang the first question.

"You got a girl?" he demanded.

It was a hell of a question. I had two reactions: why should he be concerned about my relationship with a girl; and, second, while I thought, hoped, and prayed I had a girl, the way things had been going, I was afraid she might have begun to consider me a hopeless case. I explained this to Mr. Rickey and Clyde.

Mr. Rickey wanted to know all about Rachel. I told him of our hopes and plans.

"You know, you *have* a girl," he said heartily. "When we get through today you may want to call her up because there are times when a man needs a woman by his side."

My heart began racing a little faster again as I sat there speculating. First he asked me if I really understood why he had sent for me. I told him what Clyde Sukeforth had told me.

"That's what he was supposed to tell you," Mr. Rickey said. "The truth is you are not a candidate for the Brooklyn Brown Dodgers. I've sent for you because I'm interested in you as a candidate for the Brooklyn National League Club. I think you can play in the major leagues. How do you feel about it?"

My reactions seemed like some kind of weird mixture churning in a blender. I was thrilled, scared, and excited. I was incredulous. Most of all, I was speechless.

"You think you can play for Montreal?" he demanded.

I got my tongue back. "Yes," I answered.

Montreal was the Brooklyn Dodgers' top farm club. The players who went there and made it had an excellent chance at the big time.

I was busy reorganizing my thoughts while Mr. Rickey and Clyde Sukeforth discussed me briefly, almost as if I weren't there. Mr. Rickey was questioning Clyde. Could I make the grade?

Abruptly, Mr. Rickey swung his swivel chair in my direction. He was a man who conducted himself with great drama. He pointed a finger at me.

"I know you're a good ballplayer," he barked. "What I don't know is whether you have the guts."

I knew it was all too good to be true. Here was a guy questioning my courage. That virtually amounted to him asking me if I was a coward. Mr. Rickey or no Mr. Rickey, that was an insinuation hard to take. I felt the heat coming up into my cheeks.

Before I could react to what he had said, he leaned forward in his chair and explained.

I wasn't just another athlete being hired by a ball club. We were playing for big stakes. This was the reason Branch Rickey's search had been so exhaustive. The search had spanned the globe and narrowed down to a few candidates, then finally to me. When it looked as though I might be the number-one choice, the investigation of my life, my habits, my reputation, and my character had become an intensified study.

"I've investigated you thoroughly, Robinson," Mr. Rickey said.

One of the results of this thorough screening were reports from California athletic circles that I had been a "racial agitator" at UCLA. Mr. Rickey had not accepted these criticisms on face value. He had demanded and received more information and came to the conclusion that, if I had been white, people would have said, "Here's a guy who's a contender, a competitor."

After that he had some grim words of warning. "We can't fight our way through this, Robinson. We've got no army. There's virtually nobody on our side. No owners, no umpires, very few newspapermen. And I'm afraid that many fans will be hostile. We'll be in a tough position. We can win only if we can convince the world that I'm doing this because you're a great ballplayer and a fine gentleman."

He had me transfixed as he spoke. I could feel his sincerity, and I began to get a sense of how much this major step meant to him. Because of his nature and his passion for justice, he had to do what he was doing. He continued. The rumbling voice, the theatrical gestures, were gone. He was speaking from a deep, quiet strength.

"So there's more than just playing," he said. "I wish it

meant only hits, runs, and errors—only the things they put in the box score. Because you know—yes, you would know, Robinson, that a baseball box score is a democratic thing. It doesn't tell how big you are, what church you attend, what color you are, or how your father voted in the last election. It just tells what kind of baseball player you were on that particular day."

I interrupted. "But it's the box score that really counts—that and that alone, isn't it?"

"It's all that *ought* to count," he replied. "But it isn't. Maybe one of these days it *will* be all that counts. That is one of the reasons I've got you here, Robinson. If you're a good enough man, we can make this a start in the right direction. But let me tell you, it's going to take an awful lot of courage."

He was back to the crossroads question that made me start to get angry minutes earlier. He asked it slowly and with great care.

"Have you got the guts to play the game no matter what happens?"

"I think I can play the game, Mr. Rickey," I said.

The next few minutes were tough. Branch Rickey had to make absolutely sure that I knew what I would face. Beanballs would be thrown at me. I would be called the kind of names which would hurt and infuriate any man. I would be physically attacked. Could I take all of this and control my temper, remain steadfastly loyal to our ultimate aim?

He knew I would have terrible problems and wanted me to know the extent of them before I agreed to the plan. I was twenty-six years old, and all my life back to the age of eight when a little neighbor girl called me a nigger—I had believed in payback, retaliation. The most luxurious possession, the richest treasure anybody has, is his personal dignity. I looked at Mr. Rickey guardedly, and in that second I was looking at him not as a partner in a great experiment, but as the enemy—a white man. I had a question and it was the age-old one about whether or not you sell your birthright.

"Mr. Rickey," I asked, "are you looking for a Negro who is afraid to fight back?"

I never will forget the way he exploded.

"Robinson," he said, "I'm looking for a ballplayer with guts enough not to fight back."

After that, Mr. Rickey continued his lecture on the kind of thing I'd be facing.

He not only told me about it, but he acted out the part of a white player charging into me, blaming me for the "accident" and calling me all kinds of foul racial names. He talked about my race, my parents, in language that was almost unendurable.

"They'll taunt and goad you," Mr. Rickey said. "They'll do anything to make you react. They'll try to provoke a race riot in the ball park. This is the way to prove to the public that a Negro should not be allowed in the major league. This is the way to frighten the fans and make them afraid to attend the games."

If hundreds of black people wanted to come to the ball park to watch me play and Mr. Rickey tried to discourage them, would I understand that he was doing it because the emotional enthusiasm of my people could harm the experiment? That kind of enthusiasm would be as bad as the emotional opposition of prejudiced white fans.

Suppose I was at shortstop. Another player comes down from first, stealing, flying in with spikes high, and cuts me on the leg. As I feel the blood running down my leg, the white player laughs in my face.

"How do you like that, nigger boy?" he sneers.

Could I turn the other cheek? I didn't know how I would do it. Yet I knew that I must. I had to do it for so many reasons. For black youth, for my mother, for Rae, for myself. I had already begun to feel I had to do it for Branch Rickey.

I was offered and agreed to sign later a contract with a

$3,500 bonus and $600 a month salary. I was officially a Montreal Royal. I must not tell anyone except Rae and my mother.

It was almost two months—October 23, 1945—before I was notified to go to Montreal to sign my contract and to meet Mr. Rickey's son, Branch Rickey, Jr., who was in charge of Brooklyn Dodger farm clubs. The press had been called in. They made a dash for the telephone when Hector Racine, the president of the Montreal club, announced that Jackie Robinson, a shortstop, had been signed to play for Montreal. Having phoned in the big news, the press came back to try to milk more information out of the Dodger officials and me. There was the inevitable question about the reaction of the fans to my being on the team. The Montreal president said he was confident Montreal fans were not racially biased and would judge me on my playing merit. Young Rickey told something about the talent search which had resulted in my being discovered. He added that there would undoubtedly be some reaction from sections of the United States where racial prejudice was rampant.

"My father and Mr. Racine are not inviting trouble," young Rickey said, "but they won't avoid it if it comes. Jack Robinson is a fine type of young man, intelligent and college-bred, and I think he can make it, too."

Mr. Rickey's son continued to point out that some of the Brooklyn organization's other players, particularly from certain sections of the South, would "steer away from a club with Negro players on its roster." He added, "Some of them who are with us now may even quit, but they'll be back in baseball after they work a year or two in a cotton mill."

The announcement and young Rickey's statement got a great deal of press coverage. Although some sportswriters, among them Dan Parker and Red Smith, were encouraging, there were plenty of negative comments.

Rogers Hornsby, a Texan and retired player, predicted, "Ballplayers on the road live close together. It won't work."

Fred "Dixie" Walker, a popular outfielder for Brooklyn, was quoted as saying, "As long as he isn't with the Dodgers, I'm not worried." Pitcher Bob Feller didn't see any future for me. "He is tied up in the shoulders," Feller said. "He couldn't hit an inside pitch to save his neck. If he were a white man, I doubt if they would even consider him as big league material."

Jimmy Powers, sports editor of the New York *Daily News*, wrote that I would not make the grade in the big leagues "next year or the next." I was, according to him, a thousand-to-one shot. Jack Horner of North Carolina's Durham *Herald* wrote hopefully that I would probably get out of my own accord because I would be so uncomfortable and out of place. Minor League Commissioner W. G. Bramham accused Branch Rickey of being "of the carpetbagger stripe of the white race who, under the guise of helping, is in truth using the Negro for their own self-interest, to retard the race." Bramham sneered that if the black religious leader Father Divine wasn't careful, there would soon be a Rickey Temple built in Harlem. Alvin Gardner, president of the Texas League, agreed. "I'm positive you'll never see any Negro player on any of the teams in organized baseball in the South as long as the Jim Crow laws are in force," he stated.

Overnight some of the prejudiced white owners and officials became extremely concerned about the future of the Negro leagues. They mourned because Mr. Rickey was destroying the defenseless black clubs. With some, the issue was genuine. With others, raising the issue helped cast doubt on the wisdom of taking black players from the black clubs into the major leagues.

The Kansas City Monarchs threatened to sue Rickey. They contended I had a contract with them and was their property. Some major league owners encouraged the Monarchs. These owners wanted to stop blacks from getting into the mainstream of baseball, and some were making money leasing their ball parks to the Jim Crow teams. Clark Griffith, owner of the Washington Senators, said that the Dodgers should pay the Monarchs for my services. The threatened suit came to an end suddenly when one of the Monarch owners, who, incidentally, was white, sent a telegram to Mr. Rickey saying he had been misquoted. He wouldn't dream of doing anything to keep any black player out of the major leagues. I guess the word got around that black fans would not view it kindly if the Jim Crow clubs barred the way for a black player to make the big time.

Chapter III

Breaking the
Color Barrier

Quite a while before I signed with Montreal, I had agreed to play on an all-star black team for the American National League that planned to go to Venezuela on a barnstorming tour. Rae and I had planned to be married in February. While I was in South America, we both thought it would be a good chance for Rae to begin to fulfill a lifelong dream of traveling. She wanted to go to New York to see another part of the country. She had a fear that once married she would be stuck in California as both our families were. We both had no idea that our destiny would differ significantly from our parents'. She had saved some money and her family gave her another $100. Rae had been a student nurse for five years, and the prospect of seeing New York excited her. She got a job as a hostess in a swank restaurant on Park Avenue. After a couple of months, she quit because of the way the management treated black patrons and employees. They used every kind of device to let black patrons know they weren't welcome. A black man with a turban on his head could get the best of accommodations because he wasn't a black American in the eyes of the restaurant owner.

Next, Rachel got a job as a nurse at the Hospital for Joint Diseases and lived with a friend of her mother's who had a place in Harlem. Even though she was getting a chance to see New York and had the company of her friend Janice, she was lonely. She was earning a pitifully small salary and usually had her meals at a great little restaurant on Seventh Avenue, called Jenny Lou's. As good as the food was, Rachel and Janice yearned for a home-cooked meal and for the kindness of an invitation to someone's house for dinner. The lady in whose house Rachel and Janice were staying was well-known and had many friends. But none of them thought about asking these young visitors from out of town to come to dinner. Years later, when she returned to New York as Mrs. Jackie Robinson, some of the same people who had known her before as an insignificant girl named Rachel Isum, wanted to do all sorts of things to entertain her. Rae found that quite ironic.

Rachel purchased part of her trousseau in New York, and I brought the wedding ring home from Latin America. When we were reunited in the early part of 1946, wedding plans were on the agenda. To please Rae's mother, we agreed to a big church wedding. The ceremony was beautiful and we were most pleased that our dear friend, Reverend Karl Downs, flew in from Texas to perform the ceremony.

After we had been declared man and wife, as we walked down the aisle together, I spotted some old boyhood buddies from the one-time Pepper Street gang in Pasadena. I was so happy to see them there and so happy about getting married that I stopped to shake hands with them. Rae kept walking to the end of the aisle and waited there, slightly miffed, until I caught up with her.

At the reception afterward, we had a marvelous time, but when we got ready to leave to go to a local hotel where we would be staying overnight, we found that one of my friends had "borrowed" my old car as a joke. We stood there, a brand-new bride and groom, without transportation to take us to our honeymoon hotel. Finally, the car materialized and we went to the hotel. We were lucky to be admitted because I had forgotten to make a reservation and explain that we were a bridal couple so that the management would provide the traditional flowers and extra services. Once the hotel room door closed, the minor mishaps receded before the great joy of knowing we were alone together at last.

A few weeks after the wedding, we were to fly to Daytona Beach, Florida, where I was to report for spring training with the Montreal farm club. We started out by plane from Los Angeles, arriving at New Orleans quite early in the morning. Upon arrival, I was told to go into the terminal. Rachel waited and waited. Then the stewardess came up to her and suggested that she go into the terminal and take all her things with her. I discovered we had been bumped from our flight owing to military priorities, so they said. We were not alarmed, having been assured that there would be only a brief delay. But as we argued our rights, the plane took off. Another typical black experience. After a few hours we weren't as concerned about the time we were losing as we were about the hunger we felt. Blacks could not eat in the coffee shop but could take food out. We asked where we could find a restaurant. We learned there was one that would prepare sandwiches provided we did not sit down and eat them there. Though we were both weary and hungry, we decided to skip food until we reached a place where we could be treated as human beings.

Our next project was to find a hotel where we could wait until we got another flight. The only accommodations were in a filthy, run-down place resembling a flophouse. A roof over our heads and a chance to lie down, even in a bed of uncertain sanitary condition, was better than nothing. We made the best of it and notified the airport where we could be found. They promised to call. They did. At seven in the evening, exactly twelve hours after we had been told about a "brief delay," we were in the air again. After a short flight, the plane set down at

Pensacola, Florida, for fueling. The manager of the Pensacola Airport told me that we were being bumped again. There wasn't any explanation this time. They had simply put a white couple in our seats. A black porter managed to get us a limousine. It stopped at a hotel in Pensacola, and the white driver summoned a black bellboy and asked him where we could get room and board for the night. The bellboy recommended the home of a black family. These were generous and warmhearted people who insisted on taking us in, in spite of the fact that they had a huge family and a tiny home. Their willingness to share made us forget about being sorry for ourselves. Realistically, though, there was just no room for us. We thanked them, telling them we couldn't dream of inconveniencing them and got a ride to the Greyhound bus terminal. We had decided to take the next bus to Jacksonville, thinking that at least we could relax a bit and rest our backs, but we were in for another rude jolt. We had sunk down gratefully into a couple of seats and pushed the little buttons which move you back into a reclining position. The bus was empty when we boarded, and we had taken seats in the middle of the bus. I fell fast asleep. At the first stop, a crowd of passengers got on. The bus driver gestured to us, indicating that we were to move to the back of the bus. The seats at the back were reserved seats—reserved for Negroes—and they were straight-backed. No little button to push. No reclining seats.

I had a bad few seconds, deciding whether I could continue to endure this humiliation. After we had been bumped a second time at the Pensacola Airport, I had been ready to explode with rage, but I knew that the result would mean newspaper headlines about an ugly racial incident and possible arrest not only for me but also for Rae. By giving in to my feelings then, I could have blown the whole major league bit. I had swallowed my pride and choked back my anger. Again, this time it would have been much easier to take a beating than to remain passive. But I remembered the things

41

Rae and I had said to each other during the months we had tried to prepare ourselves for exactly this kind of ordeal. We had agreed that I had no right to lose my temper and jeopardize the chances of all the blacks who would follow me if I could help break down the barriers. So we moved back to the very last seat as indicated by the driver. The bus continued to pick up passengers. They came on board the bus and filled up the choice white seats. The black section was so crowded that every other person sat forward on the edge to create more room. In the dark, Rachel was quietly crying, but I didn't know that until years later. She was crying for me and not out of self-pity. She felt badly because she knew I felt helpless. She hoped I realized that she knew how much strength it took to take these injustices and not strike back.

Finally, the bus pulled into Daytona Beach. We were relieved to reach our destination. But we had not escaped from old man Jim Crow. The white members of the team were living in a hotel; however, Rae and I had "special accommodations" at the home of Joe Harris, a local black political leader. Joe was an activist. He kept in touch with every black voter in his district to make sure they voted. His skill at organizing had enabled him to gain concessions from the power structure. He had persuaded business people in downtown Daytona Beach to treat black customers with respect and had influenced the transit people to hire black drivers on local buses. Joe and his wife Duff treated Rae and me with well-known Southern warmth. They liked to kid us, calling us the lovebirds since we were newlyweds. The one major disadvantage we had at the Harris home was that we could not cook or eat there on a regular basis except for breakfast. For our other meals, we had to depend on greasy-spoon joints.

After staying several days at Daytona Beach, the club was moved to Sanford, Florida. I would have more than two hundred teammates, the majority of them Southern. The first time we met was in the locker room and I remember being quite reticent. Most of the other players seemed intent on doing their own jobs. But there was a mutual wariness between us, a current of tension that I hoped would lessen with time.

I had my first confrontation with the press in camp. Someone asked if I thought I could "make it with these white boys." I said I hadn't had any crucial problems making it with white fellow athletes in the service or at UCLA or at Pasadena. One of the newsmen asked what I would do if one of the white pitchers threw at my head. I replied that I would duck. Noting that I was a shortstop, another newsman made the assumption that this automatically meant I wanted to replace the popular Brooklyn Dodger shortstop, Pee Wee Reese. I pointed out that Pee Wee Reese was after all with the Brooklyn Dodgers and I was trying to make the Montreal Royals. I was not in a position to go after another man's job on another team—I was going to concentrate on securing my berth with Montreal. This confrontation with the press was just a taste of what was to come. They frequently stirred up trouble by baiting me or jumping into any situation I was involved in without completely checking the facts before rushing a story into print.

Clyde Sukeforth, the scout who had taken me to Mr. Rickey, was in camp at Sanford. I was glad to see him. Clyde introduced me to Clay Hopper, the Montreal manager. I had been briefed about Hopper. What I had heard about him wasn't encouraging. A native of Mississippi, he owned a plantation there, and I had been told he was anti-black. There was no outward sign of prejudice in his manner, however, when we first met. Hopper told me I could take it easy, just hit a few and throw the ball around. This relaxed activity—or, rather, lack of activity—went on all that first day and the next. The evening of the second day, the stunning and discouraging word came that Mr. Rickey had ordered me back to Daytona Beach where I had originally reported. Naturally, I was worried about this sudden shift. Officially, I was told I was being sent ahead to Daytona a few days before the rest of the club was to arrive so that Rachel and I would have a chance to settle down. The truth I learned from Wendell Smith when en route to Daytona, was that my presence with the club in Sanford had already created racial tensions. Local civic officials had decided that mixing black and white players was apt to create trouble.

Shortly after Branch Rickey had signed me for Montreal, he had signed John Wright, a black pitcher, for the farm club. Johnny was a good pitcher, but I feel he didn't have the right kind of temperament to make it with the International League in those days. He couldn't withstand the pressure of taking insult after insult without being able to retaliate. It affected his pitching that he had to keep his temper under control all the time. Later I was very sad because he didn't make the Montreal team.

All during that spring training period in Daytona, I was conscious every minute of every day, and during many sleepless nights that I had to make good out there on that ball field. I was determined to prove to our manager, Clay Hopper, that I could make the grade. Perhaps it is a good thing that I didn't know about Hopper's initial reaction to me. Hopper had begged Mr. Rickey not to send me to his club.

"Please don't do this to me," he had pleaded. "I'm white and I've lived in Mississippi all my life. If you do this, you're going to force me to move my family and my home out of Mississippi." Clay Hopper began to come around only after I demonstrated that I was a valuable property for the club.

During this time of trial, while my fellow players were not overtly hostile to me, they made no particular effort to be friendly. They didn't speak to Wright or to me except in the line of duty, and we never tried to engage them in conversation. They seemed to have little reaction to us, one way or the other.

But the generosity and friendliness of one white teammate during those early days with Montreal stands out vividly. A young and talented player, Lou Rochelli, had been—until my arrival—the number-one candidate for second base. When I got the assignment, it would have been only human for him to resent it. And he had every right to assume that perhaps I had been assigned to second base instead of him because I was black and because Mr. Rickey had staked so much on my success. Lou was intelligent and he was a thoroughbred. He recognized that I had more experience with the left side of the infield than the right, and he spent considerable time helping me, giving me tips on technique. He taught me how to pivot on a double play. Working this pivot as a shortstop, I had been accustomed to maneuvering toward first. Now it was a matter of going away from first to get the throw, stepping on the bag, and then making the complete pivot for the throw to first. It's not an easy play to make especially when the runner coming down from first is trying to take you out of the play. Rochelli taught me the tricks, especially how to hurdle the runner. I learned readily, and from the beginning, my fielding was never in question. But my hitting record was terrible. This was obvious in practice games during that first spring training. After a good hard month of training, I had only two or three decisive hits.

Rae, Mr. Rickey, and Clyde Sukeforth were all great supporters during this period. Rae never missed watching a practice period, and Mr. Rickey became personally involved in helping me. He would stand by the base line and mumble instructions to me.

"Be more daring," he would say.

"Give it all you've got when you run. Gamble. Take a bigger lead."

While Mr. Rickey pushed me, Clyde showed his support and concern by massaging my morale and trying to get me to loosen up.

My supporters were helped by two glorious events that acted like tonic. The first was during the initial Dodgers-Royals game. On the eve of that game I experienced all kinds of mental torture. The grapevine had it that I would not be allowed to play; that the local authorities had been putting terrific pressure on Mr. Rickey. What I didn't know was that the shoe was on the other foot. The Dodger boss was the one exerting the pressure. He had done a fantastic job of persuading, bullying, lecturing, and pulling strings behind the scenes.

I had steeled myself for jeers and taunts and insulting outbursts. To my relief, when I walked out on that field, I heard nothing but a few weak and scattered boos. Holding down second, I felt a mighty surge of confidence and power. I picked up a smoking grounder that seemed certain to be a hit. Pivoting, I made an accurate throw, forcing the runner at second. My arm was in great shape and so were my legs. I had speed to spare.

That game seemed to be a turning point. The next few days in practice and intrasquad play, I began to show significant improvement. I was elated at the happiness my performance brought to Rachel and Mr. Rickey. I got my first base hit, and Rae was delighted. She had made some friends in the Agriculture Department at Bethune-Cookman College, which was close to where we lived. To celebrate, she got special permission from the Harrises to cook a victory dinner of chicken and fresh vegetables given her by her friends at Bethune. It was one of the few times she could cook for me in those days and I really enjoyed it. Our two newspaper friends, Wendell Smith and Billy Rowe of the Pittsburgh *Courier*, were our guests for dinner.

The second inspiring event occurred during the opening game of International League season in Jersey City. It was a major game and Clay Hopper had gambled on me by letting me hold down second base. Through the second inning, we kept the Jersey City team scoreless. My big moment came in our half of the third when with two men on base, I swung and connected. It felt so good I could tell it was a beauty. The ball flew 340 feet over the left field fence. I had delivered my first home run in organized baseball. Through all the cheering, my thoughts went to Rachel, and I knew she shared my joy. This was the day the dam burst between me and my teammates. Northerners and Southerners alike, they let me know how much they appreciated the way I had come through.

All these good and positive things generated a tremendous kind of power and drive inside of me. My next time at bat in the Jersey City game, I laid a bunt down the third base line. I beat it out for a hit. I got the sign to steal second, got a good jump on the pitcher, and made it with ease. When the game ended, I had four hits: a home run and three singles, and I had two stolen bases. I knew what it was that day to hear the ear-shattering roar of the crowd and know it was for me. I began to really believe one of Mr. Rickey's predictions. Color didn't matter to fans if the black man was winner.

My happiness about the three victorious games in Jersey City was soured when we got to Baltimore. There were two racist types sitting behind Rae. As soon as we emerged on the field, they began screaming all the typical phrases such as "nigger son of a bitch." Soon insults were coming from all over the stands. For me on the field it was not as bad as it was for Rae, forced to sit in the midst of the hostile spectators. It was almost impossible for her to keep her temper, but her dignity was more important to her than descending to the level of those ignorant bigots.

On the positive side Rae and I noticed in Florida and in cities like Jersey City that black fans were beginning to turn out in unprecedented numbers despite extremely adverse conditions. Fortunately, there were no racial incidents of consequence. In Southern cities, including Baltimore, segregated seating may have held down racial tension, but it was grossly unfair to blacks who had to take bleachers and outfield seats. But they turned out anyway. Their presence, their cheers, their pride, all came through to me and I knew they were counting on me to make it. It put a heavy burden of responsibility on me, but it was a glorious challenge. On the good days the cries of approval made me feel ten feet tall, but my mistakes, no matter how small, plunged me into deep depression. I guess black, as well as white, fans recognized this, and that is why they gave me that extra support I needed so badly. This was the first time the black fan market had been exploited, and the black turnout was making it clear that baseball could be made even more profitable if the game became integrated.

After Jersey City and Baltimore, the Royals moved to Montreal. It was a fantastic experience. One sportswriter later commented, "For Jackie Robinson and the city of Montreal, it was love at first sight." He was right. After the rejections, unpleasantness, and uncertainties, it was encouraging to find an atmosphere of complete acceptance and something approaching adulation. One of the reasons for the reception we received in Montreal was that people there were proud of the team that bore their city's name.

The people of Montreal were warm and wonderful to us. We rented a pretty apartment in the French-Canadian sector. Our neighbors and everyone we encountered were so attentive and kind to us that we had very little privacy. We were stared at on the street, but the stares were friendly. Kids trailed along behind us, an adoring retinue. To add to our happiness, Rachel shyly told me that very soon there were going to be three of us. There was only one sour note for me at that time. Johnny Wright, the black pitcher Mr. Rickey had signed on, was dropped from the club.

Although he never did anything overtly negative, I felt that Manager Clay Hopper had never really accepted me. He was careful to be courteous, but prejudice against the Negro was deeply ingrained in him. Much, much later in my career, after I had left the Montreal club, the depths of Hopper's bigotry were revealed to me. Very early during my first Montreal season, Mr. Rickey and Hopper had been standing together watching the team work out, when I made an unusually tricky play.

Mr. Rickey said to Hopper that the play I had just executed was "superhuman."

Hopper, astonished, asked Mr. Rickey, "Do you really think a nigger's a human being?" Mr. Rickey was furious, but he made a successful effort to restrain himself and he told me why.

"I saw that this Mississippi-born man was sincere, that he meant what he said; that his attitude of regarding the Negro as a subhuman was part of his heritage; that here was a man who had practically nursed race prejudice at his mother's breast," Mr. Rickey said. "So I decided to ignore the question."

That was one of the incidents I didn't know about, but there were others I was very well aware of because I was right in the center of them. By the time we arrived in Montreal, I had received a classic education in how it felt to be the object of bitter hatred.

Back in spring training I had had some particularly bad experiences. A game with the Jersey City Giants had been scheduled to take place in Jacksonville. But when game time came we were confronted with a padlocked ball park and told the game had been called off. The reason was obvious, and later I learned that my participation would have violated city ordinances.

In De Land, Florida, they announced that we couldn't play a game because the stadium lights weren't working. What this had to do with the fact that the game was to be played in the daytime, no one bothered to explain.

When the Royals came up against Indianapolis in Sanford, the game had begun and the crowd in the ball park had surprised us all by not registering any objection to my playing second base. In fact, the fans rewarded me with a burst of enthusiastic cheers when I slid home early in the game. I was feeling just fine about that until I got back to the dugout. Hopper came over to me and said Wright and I would have to be taken out of the game. He said a policeman had insisted he had to enforce the law that said interracial athletic competition was forbidden.

During the regular season similar incidents occurred over and over again. Surprisingly enough, it was during a game in Syracuse, New York, that I felt the most racial heat. The problem there wasn't from the fans as much as it was from the members of the Syracuse team. During the entire game they taunted me for being black. One of the Syracuse team threw a live, black cat out of the dugout, yelling loudly, "Hey, Jackie, there's your cousin."

The umpire had to call time until the frightened cat had been carried off the field. Following this incident, I doubled down the left field line, and when the next player singled to center, I scored. Passing the Syracuse dugout, I shouted, "I guess my cousin's pretty happy now."

The toll that incidents like these took was greater than I realized. I was overestimating my stamina and underestimating the beating I was taking. I couldn't sleep and often I couldn't eat. Rachel was worried, and we sought the advice of a doctor who was afraid I was going to have a nervous breakdown. He advised me to take a brief rest.

Doctor's orders or not, I just couldn't keep my mind off baseball. Winning the pennant was not a problem. It was virtually in the bag. But the trouble was that if I won the batting crown, people could say afterward that I had stayed out to protect my average. I just had to go back. The rest lasted exactly one day.

At the end of that first season, I did emerge as the league's top batter, and when we returned to play Baltimore again, there were no more taunts and epithets. Instead, I got a big standing ovation after I stole home in one of the games.

Our team won the pennant. They also won the International League play-offs that were held every year among the top four minor league teams. The Louisville Colonels won top honors in their league, the American Association. After that the Royals and Louisville would play off in the crucial little world series. The three games held in Louisville were vital baseball-wise and extremely significant racially. Louisville turned out to be the most critical test of my ability to handle abuse. In a quiet but firm way Louisville was as rigidly segregationist as any city in the Deep South. The tension was terrible, and I was greeted with some of the worst vituperation I had yet experienced. The Louisville club owners had moved to meet anticipated racial trouble by setting a black attendance quota. Many more than the prescribed number of blacks wanted to come to the game since it would be the first instance of interracial competition in baseball in the city's history. As white fans surged through the turnstiles unhampered, numbers of blacks, some of whom had come long distances, were standing outside the gates, unable to gain admittance.

I had been in a deep funk for a few days before the game. Although I didn't expect the atmosphere to be nearly as bad as it turned out to be, I knew that bad trouble lay ahead. To make matters worse I had descended into one of those deadly slumps which are the despair of any player who has ever been afflicted by them. I was playing terrible ball in Louisville. In all three games I managed one hit out of eleven tries. The worse I played, the more vicious that howling mob in the stands became. I had been booed pretty soundly before, but nothing like this. A torrent of mass hatred burst from the stands with virtually every move I made.

"Hey, black boy, go on back to Canada—and stay," a fan yelled.

"Yeah," another one screamed, "and take all your nigger-loving friends with you."

I couldn't hit my stride. With a sick heart, damp hands, a sweaty brow, and nerves on edge, I saw my team go down to defeat in two of the three games. To make up for this, we would have to win three out of the four final games to be played in Montreal. When we arrived in that city, we discovered that the Canadians were up in arms over the way I had been treated. Greeting us warmly, they let us know how they felt. They displayed their resentment against Louisville and their loyalty to us on the first day of our return to play the final games by letting loose an avalanche of boos against the Louisville players the minute they came on the field. All through that first game, they booed every time a Louisville player came out of the dugout. It was difficult to be sure how I felt. I didn't approve of this kind of retaliation, but I felt a jubilant sense of gratitude for the way the Canadians expressed their feelings. When fans go to bat for you like that, you feel it would be easy to play for them forever.

I guess the rest of the team felt that way, too. At any rate, we played as if we did. When we came on the field, our loyal Canadians did everything but break the stands down. Louisville showed some spunk as the game opened, jumping to a 2-0 lead in the first inning and going ahead 4-0 by the fifth. After that, the game changed. The confidence and love of those fans acted like a tonic to our team. In a classically hard-fought game, we won the game and tied up the series. We ended up winning three straight to win the championship. My slump had disappeared, and I finished the series hitting .400 and scoring the winning run in the final game.

I was thrilled but I was also in a hurry. I had a reservation on a plane to Detroit to take off on a barnstorming tour. The tour, starting in Detroit, was to last a month. I rushed through the happy Montreal crowds swarming over the field, got into the clubhouse, but before I could shower and dress, an usher came in to tell me the fans were still waiting to tell me good-bye. He neglected to mention that there were thousands of them. They grabbed me, they slapped my back. They hugged me. Women kissed me. Kids grinned and crowded around me. Men took me, along with Curt Davis and Clay Hopper, on their shoulders and went around the field, singing and shouting. I finally broke away, showered and dressed, and came out to find thousands still waiting. I managed to plunge through the crowd and was picked up by a private car as I ran down the street. A sportswriter, Sam Martin, described that scene succinctly. He wrote, "It was probably the only day in history that a black man ran from a white mob with love instead of lynching on its mind."

On the plane to Detroit, I had a lot to think about, most of it wonderful. One incident that occurred at the clubhouse during the beautiful madness after the game stood out. Clay Hopper was making last-minute preparations to return to his Mississippi plantation. The Montreal manager came up to me and held his hand out.

"You're a great ballplayer and a fine gentleman," he said, "It's been wonderful having you on the team."

Chapter IV

The Major Leagues

Jackie Robinson, Jr., was born in November, 1946. If there is anything to the theory that the influences affecting expectant parents have important impact on the developing child, our baby son was predestined to lead a very complicated and complex life.

Rachel had had problems during her pregnancy that I was not aware of. She accepted them with uncomplaining courage because of her conviction that, since I had a job to do in baseball that was demanding and difficult, I should be as free as possible to deal with it without the further complications of family worries. She was determined, therefore, that, while she shared my problems with me, she would keep me from knowing about her own fears and anxieties. She did a good job of keeping her problems to herself. It wasn't until after Jackie was born that I learned that Rae had occasionally experienced fevers seemingly unconnected with the normal process of pregnancy. Her temperature would rise to 103 and 104 degrees and she would take sulfa drugs and aspirin to bring her fever down. She had insisted on traveling with me during the first season with Montreal because she knew I needed her.

Often I would come home tired, discouraged, wondering if I could go on enduring the verbal abuse and even the physical provocations and continue to "turn the other cheek." Rachel knew exactly how I felt, and she would have the right words, the perfect way of comforting me. Rachel's understanding love was a powerful antidote for the poison of being taunted by fans, sneered at by fellow-players, and constantly mistreated because of my blackness.

In the eighth month of her pregnancy, I insisted that Rachel go home to Los Angeles to have the baby. Two weeks after she returned to her mother's home, I was able to get back to Los Angeles and be there the night she went into labor. When the time came, I got her to the hospital fast and our boy was born with unusual speed. We'll never forget that day—November 18, 1946.

The big question, as spring training for the 1947 season became imminent, was whether Branch Rickey would move me out of the minor league and up to the Brooklyn Dodgers. Because of my successful first season with Montreal, it was a question being asked in sportswriting and baseball circles. Even those who were dead set against a black man coming into the majors knew there was a strong possibility that Mr. Rickey would take the big step.

Mr. Rickey had to move cautiously and with skill and strategy. Rae and I never doubted that Mr. Rickey would carry out his intention, but we lived in suspense wondering when. In the latter part of January I was ordered to report back to the Montreal Royals for spring training in Cuba. I would not be able to afford to take Rachel and the baby with me. I had to go it alone.

Although we could not understand Mr. Rickey's reasons for the delay in bringing me up to the Dodgers, we believed he was working things out the best way possible. We thought it was a hopeful sign that both the Dodgers and the Royals would be training in Havana. It could be reasonably expected that the racist atmosphere I had had to face in Florida and other parts of the United States would not exist in another country of non-whites. The Royals now had three more black players—Roy Campanella, a catcher; Don Newcombe and Roy Partlow, both pitchers. I learned, on arriving in Havana, that we black players would be housed in separate quarters at a hotel fifteen miles away from the practice field. The rest of the team was living at a military academy, and the Dodgers were headquartered at the beautiful Nacional Hotel. I expressed my resentment that the Cuban authorities would subject us to the same kind of segregation I had faced in Florida and was promptly informed that living arrangements had not been made by local authorities but by Mr. Rickey. I was told that he felt his plans for us were on the threshold of success and he didn't want a possible racial incident to jeopardize his program. I reluctantly accepted the explanation.

I was told I must learn to play first base. This disturbed me because I felt it might mean a delay in reaching the majors. However, it was felt that the Dodgers, in order to become contenders for the pennant, had to strengthen the first base position.

The fact that I had been assigned to first base aroused fear in the Dodger camp. They sensed that Mr. Rickey was planning to bring me up to the Dodgers. Some of the players got together and decided to sign a petition declaring they would not play with me on the team. Ironically, the leak about the planned revolt came from a Southerner, Kirby Higbe, of South Carolina. Higbe had a few too many beers one night, and he began feeling uncomfortable about the conspiracy. He revealed the plot to one of Mr. Rickey's aides and Mr. Rickey put down the rebellion with steamroller effectiveness. He said later, "I have always believed that a little show of force at the right time is necessary when there's a deliberate violation of law. . . . I believe that when a man is involved in an overt act of violence or in destruction of someone's rights, that it's no time to conduct an experiment in education or persuasion."

He found out who the ringleaders were—Hugh Casey, a good relief pitcher from Georgia; Southerner Bobby Bragan, a respected catcher; Dixie Walker of Alabama; and Carl Furrillo. Walker had deliberately taken a trip so he wouldn't appear to be in on the scheme. The ringleaders were called in individually, and Mr. Rickey told each one that petitions would make no difference. He said he would carry out his plan, regardless of protest. Anyone who was not willing to have a black teammate could quit. The petition protest collapsed before it got started.

Mr. Rickey was very direct with me during those early 1947 spring training days. He told me I couldn't rest on the victories I'd had with Montreal. I should, in fact, forget them as much as possible. My league record meant nothing. The true test would be making the grade on the field against major league pitching.

"I want you to be a whirling demon against the Dodgers," he said. "I want you to concentrate, to hit that ball, to get on base *by any means necessary*. I want you to run wild, to steal the pants off them, to be the most conspicuous player on the field—but conspicuous only because of the kind of baseball you're playing. Not only will you impress the Dodger players, but the stories that the newspapermen send back to the Brooklyn and New York newspapers will help create demand on the part of the fans that you be brought up to the majors."

With this kind of marching order, I simply had to give my best. I batted .625 and stole seven bases during seven Royals-Dodgers games. Not even this made the Brooklyn players ask for me as Mr. Rickey had hoped. He had wanted, when promoting me, to appear to be giving in to tremendous pressure from my teammates-to-be.

When this strategy failed, Mr. Rickey, a resourceful man, arranged to have Manager Leo Durocher tell the sportswriters that his Brooklyn team could win the pennant with a good man on first base and that I was the best prospect. Leo would add he was going to try to convince Mr. Rickey to sign me.

That plan failed, too, because on April 9 before it could be carried out, Baseball Commissioner Chandler suspended Durocher for a year "for conduct detrimental to baseball." Durocher and the commissioner's office had been in conflict for some time. The commissioner's office had challenged Leo's "questionable associations" off the playing field. Durocher had hit back by noting that some very well-known gangsters had been seen near the Yankee dugout during a Dodger-Yankee game. He said no one had done anything about that. This sparked an exchange between the commissioner's office, Durocher, Mr. Rickey, and Yankee President Larry Mac-Phail. It had been common belief that the storm had blown over. Ironically, on the same April morning that Mr. Rickey hoped to make his move, Durocher was suspended.

Quickly, Mr. Rickey saw that signing the first black in the major leagues would virtually wipe the Durocher story, a negative one, off the front pages. His action would cause controversy, but he believed it would be like a shot in the arm to the club. On the morning of April 9, 1947, just before an exhibition game, reporters in the press box received a single sheet of paper with a one-line announcement. It read: "Brooklyn announces the purchase of the contract of Jack Roosevelt Robinson from Montreal. Signed, Branch Rickey."

That morning turned into a press Donnybrook. The sportswriters snatched up telephones. The telegraph wires relayed the message to the sports world.

Less than a week after I became Number 42 on the Brooklyn club, I played my first game with the team. I did a miserable job. There was an overflow crowd at Ebbets Field. If they expected any miracles out of Robinson, they were sadly disappointed. I was in another slump. I grounded out to the third baseman, flied out to left field, bounced into a double play, was safe on an error, and, later, was removed as a defensive safeguard. The next four games reflected my deep slump. I went to plate twenty times without one base hit. Burt Shotton, a man I respected and liked, had replaced Durocher as manager. As my slump deepened, I appreciated Shotton's patience and understanding. I knew the pressure was on him to take me out of the lineup. People began recalling Bob Feller's analysis of me. I was "good field, no hit." There were others who doubted that I could field and some who hoped I would flunk out and thus establish that blacks weren't ready for the majors. Shotton, however, continued to encourage me.

Early in the season, the Philadelphia Phillies came to Ebbets Field for a three-game series. I was still in my slump and events of the opening game certainly didn't help. Starting to the plate in the first inning, I could scarcely believe my ears. Almost as if it had been synchronized by some master conductor, hate poured forth from the Phillies dugout.

"Hey, nigger, why don't you go back to the cotton field where you belong?"

"They're waiting for you in the jungles, black boy!"

"Hey, snowflake, which one of those white boys' wives are you dating tonight?"

"We don't want you here, nigger."

"Go back to the bushes!"

Those insults and taunts were only samples of the torrent of abuse which poured out from the Phillies dugout that April day.

I have to admit that this day of all the unpleasant days in my life, brought me nearer to cracking up than I ever had been. Perhaps I should have become inured to this kind of garbage, but I was in New York City and unprepared to face the kind of barbarism from a northern team that I had come to associate with the Deep South. The abuse coming out of the Phillies dugout was being directed by the team's manager, Ben Chapman, a Southerner. I felt tortured and I tried just to play ball and ignore the insults. But it was really getting to me. What did the Phillies want from me? What, indeed, did Mr. Rickey expect of me? I was, after all, a human being. What was I doing here turning the other cheek as though I weren't a man? In college days I had had a reputation as a black man who never tolerated affronts to his dignity. I had defied prejudice in the Army. How could I have thought that barriers would fall, that, indeed, my talent could triumph over bigotry?

For one wild and rage-crazed minute I thought, "To hell with Mr. Rickey's 'noble experiment.' It's clear it won't succeed. I have made every effort to work hard, to get myself into shape. My best is not enough for them." I thought what a glorious, cleansing thing it would be to let go. To hell with the image of the patient black freak I was supposed to create. I could throw down my bat, stride over to that Phillies dugout, grab one of those white sons of bitches and smash his teeth in with my despised black fist. Then I could walk away from it all. I'd never become a sports star. But my son could tell his son someday what his daddy could have been if he hadn't been too much of a man.

Then, I thought of Mr. Rickey—how his family and friends had begged him not to fight for me and my people. I thought of all his predictions, which had come true. Mr. Rickey had come to a crossroads and made a lonely decision. I was at a crossroads. I would make mine. I would stay.

The haters had almost won that round. They had succeeded in getting me so upset that I was an easy out. As the game progressed, the Phillies continued with the abuse.

After seven scoreless innings, we got the Phillies out in the eighth, and it was our turn at bat. I led off. The insults were still coming. I let the first pitch go by for a ball. I lined the next one into center field for a single. Gene Hermanski came up to hit and I took my lead.

The Phillies pitcher, a knuckle expert, let fly. I cut out for second. The throw was wide. It bounced past the shortstop. As I came into third, Hermanski singled me home. That was the game.

Apparently frustrated by our victory, the Phillies players kept the heat on me during the next two days. They even enlarged their name-calling to include the rest of the Brooklyn team.

"Hey, you carpetbaggers, how's your little reconstruction period getting along?"

That was a typical taunt. By the third day of our confrontation with these emissaries from the City of Brotherly Love, they had become so outrageous that Ed Stanky exploded. He started yelling at the Phillies.

"Listen, you yellow-bellied cowards," he cried out, "why don't you yell at somebody who can answer back?" It was then that I began to feel better. I remembered Mr. Rickey's prediction. If I won the respect of the team and got them solidly behind me, there would be no question about the success of the experiment.

Stanky wasn't the only Brooklyn player who was angry with the Phillies team. Some of my other teammates told the press about the way Chapman and his players had behaved. Sports columnists around the country criticized Chapman. Dan Parker, sports editor of the New York *Daily Mirror*, reported:

> Ben Chapman, who during his career with the Yankees was frequently involved in unpleasant incidents with fans who charged him with shouting anti-Semitic remarks at them from the ball field, seems to be up to his old trick of stirring up racial trouble. During the recent series between the Phils and the Dodgers, Chapman and three of his players poured a stream of abuse at Jackie Robinson. Jackie, with admirable restraint, ignored the guttersnipe language coming from the Phils dugout, thus stamping himself as the only gentleman among those involved in the incident.

The black press did a real job of letting its readers know about the race baiting which had taken place. The publicity in the press built so much anti-Chapman public feeling that the Philadelphia club decided steps must be taken to counteract it. Chapman met with representatives of the black press to try to explain his behavior. The Phillies public relations people insisted, as Ben Chapman did, that he was not anti-Negro. Chapman himself used an interesting line of defense in speaking with black reporters. Didn't they want me to become a big-time big leaguer? Well, so did he and his players. When they played exhibitions with the Yanks, they razzed DiMaggio as "the Wop," Chapman explained. When they came up against the Cards, Whitey Kurowski was called "the Polack." Riding opposition players was the Phils' style of baseball. The Phils could give it out and they could take it. Was I a weakling who couldn't take it? Well, if I wasn't a weakling, then I shouldn't expect special treatment. After all, Chapman said, all is forgotten after a ball game ends.

The press, black and white, didn't buy that argument. They said so. Commissioner Happy Chandler wasn't having any either. His office warned the Phils to keep racial baiting out of the dugout bench jockeying.

A fascinating development of the nastiness with the Phils was the attitude of Mr. Rickey and the reaction of my Brooklyn teammates. Mr. Rickey knew, better than most people, that Chapman's racial prejudice was deeper than he admitted. Bob Carpenter, the Phils' president, had phoned Rickey before game time to try to persuade him not to include me in the lineup. If I played, Carpenter threatened, his team would refuse to play. Mr. Rickey's response was that this would be fine with him. The Dodgers would then take all three games by default. The Dodgers' president wasn't angry with Chapman or his players. As a matter of fact, in later years, Mr. Rickey commented, "Chapman did more than anybody to unite the Dodgers. When he poured out that string of unconscionable abuse, he solidified and unified thirty men, not one of whom was willing to sit by and see someone kick around a man who had his hands tied behind his back—Chapman made Jackie a real member of the Dodgers."

Privately, at the time, I thought Mr. Rickey was carrying his "gratitude" to Chapman a little too far when he asked me to appear in public with Chapman. The Phillies manager was genuinely in trouble as a result of all the publicity on the racial razzing. Mr. Rickey thought it would be gracious and generous if I posed for a picture shaking hands with Chapman. The idea was also promoted by the baseball commissioner. I was somewhat sold—but not altogether—on the concept that a display of such harmony would be "good for the game." I have to admit, though, that having my picture taken with this man was one of the most difficult things I had to make myself do.

There were times, after I had bowed to humiliations like shaking hands with Chapman, when deep depression and speculation as to whether it was all worthwhile would seize me. Often, when I was in this kind of mood, something positive would happen to give me new strength. Sometimes the positive development would come in response to a negative one. This was exactly what happened when a clever sports editor exposed a plot that was brewing among the St. Louis Cardinals. The plan was set to be executed on May 9, 1947, when Brooklyn was to visit St. Louis for the first game of the season between the two clubs. The Cards were planning to pull a last-minute protest strike against my playing in the game. If successful, the plan could have had a chain reaction throughout the baseball world—with other players agreeing to unite in a strong bid to keep baseball white. Stanley Woodward, sports editor of the New York *Herald Tribune,* had learned of the plot and printed an exclusive scoop exposing it. Ford Frick reacted immediately and notified the Cardinal players in no uncertain terms that they would not be permitted to get away with a strike.

"If you do this you will be suspended from the league," Frick warned. "You will find that the friends you think you have in the press box will not support you, that you will be outcasts. I do not care if half the league strikes. Those who do it will encounter quick retribution. They will be suspended and I don't care if it wrecks the National League for five years. This is the United States of America, and one citizen has as much right to play as another.

"The National League," Frick continued, "will go down the

line with Robinson whatever the consequence. You will find if you go through with your intention that you have been guilty of complete madness."

The hot light of publicity about the plot and the forthright hard line that Frick laid down to the plotters helped to avert what could have been a disaster for integration of baseball. Many writers and baseball personalities credited Woodward with significant service to baseball and to sportsmanship.

While some positive things were happening, there were others that were negative. Hate mail arrived daily, but it didn't bother me nearly as much as the threat mail. The threat mail included orders to me to get out of the game or be killed, threats to assault Rachel, to kidnap Jackie, Jr. Although none of the threats materialized, I was quite alarmed. Mr. Rickey, early in May, decided to turn some of the letters over to the police.

That same spring the Benjamin Franklin Hotel in Philadelphia, where my teammates were quartered, refused to accommodate me. The Phillies heckled me a second time, mixing up race baiting with childish remarks and gestures that coincided with the threats that had been made. Some of those grown men sat in the dugout and pointed bats at me and made machine-gunlike noises. It was an incredibly childish display of bad will.

I was helped over these crises by the courage and decency of a teammate who could easily have been my enemy rather than my friend. Pee Wee Reese, the successful Dodger shortstop, was one of the most highly respected players in the major leagues. When I first joined the club, I was aware that there might well be a real reluctance on Reese's part to accept me as a teammate. He was from Ekron, Kentucky. Furthermore, it had been rumored that I might take over Reese's position on the team. Mischief-makers seeking to create trouble between us had tried to agitate Reese into regarding me as a threat—a black one at that. But Reese, from the time I joined Brooklyn, had demonstrated a totally fair attitude.

Reese told a sportswriter, some months after I became a Dodger, "When I first met Robinson in spring training, I figured, well, let me give this guy a chance. It may be he's just as good as I am. Frankly, I don't think I'd stand up under the kind of thing he's been subjected to as well as he has."

Reese's tolerant attitude of witholding judgment to see if I would make it was translated into positive support soon after we became teammates. In Boston during a period when the heckling pressure seemed unbearable, some of the Boston players began to heckle Reese. They were riding him about being a Southerner and playing ball with a black man. Pee Wee didn't answer them. Without a glance in their direction, he left his position and walked over to me. He put his hand on my shoulder and began talking to me. His words weren't important. I don't even remember what he said. It was the gesture of comradeship and support that counted. As he stood talking with me with a friendly arm around my shoulder, he was saying loud and clear, "Yell. Heckle. Do anything you want. We came here to play baseball."

The jeering stopped, and a close and lasting friendship began between Reese and me. We were able, not only to help each other and our team in private as well as public situations, but to talk about racial prejudices and misunderstanding.

At the same time Mr. Rickey told me that when my teammates began to rally to my cause, we could consider the battle half won; he had also said that one of my roughest burdens would be the experience of being lonely in the midst of a group—my teammates. They would be my teammates on the field. But back in the locker rooms, I would know the strain and pressure of being a stranger in a crowd of guys who were friendly among themselves but uncertain about how to treat me. Some of them would resent me but would cover the resentment with aloofness or just a minimum amount of courtesy. Others genuinely wouldn't know how to be friendly with me. Some would even feel I preferred to be off in a corner and left out. After the games were over, my teammates had normal social lives with their wives, their girls, and each other. When I traveled, during those early days, unless Wendell Smith or some other black sportswriter happened to be going along, I sat by myself while the other guys chatted and laughed and played cards. I remember vividly a rare occasion when I was invited to join a poker game. One of the participants was a Georgia guy, Hugh Casey, the relief pitcher. Casey's luck wasn't too good during the game, and at one point he addressed a remark directly to me that caused a horrified silence.

"You know what I used to do down in Georgia when I ran into bad luck?" he said. "I used to go out and find me the biggest, blackest nigger woman I could find and rub her teats to change my luck."

I don't believe there was a man in that game, including me, who thought that I could take that. I had to force back my anger. I had the memory of Mr. Rickey's words about looking for a man "with guts enough not to fight back." Finally, I made myself turn to the dealer and told him to deal the cards.

Traveling had its problems but being at home with Rachel and little Jackie was great even if our living conditions left something to be desired. If we had been living away from our home base, the club would have found some type of separate living arrangement for us. But in the excitement of converting me into a Dodger, no one seemed to have given a thought to our accommodations. We were living—three of us—in one room in the McAlpin Hotel in midtown Manhattan. It was miserable for Rae. In that one room that seemed constantly overrun with newsmen, she had to fix the baby's formula, change his diapers, bathe him, and do all the things mothers do for small babies. We had no relatives in New York and no one to turn to for babysitting. Rae brought our son out to the ball park for the first game I played with the Dodgers. She was determined not to miss that game. Never having lived in the East, she brought little Jackie dressed in a coat which, in

California, would have been a winter coat. He would not have been able to stand the cold, dressed as he was, if Roy Campanella's mother-in-law hadn't kept him with her under her fur coat. Rae warmed bottles at a hot dog stand. At four and a half months, Jackie began what was to be the story of his young life—growing up in the ball park. He came to many games with his mother, and when he was old enough, he became very popular with some of the Dodger players who would keep him on their laps and play with him.

Before the season ended, we did manage to escape from the hotel. We found a place in Brooklyn where there was a small sleeping room for little Jackie, a bedroom, and use of a kitchen for us. We had no place to entertain the few friends we were making, but it certainly beat living in the hotel and we were grateful.

We were glad, too, that we could see some tangible results from our sacrifices. Not only were the other black players on the Dodger team winning acceptance, but other teams started to follow Mr. Rickey's example. Larry Doby became the first black player in the American League, signing on with the Cleveland Indians, and Willard Brown and Henry Thompson had been hired by the St. Louis Browns.

The Dodgers won the pennant that year, and when our club came home in September from a swing across the West, we were joyfully received by our fans. Their enthusiasm for me was so great that I once went into a phone booth to call Rae and was trapped in that phone booth by admirers who let up only when policemen arrived on the scene to liberate me.

Getting a hero's welcome in September made me remember how bad the beginning of my first season with the Dodgers had been. At that time I still wasn't looking like any kind of winner, even though the increasing acceptance of my teammates had begun to help me out of a terrible slump. I seriously wondered if I could ever make the Rickey experiment a success. Both Manager Burt Shotton and Mr.

Rickey believed I would eventually come through. Clyde Sukeforth with his quiet confidence helped as much as anybody else.

During the season I was under even greater pressure than in my Montreal days. It was there that I had earned a reputation for stealing bases, and the pressure eased when I began stealing them again. Late in June, in a night game at Pittsburgh, with the score tied 2-2 I kept a careful eye on pitcher Fitz Ostermueller. I noticed he had become a little careless and relaxed. I began dancing off third base. Ostermueller paid me the insult of winding up, ignoring my movements as antics. The pitch was a ball. Easing open my lead off third, I made a bold dash for home plate and slid in safe. That put us in the lead 3-2. It was the winning run of the game. As I ran I heard the exhilarating noise that is the best reward a player can get. The roar of the crowd.

After I made that comeback, I think Mr. Rickey was as happy as I was. He said to some friends at the time, "Wait! You haven't seen Robinson in action yet—not really. You may not have seen him at his best this year at all, or even next year. He's still in his shell. When he comes out for good, he'll be compared to Ty Cobb."

Mr. Rickey's words meant a great deal to me but not as much as something he did. Howie Schultz, the player who had been mentioned as a possible replacement for me during the bad days of my slump, was sold by the club.

That 1947 season was memorable in many ways. Some of the incidents that occurred resulted in far-reaching changes for the club. In late August we played the St. Louis Cardinals. In one of the last games, Enos Slaughter, a Cards outfielder, hit a ground ball. As I took the throw at first from the infielder, Slaughter deliberately went for my leg instead of the base and spiked me rather severely.

It was an act that unified the Dodger team. Teammates such as Hugh Casey of the poker game incident came charging out on the field to protest. The team had always been close to first place in the pennant race, but the spirit shown after the Slaughter incident strengthened our resolve and made us go on to win the pennant. The next time we played the Cards, we won two of the three games.

I had started the season as a lonely man, often feeling like a black Don Quixote tilting at a lot of white windmills. I ended it feeling like a member of a solid team. The Dodgers were a championship team because all of us had learned something. I had learned how to exercise self-control—to answer insults, violence, and injustice with silence—and I had learned how to earn the respect of my teammates. They had learned that it's not skin color but talent and ability that counts. Maybe even the bigots had learned that, too.

The press had also changed. When I came up to the majors, the influential *Sporting News* had declared that a black man would find it almost impossible to succeed in organized baseball. At the end of the season, when they selected me as Rookie of the Year, that same publication said:

> That Jackie Roosevelt Robinson might have had more obstacles than his first year competitors, and that he perhaps had a harder fight to gain even major league recognition, was no concern of this publication. The sociological experiment that Robinson represented, the trail-blazing that he did, the barriers he broke down, did not enter into the decision. He was rated and examined solely as a freshman player in the big leagues—on the basis of his hitting, his running, his defensive play, his team value.
>
> Dixie Walker summed it up in a few words the other day when he said: "No other ballplayer on this club with the possible exception of Bruce Edwards has done more to put the Dodgers up in the race than Robinson has. He is everything Branch Rickey said he was when he came up from Montreal."

Rachel and I moved again. She had managed to find more satisfactory living quarters in Brooklyn, where we had our own kitchen and living room and even a guest bedroom. I was delighted when I learned that the man I had admired so much as a youngster, the Reverend Karl Downs, wanted to visit us. I had kept in touch with Karl over the years. Before I'd gone into service, he had left Pasadena to become president of Sam Houston State College in Texas. When I left UCLA, I heard from Karl who said he was on the spot. He needed a coach for his basketball team. There was very little money involved, but I knew that Karl would have done anything for me, so I couldn't turn him down. I went to Texas and took the job but could only stay for a few months before financial pressures caught up with me. When Rachel and I were married, Karl, insisting on paying his own expenses, had set aside all his duties in Texas to fly to Los Angeles and officiate at our wedding. I was delighted by the prospect of his visit to Brooklyn.

One day, during his visit, Karl had come out to see one of the games. Suddenly he felt sick and decided to go back home to rest and wait for us. I had no idea his sickness was serious. That evening when I reached home, Rachel had taken him to the hospital. Several days later, apparently recovered, Karl had returned to Texas. In a few days, he was dead.

Karl's death, in itself, was hard enough to take. But when we learned the circumstances, Rae and I experienced the bitter feeling that Karl Downs had died a victim of racism. We are convinced that Karl Downs would not have died at that time if he had remained in Brooklyn for the operation he required.

When he returned to Texas, Karl went to a segregated hospital to be operated on. As he was being wheeled back from the recovery room, complications set in. Rather than returning his black patient to the operating room or to a recovery room to be closely watched, the doctor in charge let him go to the segregated ward where he died. We believe Karl would not have died if he had received proper care, and there are a number of whites who evidently shared this belief. After

Karl's death the doctor who performed the operation was put under such pressure that he was forced to leave town.

Karl Downs ranked with Roy Wilkins, Whitney Young, and Dr. Martin Luther King, Jr., in ability and dedication, and had he lived he would have developed into one of the front line leaders on the national scene. He was able to communicate with people of all colors because he was endowed with the ability to inspire confidence. It was hard to believe that God had taken the life of a man with such a promising future.

I especially missed Karl at the opening day of the 1947 world series. Seventy-five thousand fans, many of whom were black, turned out for that first series game. During the game, the fans were very kind to me, and there was an avalanche of crowd approval in the first inning as I drew a base on balls from Frank Shea and stole second. Pete Reiser hit a ground ball to shortstop and I tried for third, but I was caught in the run down. Fortunately my stops and starts gave Reiser a chance to reach second and, from that position, to score the first run of the game. In that series, our team was the underdog. We were up against that spectacular New York Yankees team that included some of the greats in baseball: Joe DiMaggio, Tommy Henrich, Yogi Berra, Johnny Lindell, Phil Rizzuto, and George McQuinn. We fought hard, but the Yankees were a great baseball club. Even though we lost we still felt we had acquitted ourselves well.

During the winter I went on a speaking tour of the South. It was a successful tour except for the fact that almost every night we were treated to some of the best Southern cooking available in private homes. We ate like pigs, and for me it was disastrous.

Chapter V

"Just Another Guy"

When I reported for spring training in the Dominican Republic in 1948, I was twenty-five pounds over playing weight. Leo Durocher was manager and Leo has always been long on sarcasm. He had every right to be angry, and he wasn't going to resist making cracks about my weight whenever they occurred to him. He made several in the presence of newsmen who gleefully reported that my overeating was eating Durocher. In fact, the press had a field day with my excess poundage and Leo's remarks. I couldn't blame them.

To get me in shape, Leo put me through some furious physical paces. They were humiliating because rookies, reporters, and teammates were all onlookers. Leo also kept after me verbally, and as the world knows, he is a magnificent tongue-lasher. At the time I thought he was being excessive, but later I realized he was only doing what was necessary, and even though his comments hurt, I could not forget that Durocher had done all he could the previous year to help ease my way into the majors.

Mr. Rickey had booked several exhibition games in the Southwest and Deep South during spring training and the turnout at these games established new attendance records. In Fort Worth, Texas, close to 16,000 fans came out to one Sunday game. In Dallas, it was 12,000, and half of the fans were black. This was proof that Southerners were accepting black players, and that black fans in large numbers would attend integrated games, not only in the North, but all around the country.

I wasn't hitting, and, in fact, the whole season started badly for the Dodgers. The experience of being out of shape was a sobering one. After that I vowed it would never happen again. Almost any athlete who has had the same experience knows how grim it can be.

As late as the middle of the season we were still struggling. I wasn't hitting. However, Leo's urging and my response to it had just begun to tell. I was starting to hit again when Leo left us and took over our long-time enemies, the Giants. Burt Shotton came back as manager just at the time my weight had come under control and I got back into stride. The effort and determination I had put into whipping myself into shape while Leo was still with us had paid off, but the seemingly sudden transition the minute Burt Shotton reappeared made Leo madder than ever. I think that Leo felt I had not given him my best effort and was working harder for Shotton. That wasn't true, but on the playing field Leo and I got into a number of hassles that were picked up by the press. Leo and I were alike in many ways, and that could have been part of our problem. But no matter how many verbal insults we exchanged, I believe we never lost the respect we had for each other's abilities.

At the time Leo left in July, Rachel, Jackie, and I moved into half of a very pleasant duplex in the Flatbush section of Brooklyn. Although we were much more at ease here, we soon learned that when our black landlady rented us part of her place, she had been in trouble herself. There had been a petition by the predominantly Jewish neighbors to try to keep her from occupying the house.

Rachel and I are both proud. It wouldn't occur to us to run after people who might be unreceptive to us. Therefore we largely ignored the neighbors. Jackie, however, with the innocent purity of a child, was sometimes the cause of breaking the ice between us and our hostile neighbors. He would disappear into one of their backyards, knock on a door, ask for a cookie. Rae or I would go looking for our wandering son only to find that Jackie had enchanted another white person out of his hang-up about their black neighbors.

There was one white youngster—a little guy of maybe nine—who was a big Jackie Robinson fan. Every day, when I came out of the house, he would be right there, staring at me. At first, this puzzled me, until I began to understand that he was just like a lot of other people—many much older than he. He just wanted some attention. Once I knew that he was not one of our hostile neighbors, I began to talk to him and cultivate his friendship. After a few days of this, I couldn't have had a better little buddy.

We had another neighbor, Mrs. Sarah Satlow, who lived two houses from us on Tilden Avenue in the Flatbush section of Brooklyn. Sarah was one of the whites on the block who had refused to sign the petition protesting our black landlady's presence. The Satlow family and the Robinson family became very close friends and still are today. Sarah had children also who loved little Jackie and played with him almost every day. One Christmas Eve Rachel and I were decorating the Christmas tree with Jackie doing his share. Sarah's children were at our house, and suddenly I was aware of how wistful they looked as they watched us hang ornaments and lights. It occurred to me that perhaps the Satlows couldn't afford to have a tree. I slipped out of the house and drove around the neighborhood until I found one of those Christmas Eve hucksters who still has trees left. I went home and split up half of the lights and decorations and delivered tree and trimmings to Sarah's house. She was flabbergasted, and I felt like a true Good Samaritan. I returned home, and then the thought came to me that maybe we should have volunteered to help the Satlows decorate their tree. I mentioned it to Rae and she immediately agreed to go over and see. When Rachel got to our friends' home, she was puzzled to find the whole family sitting around staring at the tree. They seemed fascinated, but they hadn't begun to set the tree up, or decorate it. After an uncomfortable silence, Sarah leveled with Rae. "Rachel," she said, "we have a problem. We appreciate your thoughtfulness but, you see, you and Jack must have forgotten that we don't celebrate Christmas exactly like you do—you know, being Jewish."

Rachel's eyes widened and then she realized how funny the situation was. So did all the Satlows, and everybody started laughing. The payoff was, however, that Sarah Satlow decided to throw caution to the winds.

"We're putting that tree up," she said. "If my mother and father come by to visit, they'll have a fit, but this is one Christmas this Jewish family is going to have a Christmas tree."

And they did.

During that unspectacular 1948 season there was one valuable development. Pee Wee Reese was at shortstop and I had been moved to second base. We worked together exceptionally well and developed into a magnificent double-play combination.

I had had a miserable start, but I ended the season batting .296 with twelve home runs and eighty-five runs batted in. I led the league in being hit with seven pitched balls (a dubious distinction) and in fielding average for a second baseman with a .983.

The most important thing that happened to me in 1948, as far as I am concerned, is that I got thrown out of a game for heckling an umpire. It happened in Pittsburgh. The umpire was Butch Henline. In the fourth Henline called a strike on Gene Hermanski. Along with other Dodgers on the bench, I gave Henline what we called the bench jockey treatment, booing and raucously protesting what we felt was a bad decision.

Henline gave us a warning to quit. I continued the heckling.

He whirled around, snatched off his mask, and pointed at me. "You! Robinson. Yer out of the game."

He didn't pick on me because I was black. He was treating me exactly as he would any ballplayer who got on his nerves. That made me feel great, even though I couldn't play anymore that day. One of the newspapers said it in the best headline I ever got: JACKIE JUST ANOTHER GUY.

I certainly could use it. Because the next season, in 1949, there were going to be some pretty rough headlines.

I thought I had learned the worst there was to learn about racial hatred in America. The year 1949 taught me more. A black man, even after he has proven himself on and off the playing field, will still be denied his rights. I am not talking about the things that happened to me in order to portray myself as some kind of martyr. I am recording them because I want to warn the white world that young blacks today are not willing—nor should they be—to endure the humiliations I did. I suffered them because I hoped to provide a better future for my children and for young black people everywhere, and because I naïvely believed that my sacrifices might help a little to make America the kind of country it was supposed to be. People have asked me, "Jack, what's your beef? You've got it made." I'm grateful for all the breaks and honors and opportunities I've had, but I always believe I won't have it made until the humblest black kid in the most remote backwoods of America has it made.

It is not terribly difficult for the black man as an individual to enter into the white man's world and be partially accepted. However, if that individual black man is, in the eyes of the white world, an "uppity nigger," he is in for a very hard time indeed. I can just hear my liberal white friends and a lot of Negroes who haven't yet got the word that they are black, protesting such an observation.

The late Malcolm X had a very interesting comment on the "progress" of the Negro. I disagreed with Malcolm vigorously in many areas during his earlier days, but I certainly agreed with him when he said, "Don't tell me about progress the black man has made. You don't stick a knife ten inches in my back, pull it out three or four, then tell me I'm making progress."

Malcolm, in a few well-chosen words, captured the essence of the way most blacks, I believe, think today. Virtually every time the black stands up like a man to make a protest or tell a truth as he sees it, white folks and some white-minded black folks try to hush or shame him by singing out that "You've come a long way" routine. They fail to say that we've still got a long way to go because of the unjust headstart the founding fathers of this country had on us and the handicaps they bestowed on the red men they robbed and the blacks they abducted and enslaved.

Whites are expert game-players in their contests to maintain absolute power. One of their time-honored gimmicks is to point to individual blacks who have achieved recognition: "But look at Ralph Bunche. Think about Lena Horne or Marian Anderson. Look at Jackie Robinson. They made it."

As one of those who has "made it," I would like to be thought of as an inspiration to our young. But I don't want them lied to. The late Dr. Ralph Bunche, a true black man of our time, felt the same way. The "system supporters" will point to the honors heaped on a Ralph Bunche. They will play down the fact that he and his son were barred from membership in the New York Tennis Club because of blackness. They will gloss over the historical truth that Mr. Bunche was once offered a high post in the State Department and did not accept because it would have meant Jim Crow schools for his children. Look at Lena Horne, they say. The show business world took this lovely woman and tried to make her into a sepia Marilyn Monroe. They overlooked her dramatic ability and her other talents and insisted that she be cast only in the role of a cheap sexpot. When she refused they white-listed her out of the film colony. They point to her as a success symbol, but they will go easy on reminding you that she defied the United States Army when she was programmed to sing Jim Crow concerts for black troops and separate concerts for whites and German prisoners of war in a Southern installation. Lena sang for the black troops only.

If a black becomes too important or too big for his racial britches or if he has too much power, he will get cut down. They will cut him down even when the power the black has doesn't come from the white man, but from grass-roots black masses, as was the case of Harlem Congressman Adam Clayton Powell. With all his faults, Adam was a man who rocked the establishment boat, and the establishment lynched him politically for it. I don't think anyone in or out of sports could ever seriously accuse Willie Mays of offending white sensitivities. But when he was in California, whites refused to sell him a house in their community. They loved his talent, but they didn't want him for a neighbor.

Name them for me. The examples of blacks who "made it." For virtually every one you name, I can give you a sordid piece of factual information on how they have been mistreated, humiliated.

Not being able to fight back is a form of severe punishment. I was relieved when Mr. Rickey finally called me into his office and said, "Jackie, you're on your own now. You can be yourself now."

Chapter VI

My Own Man

All along, the Brooklyn Dodger president had been very sensitive to the inner pressures that had been bugging me. He knew that I believed in fierce competition and swift retaliation for mistreatment. Several years after he told me I was on my own, he explained his decison in these words.

"I realized the point would come when my almost filial relationship with Jackie would break with ill feeling if I did not issue an emancipation proclamation for him. I could see how the tensions had built up in two years and that this young man had come through with courage far beyond what I asked, yet, I knew that burning inside him was the same pride and determination that burned inside those Negro slaves a century earlier. I knew also that while the wisest policy for Robinson during those first two years was to turn the other cheek and not fight back, there were many in baseball who would not understand his lack of action. They could be made to respect only the fighting back, the things that are the signs of courage to men who know courage only in its physical sense. So I told Robinson that he was on his own. Then I sat back happily, knowing that, with the restraints removed, Robinson was going to show the National League a thing or two."

Very soon after my talk with Mr. Rickey, I learned that as long as I appeared to ignore insult and injury, I was a martyred hero to a lot of people who seemed to have sympathy for the underdog. But the minute I began to answer, to argue, to protest—the minute I began to sound off—I became a swellhead, a wise guy, an "uppity" nigger. When a white player did it, he had spirit. When a black player did it, he was "ungrateful," an upstart, a sorehead. It was hard to believe the prejudice I saw emerging among people who had seemed friendly toward me before I began to speak my mind. I became, in their minds and in their columns, a "pop-off," a "troublemaker," a "rabble-rouser." It was apparent that I was a fine guy until "Success went to his head," until I began to "change."

It is true that I had stored up a lot of hostility. I had been going home nights to Rachel and young Jackie, tense and irritable, keyed up because I hadn't been able to speak out when I wanted to. In 1949 I wouldn't have to do this. I could fight back when I wanted. That sounds as though I wanted to get even, and I'm sure that is partly true. I wouldn't have been human otherwise. But, more than revenge, I wanted to be Jackie Robinson, and for the first time I would be justified because by 1949 the *principle* had been established: the major victory won. There were enough blacks on other teams to ensure that American baseball could never again turn its back on minority competitors.

When I reported for spring training I was right on target, weightwise, in excellent condition, and my morale was high. On the first day a sportswriter who interviewed me, quoted me as saying, "They'd better be rough on me this year because I'm sure going to be rough on them."

Baseball Commissioner Happy Chandler had me on the carpet for that statement. I couldn't help wondering if he would have called up Ty Cobb, Frankie Frisch, or Pepper Martin—all white and all given to sounding off—for the same thing. I told the commissioner exactly how I felt and that, while I had no intention of creating problems, I was no longer going to turn my cheek to insults. Chandler completely understood my position, and that was the end of our interview.

During spring training it looked as though there would be definite racial trouble ahead. We were scheduled to play in Atlanta in April. The Atlanta newspapers announced that the Grand Dragon of the Klan had warned the Dodgers that Roy Campanella and I would not be allowed to play because interracial games were against the laws of the state. Dr. Samuel Green was the top Klansman and Earl Mann ran the Atlanta Crackers team. Green and his bedsheet brigade were assailed in the local press for indicating that, if black players came to Atlanta with the Dodgers, there would be bloody violence.

Mr. Rickey predicted that there would be an assault of enthusiasm instead of violence and that we would be threatened by hoards of autograph seekers rather than Klansmen. It was another Rickey prediction that was right on target. The autograph-seeking crowds after that first game were tremendous. Almost 50,000 turned out for each of the three games, and for the Sunday game there were about 14,000 black fans. I don't know whether that disheartened the Klan or not, but there was absolutely no trouble. In a number of other Southern cities that season, we didn't even encounter threats. The fans were accepting integrated baseball, but there were other problems to contend with.

In one game at Vero Beach I had gotten into a hassle with a young Brooklyn farmhand which almost came to blows. Later, during the season, I was thrown out of a game for the second time. The penalty was for grabbing at my throat—a sign that signified an umpire was choking up. "Choking up" meant that the umpire was favoring home teams on decisions.

In acting like this, I wasn't doing anything that players hadn't been doing for years. All typical players with spirit act that way. They throw their hands in the air in disgust, kick bitterly at the ground or at a glove. They shake their heads in disbelief at decisions. They react. Sometimes they get fines.

Most of the time, unless they do something terribly violent, there just isn't any aftermath at all.

I received a great deal of personal publicity in 1949. Sometimes, in the dressing room, in the midst of a group of Dodgers, all of us would sound off about something we didn't approve of. A writer outside the door who had heard what we were saying would do a piece telling the world what Robinson was "popping off" about. That was one of the reasons for the excess publicity. Another was that I said pretty much what was on my mind whenever the press interviewed me. Sports-writers seemed to come directly to me whenever there was a hint of a story. They knew I would say what I thought. One of them once told me I represented the difference between steak and hamburger on the dinner plates of some writers. The sportswriters knew I wouldn't back down if I got into trouble—that I wouldn't whine that "I was misquoted."

It felt good to be able to breathe freely, to speak out when I wanted to. There was also another good element. Many times when I made strong or controversial statements, I was not fighting for a personal thing. I was standing up for my team. I was saying things some of my teammates felt but were reluctant to say. The Dodgers appreciated this, and it was a refutation of the charge that I was making verbal grandstand plays to promote myself.

In July, 1949, I was asked to testify before the House Un-American Activities Committee headed by Georgia Congressman John S. Wood. He sent me a telegram asking me to come to Washington to testify before his committee "to give the lie to statements by Paul Robeson." I learned that the committee had also invited other blacks, some prominent lawyers, sociologists, ministers, and educators. I was impressed by the fact that a Congressional committee had asked for my views, but I realized that they must have felt my popularity with black and white sports-loving masses would help them refute the Robeson statement. I was in a dilemma because the statement was disturbing to me in some ways, although I believed I knew why it had been made.

Paul Robeson, the noted singer, an active fighter against racism, had been quoted in the world press as saying that American Negroes would not fight for America in case of a war against Russia. It was not the first time Robeson had troubled the establishment. He was a black man who, in white eyes, "had it made." But he was an embattled and bitter man. He looked back on a childhood in a city where white people pushed blacks off the sidewalk. He grew up, not in the South, but in Princeton, New Jersey. He had gone to Rutgers University, become Phi Beta Kappa and the captain of a record-making football team. Robeson remembered sitting on the bench during certain football games even though he was the star because a Southern college was playing his team and would not countenance the presence of a black man on the field. Paul was a brilliant law student. When he was graduated from law school and looked for jobs with white law firms (there were few black firms in those days), he found he was discriminated against. Even after he became an eminent artist, he learned with resentment and sorrow that after the applause had died, he was once again a nigger. When he was on tour, hotels found polite excuses—sometimes not polite— for not taking him in. In others that did give him accommodations, he was asked to take his meals in his room.

In 1931 Robeson left his country, announcing that he would live in England. He took his son, Paul, to Russia to be educated. In Russia he found a country where "I walked the earth for the first time with complete dignity." He had not yet officially espoused Communism, but his statement, from Paris, declaring blacks would not fight Russia for America, had aroused Congress and the press.

I was not sure about what to do. Rachel and I had long talks about it. She felt I should follow my instincts. I didn't want to fall prey to the white man's game and allow myself to be pitted against another black man. I knew that Robeson was striking out against racial inequality in the way that seemed best to him. However in those days I had much more faith in the ultimate justice of the American white man than I have today. I would reject such an invitation if offered now.

The newspaper accounts seemed to picture the great singer as speaking for the whole race of black people. With all the respect I had for him, I didn't believe anyone had the right to do that. I thought Robeson, although deeply dedicated to his people, was also strongly influenced by his attraction to Soviet Russia and the Communist cause. I wasn't about to knock him for being a Communist or a Communist sympathizer. That was his right. But I was afraid that Robeson's statement might discredit blacks in the eyes of whites. If his statement meant that *all* black people—not just *some* blacks—would refuse to defend America, then it seemed to me that he had been guilty of too sweeping an assumption. I was black and he wasn't speaking for me. I had served in the Armed Forces and had been badly mistreated. When I couldn't defend my country for the injustice I suffered, I was still proud to have been in uniform. I felt that there were two wars raging at once—one against foreign enemies and one against domestic foes—and the black man was forced to fight both. I felt we must not back down on either front. This land belongs to us as much as it belongs to any immigrant or any descendant of the American colonists, and slavery in this country—in whatever sophisticated form—must end. There are whites who would love to see us refuse to defend our country because then we could relinquish our right to be Americans. It isn't a perfect America and it isn't run right, but it still belongs to us. As my friend the Reverend Jesse Jackson says, "It ain't our government, but it's our country."

After word got out that I had been asked to testify, Rae and I received an overwhelming amount of letters, wires, and telephone calls. Some sought to dissuade me from going to Washington, others gave advice on what I should say, and still others threatened me with a loss of popularity in the black community and charged I would be a "traitor" to my people if I testified. Obviously some of the mail had been organized by the Communist Party, but there was a considerable amount that Rachel and I judged was sincerely free of political motivation. After we considered all the factors, I decided to testify.

The speech I gave in front of the committee was well-received. However, many of the newspaper articles praising it, also gave the impression that I had put down Robeson hard. That wasn't true. The major points I made were these:

I said that the question of Communist activity in the United States wasn't a matter of partisan politics. I mentioned that some of the policies of the committee itself had become political issues.

I told the committee that I didn't pretend to be an expert on Communism or any other kind of political "ism," but I was an expert on being a colored American, having had thirty years of experience at it, and I knew how difficult it was to be in the minority. I felt that we had made some progress in baseball and that we could make progress in other American fields provided we got rid of some of the misunderstandings the public still suffered from. There had been a lot of misunderstanding on the subject of Communism among Negroes in this country that was bound to hurt my people's cause unless it was cleared up. Every Negro worth his salt hated racial discrimination, and if it happened that it was a Communist who denounced discrimination, that didn't change the truth of his charges. It might be true that Communists kicked up a big fuss over racial discrimination because it suited their purposes. However that was no reason to pretend that the whole issue was a creation of the Communist imagination. This talk about "Communists stirring up Negroes to protest" only made present misunderstandings worse.

I then said I had been asked to express my views on Paul Robeson's statement to the effect that American Negroes would refuse to fight in any war against Russia because we loved Russia so much. I commented that if Mr. Robeson actually made that statement, it sounded very silly to me but that he had a right to his personal views. People shouldn't get scared and think that one Negro among 15,000,000 of us, speaking to a Communist group in Paris, could speak for the rest of his race.

I wound up my statement by saying:

"I can't speak for any fifteen million people any more than any other person can, but I know that I've got too much invested for my wife and child and myself in the future of this country, and I and other Americans of many races and faiths have too much invested in our country's welfare, for any of us to throw it away because of a siren song sung in bass.

"I am a religious man. Therefore I cherish America where I am free to worship as I please, a privilege which some countries do not give. And I suspect that nine hundred and ninety-nine out of almost any thousand colored Americans you meet will tell you the same thing.

"But that doesn't mean that we're going to stop fighting race discrimination in this country until we've got it licked. It means that we're going to fight it all the harder because our stake in the future is so big. We can win our fight without the Communists and we don't want their help."

That statement was made over twenty years ago, and I have never regretted it. But I have grown wiser and closer to painful truths about America's destructiveness. And I do have an increased respect for Paul Robeson who, over the span of that twenty years, sacrificed himself, his career, and the wealth and comfort he once enjoyed because, I believe, he was sincerely trying to help his people.

During the 1949 season there was a tremendous improvement in the closeness of the Dodger team. Racial tensions had almost completely dissipated, and the team cared most about acquiring talented players. The club had been strengthened by the addition of several players, among them Roy Campanella and Don Newcombe. The year 1949 wound up being a truly great one. Once again, we became the National League pennant winners. We lost the series to the Yankees, but it was a hard-fought series.

The year 1949 was also a banner year for me personally because the sportswriters named me Most Valuable Player. I signed a 1950 contract for $35,000, which in those days was a very good paycheck. I was happy as the season ended and happily unaware of the trouble that lay ahead.

Chapter VII

The Price of Popularity

To our great joy we had another addition to the family in 1950. Sharon Robinson was born on January 13 in Flower Fifth Avenue Hospital in New York. We had finally bought our own home in the St. Albans section of Long Island. There were some modestly priced good-looking homes in our immediate neighborhood, homes that were mainly white-owned. Located in the neighborhood were the Roy Campanellas; Count Basie and his wife, Catherine; Herbert Mills of the Mills Brothers; and others from the entertainment world and field of education.

A movie, *The Jackie Robinson Story*, was to be filmed that year. The producers wanted to make it before spring training, but I had been holding them up until the birth of my daughter. When Sharon was born, I planned to take Jackie out to Hollywood with me while Rachel stayed home with the baby and my mother, who had come East to help us during the last stages of Rae's pregnancy.

Two weeks after I'd been on the set in my unaccustomed role of actor, I confessed to Rachel that not only did I miss her a lot but I wanted to see Sharon and I'd probably learn my script much faster if she came out to join me. When Sharon was just three weeks old, she was en route to Hollywood with her mother. Rae said that our daily life during those few weeks when they rushed to put the picture together in record time, reminded her of my first baseball days. There was a lot of difference, though. Every morning a limousine came to pick up the four of us and we would all spend the day on the lot. Ruby Dee, who played the role of Rachel in the picture, paid a lot of attention to our baby. Jackie had spent a lot of his infant hours on the knees of baseball players, and little Sharon was getting the same kind of treatment from movie stars. That same old *Jackie Robinson Story* is still turning up here and there on television. It was exciting to participate in it. But later I realized it had been made too quickly, that it was budgeted too low, and that, if it had been made later in my career, it could have been done much better.

I left Rachel and the children with her mother and went on to spring training. Often, during that spring training season, I thought about how much fun it had been when Rae and I had Jackie with us during spring training at Vero Beach. He loved that place. He had his own ball then and would play out on the field every day, running back and forth to Rae to get his ration of freshly squeezed orange juice. Ballplayers and some of the fans gave him a lot of attention, and at times he was surprisingly responsive. One day, unknown to Rae and me, he got out on the field and started hamming it up. It was during an exhibition game warm-up and people were throwing money at him from the stands. He was happily giving his fans autographs and before I realized what was going on, he had collected quite a little hoard of change for himself.

Watching little Jackie being so outgoing delighted Rae and me, but at the same time it gave us a sober awareness of the serious problem he would have in asserting himself as an individual. We had heard and read about the conflicts children face whose parents live in the spotlight. We became more aware of the problem each day as Jackie grew older.

There are any number of well-intentioned people who inflict problems on the kids of famous fathers. Jackie became a victim of these problems when he was still a very small boy. Almost as soon as he could say his name, people would come up with brilliant statements such as, "Oh, so you're little Jackie Robinson, huh? You think you'll ever be as famous as your father?" Or, "Oh, are you going to be a ballplayer too? You know you'll never be able to do what your daddy has done."

There were dozens of approaches, all meant to be teasing or affectionate and all chipping away at this little boy's self-esteem. They also convinced him that probably he and I were or should be in some sort of competition.

He was a loving and lovable youngster and sunny in disposition. There was very seldom any outward sign that this kind of thing bothered him. But it did and we knew it did. We knew that when he was very young, he began to feel exploited, to sense that perhaps people were making much of him, not because of himself, but because he was my son.

I recall one instance when his resentment showed. Jackie was about three and we were living in Brooklyn. *Life* magazine was doing a cover piece on the Robinson family. The cover picture was to show Rae and myself sitting on the stoop with Jackie riding around in front of us on his bicycle. Something in Jackie's little boy psyche told him that he should refuse to pose. Nothing was going to change his mind, and, of course, we were not about to tell him he must pose. The picture came out with Rae and me sitting on the step and Jackie on his tricycle with his back to the camera. It was then that Rae decided there had been too much pressure on him and that we would declare a moratorium on any picture-taking of Jackie until and unless he wanted it. Shortly after that, he went through an exhibitionist stage, and we couldn't keep him out of things when the photographers were around.

Jackie certainly seemed to be proud of me, but he had an interesting problem when he was first attending school. We think he was a bit confused as to why I spent my time playing ball and being away from home instead of having a normal job like those of his classmates' fathers who were policemen, teachers, businessmen. Playing ball didn't seem too much like an occupation to him, and his teachers reported that he very seldom spoke about what I did for a living.

He must have been confused also about the kinds of places where we lived as a family. When he and his mother were with me during spring training, he lived in a rigidly segregated atmosphere. He hardly ever saw a white person then. Later, when we moved to Stamford, Connecticut, we lived in a totally white neighborhood. When Jackie was growing up, Rae and I mistakenly tried to shield him from knowledge of racial prejudice. Later when his sister Sharon and his brother David came along, the subject of racial differences was all over television and we discussed it openly as a family.

There was an episode in Vero Beach in 1949 that was symbolic of the kind of ordeal Rachel and little Jackie had to face, mainly in Southern communities. I don't think Jackie was old enough to really understand how ugly and bigoted it was, but youngsters are peculiarly attuned to the stress of parents, particularly when they are as close as Rachel and Jackie were. Some of the annoyances Rachel had to put up with may seem petty, but they were terribly difficult for a proud black woman. In the Vero Beach days black women had their hair done in a black beauty shop in a black neighborhood. Since Rae didn't know the town well—and we were almost always strangers in town—she needed a taxicab because she didn't want to take the chance of getting lost on public transportation. One day, with Jackie, Rae set out for the beauty shop. She saw a taxi stop a few feet away from her and discharge a passenger. She walked over to the cab only to be informed that it was a "white cab." The driver gave her a telephone number to call to get a "colored cab."

Rae and Jackie sat on the lawn in front of the main building, waiting for the "colored cab." After a while, along came a huge bus that was empty except for a black driver. It was dilapidated and had broken windows. As soon as she realized this was the "colored cab" Rae got on the bus. Jackie scrambled along after her, undoubtedly thinking he was about to embark on a remarkable adventure. The "bus" circled and passed the swimming pool where all the other baseball wives and their children were relaxing. They all stared. Rachel, of course, felt humiliated. Jackie, happily innocent, was waving good-bye to the white children and their mothers. The bus let them off at a little shack somewhere in the vicinity of the beauty shop. Rachel was so furious that she vowed they would not take that bus back. There was no place to eat in the vicinity, and when they started back, they set out down a long dusty road. Suddenly, Rachel looked down at our son manfully puffing along, tired, hungry, and probably puzzled, but not complaining. She realized that she was giving vent to her hurt and pride and that little Jackie was suffering for it. She stopped, waited, and, in due time, along came the "colored cab" bus, bringing back the black workers from the village to do the evening meal for the ballplayers and their families. Rae was still pretty angry, and she had to find some way to express herself so she simply did not put any fare in the box.

We were living on an Army base then. It was like being confined to a reservation, and it was the only reason we were quartered along with the whites. That, too, was difficult for Rae. Her relationships with the other wives were tense and uncomfortable for her and for them. She didn't know how to relate to them, and they quite clearly did not know how to relate to her. Certainly Jackie absorbed some of these tensions, and later on we felt it had affected him.

The news that Branch Rickey would be leaving the Dodgers at the end of the 1950 season to take over the Pittsburgh Pirates hit me hard. Walter O'Malley, an officer of the corporation, had the first option to buy Mr. Rickey's stock. As soon as O'Malley took over the presidency of the club, he made it clear that he was anti-Rickey. At the time, I didn't know whether O'Malley was jealous of the man or down on him because he had brought integration into the game. All I knew in 1950 was that he seemed to become furious whenever he heard the name Rickey. He knew that I felt very deeply about Mr. Rickey, and, consequently, I became the target of his insecurity. I didn't act like some sorehead who has lost his protector. I didn't need a protector at this point.

O'Malley's attitude toward me was viciously antagonistic. I learned that he had a habit of calling me Mr. Rickey's prima donna and giving Mr. Rickey a hard time about what kind of season I would have. I also learned that O'Malley and some of the other Dodger stockholders had squeezed Rickey out at the end of 1950. They wouldn't sign a new contract for him, and they arranged it so he would have to sell his stock.

My troubles with the Dodger front office in the early fifties—particularly 1951 and 1952—combined with my spirited response on the playing field whenever I felt that either my team or I was being shoved around inflamed the relationship between me and some members of the press.

There were more than a few sportswriters who were willing to sacrifice principle for a scoop. During the 1951 season, for instance, we were losing a vital game with the Braves and all of us were feeling low. Our outlook didn't improve when umpire Frank Dascoli called what we saw as a bum decision against the team. Toward the end of the game, with the score tied, we needed to keep them from scoring and going into extra innings. The ball was grounded to me. I threw it to Roy at home. It seemed to us that Roy had the plate blocked and the runner was out. Nevertheless, Dascoli called him safe. Roy jumped up to protest, and Dascoli immediately threw him out of the game. Our whole team was furious. We let the umpires know it as we walked back toward the clubhouse. Preacher Roe stopped at the umpires' dressing room door and kicked it so hard that he knocked a hole in it. Imagine my astonishment when, that evening, I saw a newspaper with a big page-one headline saying that Jackie Robinson had blown his top and kicked in the door. I called the paper and spoke to the man who had by-lined the story. I told him I could prove the story was a lie and demanded to know how he got this phony information. He hemmed and hawed and finally told me that a private policeman had told him and he didn't have time to verify it with me because he had to make his deadline.

I was pretty angry at this lame excuse. The following day the writer ran a tiny story retracting the lie the paper had used to create such a big sensation. Retractions never catch up with headlines.

The sportswriter who seemed to be doing his best to make me revert to the old cheek-turning, humble Robinson was Dick Young of the New York *Daily News*. Dick and I have had, for a number of years, a strange relationship. I used to think he was a nice guy personally, and I knew he was a good sportswriter. As time went by, Young became, in my book, a racial bigot. My trouble with Dick began right after 1949 when he first warned me that I should refrain from sounding off because I was offending sportswriters like himself. He pointed out that there were a lot of awards and advantages I might miss out on if I antagonized sportswriters since they have a great deal of power. In his way, I believe that Dick was trying to help me at that time. He genuinely did not understand that as much as I liked awards and being popular, these things were not as important to me as my own integrity. When I told Dick this and that I was infinitely more interested in being respected as a man than in being liked, he apparently took it as a personal insult. Although he seemed to stand up for me occasionally in later years, he often seemed to use his column to attack me, and relations between us have often been strained.

Milton Gross proved to me several times that he was a writer with perspective and a sense of objectivity. Once I suddenly found myself in a hassle with Buzzy Bavasi who had become vice-president and general manager of the club after Branch Rickey left. Walter O'Malley had signed a deal that would mean playing a certain number of games in Jersey City. Our team didn't like it because, in order to attract just a little more business, we were being subjected to playing in less than major league conditions. A number of players made angry statements about it and the writers placed the most emphasis on mine. The press made the same old, tired comments, condemning me again for sounding off.

Milt Gross wrote:

> Anybody else may say anything and it's disregarded. Jackie opens his mouth and everybody rushes to put their feet into it. The tempest evoked by Robinson last week would have been nothing if any other Dodger had said what Jackie did about Walter O'Malley's Jersey City junket. As a matter of fact, they did. There wasn't a Dodger in the clubhouse who didn't pop off as much or more. But it was Robinson who found himself embroiled with a needling newspaperman, exchanging cross words with Bavasi and being falsely accused by another member of the press of wanting to beat up an interviewer as an aftermath of his expression of an honest opinion.
>
> The sorry conclusion must be that honesty in baseball is no longer a virtue and Jackie's reward will be that he remains a target for the agitators who, unfortunately, include a number of men in my own business.

Dick Young was responsible for starting another rhubarb with O'Malley. Young printed a report about some young Dodger players who had allegedly discussed me negatively in a few of the Brooklyn drinking spots. Dick was not even on the scene when these conversations supposedly took place, and somebody apparently brought a story to him which he promptly presented to the public. His article indicated that these players were unhappy with me because I was too "aggressive" in protesting plays and that I acted "as though I was running the team."

Dick's article gave O'Malley another opportunity to go around criticizing me. But I knew what O'Malley's problem was. To put it bluntly, I was one of those "uppity niggers" in O'Malley's book.

I responded normally when some newspaper reporters asked me what I thought of churches and synagogues being bombed in the South in protest against the Supreme Court ruling on school desegregation. I said that the people who would bomb a church had to be sick and that our federal government ought to use every resource to prosecute them. The writer interviewing me made me feel very sad when he claimed that Roy Campanella had observed that the way to prevent such incidents was for blacks "to stop pressing to get too far too fast."

Campy was, after all, a father, just as I was. If I had a room jammed with trophies, awards, and citations, and a child of mine came to me into that room and asked what I had done in defense of black people and decent whites fighting for freedom—and I had to tell that child I had kept quiet, that I had been timid, I would have to mark myself a total failure in the whole business of living.

Another incident pointing up differences between Campy and me involved the Chase Hotel in St. Louis. I took a stand and said I was tired of having special, Jim Crow living arrangements made for me while white players slept in the air-conditioned Chase Hotel rooms. That made the hotel back down, and they announced that from then on, I could stay with the team. Roy told me he didn't want to stay at the Chase. He said it was a matter of pride since they hadn't wanted him in the past.

I told him that he had no monopoly on pride, that baseball hadn't wanted him in the past, but that he was in it now. I added that winning a victory over the Chase Hotel prejudice meant we were really becoming a team—members would all be treated equally. Also, now that we had broken the barriers at the Chase, other blacks, not in baseball, who wanted to stay in a decent hotel would begin to find acceptance.

I'll never forget Campy's answer to all of that.

"I'm no crusader," he said.

That was the kind of attitude a Dick Young—and many other whites—approved of. During a conversation in which Dick Young and I were trying to define our differences, Dick said, "The trouble between you and me, Jackie, is that I can go to Campy and all we discuss is baseball. I talk to you and sooner or later we get around to social issues. It just happens I'm not interested in social issues."

I told him that I was and added that if I had to stop saying anything to him about race relations or discrimination against black people or injustices in the game, then we'd probably just have to stop any serious discussions.

"I'm telling you as a friend," Dick insisted, "that a lot of newspapermen are saying that Campy's the kind of guy they can like but that your aggressiveness, your wearing your race on your sleeve, makes enemies."

"Dick, we might just as well get this straight," I answered. "I like friends just as much as other people. But if it comes down to the question of having a choice between the friendship of some of these writers and their respect, I'll take their respect. I know that a lot of them don't like me because I discuss things that get in the way of their guilt complexes, but I'll bet you they respect me."

"Personally, Jackie," Dick persisted, "when I talk to Campy, I almost never think of him as a Negro. Any time I talk to you, I'm acutely aware of the fact that you're a Negro."

I tried patiently to explain that I want to be thought of as what I am, that I am proud of my blackness, proud of the accomplishments of black people.

"If you tell me that when you think of me, you think of a whining, cringing, handkerchief-head standing before you with his hat in his hand expressing eternal gratitude for the fact that you only had nine little digs in yesterday's story when you could have had ten, that's one thing," I replied. "If you think of me as the kind of Negro who's come to the conclusion that he isn't going to beg for anything, that he will be reasonable but he damned well is tired of being patient, that's another thing. I want to be thought of as the latter kind of Negro and if it makes some people uncomfortable, if it makes me the kind of guy they can't like, that's tough. That's the way the ball bounces."

I knew that my message didn't get through to Dick; either that or it was a message he wasn't willing to accept. I was sorry he felt he had to compare Campy and myself, but I did feel strengthened in my convictions because of the approval I received from the black press which had been in my corner from the very beginning of my career. A. S. "Doc" Young, for instance, who is one of the most brilliant black sportswriters in the country, sized up the Robinson-Campanella situation like this:

> Background for this feud is found in the differences in personalities between these two stars. Campy is a Dale Carnegie disciple who believes in "getting along" at all costs, in being exceedingly grateful for any favor or any deed interpreted as a favor.
>
> Jackie, on the other hand, is an aggressive individualist who is willing to pay the price and, once having paid it in full, does not believe that effusive thank you's are a necessary tip.
>
> Campy believes Jackie owes baseball everything. Jackie knows that baseball was ready to put the skids under him without his knowledge after having lived handsomely on him for years. Jackie knows that baseball never has been overly concerned about its unpaid debts to all the great Negro players who lived from 1887 to 1945, without a mere look-in on organized ball. . . . I like both players and I'm sorry this kind of thing must come up.

I liked what Doc had to say because I thought he was trying to be fair. He wasn't tackling Roy or calling him an Uncle

Tom. He wasn't hitting me as some kind of troublemaker. He was just saying we were two different people with two different points of view. I am glad to say that I never had a personal quarrel with Campy. I have always respected him, and I regard him as a guy worthy of great admiration. Our friendship was one thing that many white writers didn't want to see.

Joe Reichler of the Associated Press reported a supposed Campanella remark which he said Roy made early in his career, during an altercation with an umpire in which the fierce Jackie Robinson was involved. The supposed remark was: "I like it up here. Don't spoil it." The implication was that Campanella was happy to be in the major leagues after so many years of struggling in the Negro leagues, and he didn't want anything to jeopardize his chances of remaining there.

All the attention I was getting from the press seemed to compound O'Malley's antagonistic attitude toward me. I found out just what kind of person Walter O'Malley was in 1952 when he called me on the carpet for not being able to show up at exhibition games owing to the fact that I had been injured. He asked Rae to come along with me to his office. She had never become involved with matters concerning me and the team except for our own discussions at home. But that day I saw Rae really lose her temper.

Rae sat there fuming as O'Malley charged me with being unfair to the fans by missing the exhibition games, and while he was getting his complaints in, he indicated that I had no right to complain about being assigned to a separate hotel. A separate hotel had been good enough for me in 1947, hadn't it?

That burned me up. I told O'Malley that if he thought I intended to tolerate conditions I had been forced to stand for in the past, he was dead wrong. I added that it seemed to me that if the owners had a little more guts, black players wouldn't have to be forced to undergo so many indignities. I said that I resented being suspected of pretending to be in-

jured and that my injuries could be easily checked with the
trainer. I observed that he seemed more interested in the few
extra dollars to be gained out of exhibition games than in
protecting the health and strength of his team for the season.

It was then he called me a prima donna and said I was
behaving like a "crybaby" over a sore leg.

That's when Rachel's rage broke. She started off saying she
felt she had to express herself. She said she resented my being
called a prima donna.

"I've seen him play with sore legs, a sore back, sore arms,
even without other members of the team knowing it," Rachel
declared. "Doing it not for praise, but because he was
thinking about his team. Nobody worries about this club more
than Jackie Robinson and that includes the owners. I live with
him, so I know. Nobody gets up earlier than Jackie Robinson
to see what kind of day it's going to be, if it's going to be good
weather for the game, if the team is likely to have a good
crowd. Nobody else spends more time worrying about Pee
Wee Reese's sore foot or Gil Hodges' batting slump or Carl
Erskine's ailing arm. Jack's heart and soul is with the baseball
club, and it pains me deeply to have you say what you just
said."

Rachel was just warming up.

"You know, Mr. O'Malley," she continued, "bringing Jack
into organized baseball was not the greatest thing Mr. Rickey
did for him. In my opinion, it was this: Having brought Jack
in, he stuck by him to the very end. He understood Jack. He
never listened to the ugly little rumors like those you have
mentioned to us today. If there was something wrong, he
would go to Jack and ask him about it. He would talk to Jack
and they would get to the heart of it like men with a mutual
respect for the abilities and feelings of each other."

Then, I told O'Malley that I could have made a lot of
legitimate complaints about the crummy hotel we were living
in and about a number of other things. "It doesn't strike me
as fair to have people who are sitting in comfort in an air-

conditioned hotel lecture me about not complaining," I said.

O'Malley abruptly changed his tune. He began to apply the soft soap, telling us he had meant no harm and pleading with me to "just try to come out and play today."

He backed down because he had found out he couldn't bully us. O'Malley never really let up. He continued to make anti-Rickey remarks that he knew would get under my skin, and he knew, because I had told him, that I would always be loyal to Mr. Rickey.

My troubles continued. In 1953 I had unwittingly detonated an explosion. I appeared on a television program: *Youth Wants to Know*, moderated by Faye Emerson. During the show, where members of the studio audience ask unrehearsed questions, one young lady asked me if I thought the Yankees were discriminating in their hiring practices. It was a loaded question because the Yankees, at the time, had a lily-white team. I replied that the Yankee players were tops in my book as sportsmen and good guys. However, since I couldn't duck the real thrust of her question, I added that I thought the Yankee front office was discriminating against blacks and pointed out that they were the only team in New York which had not hired even one.

I had no idea—and I am sure that girl never dreamed—that her innocent question and my candid reply would cause all hell to break loose. The next day headline stories were published. A Cleveland writer tried to take me apart in an article in which he described me as a "soap box orator" and a "rabble-rouser." Many hate letters, a lot of them anonymous, came into our club attacking me. When Commissioner Frick sent for me, I anticipated a strong verbal rebuke and possibly disciplinary measures. I was ready, however, because I had said what I meant. I told the commissioner as soon as I faced him that I would repeat what I had said to anyone who asked me the question again. If the Yankees were so concerned, why didn't they answer in the only convincing way they could, by hiring some black players?

The commissioner surprised me. He said he was not trying to protect or defend the Yankees. He merely wanted to get to the bottom of the matter because to do so was his responsibility. He agreed when I said that he might do well to request the script of the show and see what I had actually said. When we finished our talk, Commissioner Frick made a statement which I will never forget.

"Jackie," he said, "I just want you to know how I feel personally. Whenever you believe enough in something to sound off about it, whenever you feel strongly that you've got to come out swinging, I sincerely hope you'll swing the real heavy bat and not the fungo."

Without that kind of support from some of the people in baseball who had power, I could not have made it, no matter how well I performed, no matter how loyal black people were. I am well aware that there were countless other whites, not as well-known or influential, who were in my corner.

I remember the fans in Montreal who rocked the Louisville team by giving them a tremendous booing in retaliation for the way Louisville had heckled me when I played there. Those same Canadians made life for Rachel and me comfortable and warm with affection. They spared no effort in showing me that they were proud that I belonged to their home team. They were not black people.

This is one of the reasons I cannot buy the "black only" package being peddled by segregationists who are white and separatists who are black. There are those who sincerely believe that the racial problem can be solved if an all-black society is created. They are flattering the black masses, making them believe an impossible dream will come true. The best opportunity for genocide the bigoted white man could have is to help blacks establish an all-black society in this country. It would be much more convenient to wipe out blacks if they were all collected in one place. It seems to me wrong— in fact, evil—for "leaders" to envision an all-black paradise, to mislead a people starving for hope.

I am not a fanatical integrationist. I don't think there is any particular magic in a white kid sitting next to a black kid in a classroom. I simply don't want all-black classrooms and all-black schools in a system where the best teachers and the best equipment and the best administration go to the white school and the worst to the black. I see more value in making a ghetto school great enough to induce parents of all races to send their children to it. I also believe both black and white children can gain something by being able to relate to each other.

I am opposed to enforced separatism and I am opposed to enforced segregation. The first freedom for all people is freedom of choice. I want to live in a neighborhood of my choice where I can afford to pay the rent. I want to send my children to school where I believe they will develop best. I want the freedom to rise as high in my career as my ability indicates. I want to be free to follow the dictates of my own mind and conscience without being subject to the pressures of any man, black or white. I think that is what most people of all races want. Unfortunately, it is not what black people in this country have. Until we do we will continue to live in a farcical society, and the high principles on which America was founded will continue to be distorted. Finally, although I am opposed to complete separatism, there is a valid necessity for blacks to stand apart and develop themselves independently. We must have a sense of our own identity and we must develop an economic unity so we can built an independent power base from which to deal with whites on a more equal basis. This is what I tried to do later in my life when I got involved in the Freedom Bank venture. It is only through such accomplishments as these that we can negotiate from strength and self-respect rather than from the weak position of trying to be included in already existing white institutions.

Chapter VIII

The Growing Family

After the birth of Sharon in 1950, our house in St. Albans had become increasingly inadequate. In addition to being too small, it was located right on the street without any room for privacy. Well-meaning people constantly harassed us. They would pull up in their cars, walk boldly into our front yard and start taking pictures. When they rang the bell, Rae would go to the door, dressed for housework, to find people insistent on taking her picture. Usually they would demand that Rae produce the children for a picture. If Rae insisted on the right to privacy, they would leave grumbling that the Robinsons were stuck up and didn't appreciate what the public had done for them. Inevitably, the public both idolizes and abuses celebrities and their families. We understood and were grateful for their interest. On the other hand, anyone like me who can't abide discourtesies, such as being expected to stop in the middle of a meal in a restaurant to sign an autograph, runs the risk of being called ungrateful. Usually, Rachel was very diplomatic with the intruders, but some of the liberties people took got on her nerves.

By the time David was born on May 14, 1952, we were

determined to leave Long Island and we wanted to either find or, preferably, build another house. Considering all the traveling I did in baseball, I was really blessed to be able to be home for the births of each of our three children. I came in from St. Louis in time for David's arrival on the scene. Rachel had never had any trouble after births before, but this time she developed acute nephritis, which was quickly brought under control, but David had to be brought home before she was released. Willette Bailey, a family friend, was our salvation then. She agreed to become nurse for the new baby and generally help with the children. She continued to help us out for a number of years.

While Rachel was house-hunting in 1952 and 1953, we became even more acutely aware that racial prejudice and discrimination in housing is vicious. It doesn't matter whether you are a day laborer or a celebrity, as long as you are black. There were numerous instances which proved that. Once Rachel found property in Purchase, New York. We liked it so much that we wanted to put a deposit on it. Suddenly, it was taken off the market. In other cases, the places we could have bought zoomed upward in price when the owners learned my identity. Sometimes it was hard to tell whether we were being subjected to color prejudice or celebrity prejudice or both. Whatever the reason, being treated differently from others is very frustrating.

We were having a bad time trying to find the kind of place we wanted. We were looking for a big house with rooms for each of our children. We wanted them to be able to play outdoors with plenty of space, a minimum of risk from traffic, and we wanted water that we could see and perhaps use for swimming and rowing. We passionately wanted our children to be educated in integrated schools.

Our neighborhood associations at St. Albans had been pleasant and we had been proud to see that the blacks who had moved into the community were enhancing property values rather than depreciating them. They cared for their homes and grounds. They spent significant sums of money refurbishing inside and outside. However, there was one factor which alarmed us. Younger families were replacing older couples. Teachers, who were all white and older, were unhappy and unprepared to deal with black children or with the increase in the size of their classes. Remember, this was twenty years ago and the passion for integration in schools was growing to a fever pitch, culminating in the triumphant Supreme Court decision in 1954. Like so many parents then, we knew our children were growing up in a society where they would have to deal with people of all colors; therefore, we wanted them to learn about people of other races while they were still young. However conditions in the school got worse, and it seemed to us that Jackie was not getting the education we wanted for him. This was the conflict we faced—wanting to be part of the great integration movement and yet fearing for our son's education. When the school went on double sessions because of the overcrowding and shortage of teachers, we reluctantly withdrew Jackie and put him in a private school.

Meanwhile, just when our house-hunting was at its most discouraging, a newsman from the Bridgeport *Herald* in Bridgeport, Connecticut, stepped into the picture. He was working on a series on housing discrimination and had heard we were having trouble locating. He telephoned Rachel and asked to interview her. After the interview, he did a major piece about all the obvious, subtle, and sophisticated methods that had been used to tell us, "We don't want you for a neighbor." His article made it appear that the North Stamford, Connecticut community had been exceptionally guilty. This wasn't really accurate and it did not reflect what Rae had said about that particular community, but it was most effective in mobilizing North Stamford ministers who did not appreciate being pictured as racists and were prepared to assist. We received several offers to inspect properties in North Stamford and surrounding areas. Some were white elephants in Greenwich which the owners were trying to unload on anyone.

We had to turn them down. One real estate man, either ill-intentioned or ignorant, had spread the rumor that we didn't really want to buy a house since we had turned down a few that had been offered us; that we were actually agitators trying to stir up racial trouble.

Tom Gaines, a liberal builder and developer, and a group of ministers, apparently in reaction to the newspaper piece, set up a committee in North Stamford to fight housing bias. Andrea Simon, one of the key members, phoned Rachel and said the ministers on the committee would like to talk to her at a meeting at the Simon home. Rachel very quickly disposed of the rumor that we were agitators when she met with the committee. The ministers agreed to take up the issue with their congregations.

A real estate broker had been invited by Andrea Simon to attend the meeting. Immediately afterwards he arranged to show Rachel and Andrea available properties. The first few places were interesting but lacked one or more of the elements we desired. Finally, the broker said she had one more place, but she was reluctant to show it. She felt it was exactly what Rae and I were looking for. However, she didn't want Rae to see it and get excited about it only to find that we couldn't have it. She said the builder had a financial problem and that the banks and local merchants would have to be checked before we could have it.

The minute she arrived at the place, Rachel fell in love with it. The expanse of land, the beautiful private lake, the majestic trees—and the foundations for the house to be built on—all were perfect. The builder after a talk with the broker announced that we had a deal. A year's search was over.

We bought the Stamford property in 1954 but were unable to occupy it until 1955. There were some fascinating developments involving the builder. He was a character—lovable but sometimes difficult. He had his problems and we had ours.

Rachel and I have constantly tried to assess how wise we

were in depriving our children of black companionship. When we were in St. Albans, the private nursery school we sent Jackie to was all-white at first. I think we were unaware of how detrimental that was to him. We were simply determined to send our children to a good school. We hoped Jackie's school would become better balanced racially than it did. Then, when we moved to North Stamford, which was predominantly white at the time, we fervently hoped that other black families would follow us. We wanted our children in good schools, and we wanted the neighborhoods and schools to be integrated so they could have black companionship. This did not occur soon enough for our children.

We now realize how much being "the only black" can hurt. In talks with us as they grew up, our children made us realize what a heavy burden had been placed on them. Sharon, as well as David and Jackie, went through a loss of identity. Parents often don't know what their youngsters are exposed to—the name-calling, the slights, the feeling of being excluded, even the feeling of being patronized, and the realization that there is nobody in your class or school who looks like you. We learned belatedly that a "good school" involves much more than excellent teaching.

When the time came for Rachel to take Jackie, Jr., to school in Connecticut she was deeply concerned. She says she began to recognize some of the hesitation that black parents in the South are subject to: wondering whether or not to put their children in white schools. In addition to being the only black youngster in the school, our son would face other serious disadvantages. In the private school on Long Island, said to be a very fine one, he had learned to print but not to write, and he could scarcely read. Socially and academically, he was going to have adult-sized barriers to climb. Rachel says, in no uncertain terms, that if we had it to do all over again, she would elect to remain in an all-black community rather than go through the frustrating year-long search to find an integrated community and then finally to have to settle for an all-white community. We thought we were pioneering. Today, blacks are moving into the suburbs at a rapid rate. That wasn't true eighteen years ago when our kids needed it. We did better with Sharon and David when their school time came along because by that time we were more aware. But when Jackie first entered school, it was different. The builder promised us our home would be ready by the time school opened. We had already moved out of our old house, and our dear friends, Andrea and Richard Simon, had loaned us their summer home in Stamford. Jackie had been friends with the Simons' son for some time. They were the same age and he had been visiting them all summer. But the Simons went back to Riverdale when we took over their place temporarily. So Jackie had to go it alone.

Jackie's first day of school is a day Rachel will never forget. When she arrived at the Martha Hoyt School with our son, the other kids were all standing in line. They had just alighted from the bus and were ready to go into the school. As Rae went up the steps, she could hear them whispering. She couldn't hear what they were saying, but it was obvious that they were discussing Jackie. It was a long climb up those steps to where the principal stood. Rachel hoped desperately that Jackie couldn't hear the comments about this strange, little colored boy who had arrived on the scene. Rae kept hoping she would see at least one other black kid in the school. There were none and there were no other public schools near us. This meant there was no choice and Jackie had to go to Martha Hoyt. Rae was sure that first day that Jackie sensed that the whispers and stares meant he was somehow different and that he was aware of the tension surrounding him and his mother.

During his first year at the Stamford school, Jackie had one very good break. There was a marvelous teacher, a Miss Carlucci, who won Jackie's heart and interest. She was concerned about him and determined to do something about his reading deficiency. In later years Jackie referred to her as the only teacher who really cared about him. She kept him after school without making it seem like a punishment. She used to say to him, "Jackie, you and I are going to work this afternoon. We'll play a little ball first." He respected her because she could fire a baseball at him. Afterward she took him inside and did some reading with him. The extra time Miss Carlucci spent with Jackie helped tremendously.

Because of her efforts, Jackie did catch up by the end of the year. The school had made Jackie part of what was called the tracking system. This is a system of judging a child's ability and assigning him to a certain track within a grade, used by many schools. Often the child gets stuck in a low track with the slow learners at an early age and is then convinced he is not bright. Rae feels the system is particularly damaging to black kids who have already started out handicapped by a society that damages their self-esteem early in life. Children in a low track can begin not to care and lose any desire to rise above that track, and sometimes their teachers are certain that such youngsters never can and never will learn above a certain level. If a kid is convinced that he's dumb, it doesn't take much for him to decide to prove it. He is apt to always live with a low ceiling of expectation and frequently the teacher won't try to change this. In most black communities, knowledgeable parents are beginning to fight this stultifying system.

At the end of Jackie's first year, Miss Carlucci was terribly proud of him. He had worked hard with her, reacting beautifully to the special attention she gave him. It was the kind of attention that had nothing to do with being the son of a well-known father. Jackie knew Miss Carlucci liked him for himself.

There weren't any more Miss Carluccis.

As the school years passed, Jackie developed the habit of not concentrating. Not bringing his homework home. He was an attractive, winning child, but we began to notice that he was very dependent. Rachel thinks that we contributed heavily toward making him that way.

"People around this house were always doing things for him," Rachel remembers. "He'd get up in the morning and someone would be pressing his pants. He always wanted to look neat in well-pressed pants. Someone else would be getting his breakfast. Maybe he'd leave home without his books and someone would run after him with them. He hardly had to do anything for himself. You know, when you come right down to it, you're never prepared to be a parent to the first child. Very few people are really ready. I think we were— all of us, including his Grandmother Isum—very sensitive to the identity crisis he had owing to his dad's fame, and we were making it up to him, in little ways, showing our love by taking care of him, doing special things for him. Waiting on Jackie even carried over to his school. He'd start out of his classroom after school and just hold out his arms. Someone would pile on his books. Someone would remember to give him his sneakers, his lunch box. People just did things for him. I think all that catering to Jackie caught up with him in later years. He wasn't independent enough. He'd been told time and again he couldn't be better than his dad. So he didn't have the fierce competitive spirit that his dad had."

Some of the lessons we learned from Jackie's early school experiences helped us to do a little better with Sharon and David. As we got out of the car the first day we brought Sharon to kindergarten, an extremely friendly lady came over to me and said, "I'm Sandy Ammussen. Will your little girl be in kindergarten with my son Chris?" I could tell that Sharon would have at least one little pal in school.

Sharon was the middle child, and during her early years she was apparently unscathed by the identity problem. But Rachel and I learned, after she had become a teen-ager, that she had taken her lumps, too, and somehow managed to keep most of her serious concerns to herself. This is not to say that Sharon did not communicate with us. She did. But she was just such an ideal and perfect child in our eyes and in the opinion of virtually everyone who came in touch with her that she sometimes seemed a little too good to be true. While fathers may be crazy about their sons, there is something extraordinarily special about a daughter. It's still the same—our relationship—perhaps even deeper. Only I understand her better and I'm amazed at some of the crises she faced as a child and later as a young girl without letting us in on them. Everybody thought about our daughter as shy, sweet Sharon. She was shy, but not painfully so. We felt guilty because we let our interest in the boys consume us. Rachel had been brought up with the same family pattern—a girl in the middle of two boys. She was the busy, loving, but not necessarily always happy, mainstay of her family who took care of her younger brother. With a kind of grim amusement, I recall our assumption that Sharon was strong enough to cope well with whatever she was confronted with. We took her development for granted for many years. She rarely signaled distress or called attention to her problems by being dramatic. We didn't know that much about Sharon's problems in childhood until she reached adolescence, and then she began to let us know— by rebelling and refusing to do certain things we wanted her to do. Love for her family was still there even when she became a determined young rebel, but she let us know, in no uncertain terms, that she, too, had strong desires to be an individual and to be 'accepted as such. Her smooth progress in school had helped to deceive us about her inner conflicts. Sharon remembers, even as a small child, that when she went into a restaurant with me she was aware that the treatment was different and special. She too had the feeling that she was not appreciated for herself.

David was about eighteen months old when we moved to Stamford. I don't think anyone in the family enjoyed our new place more than he did. He was such an active, curious, adventuresome little guy. Rachel had to keep constant watch over him. The builder had left the grounds full of cavernous holes where he had dug up gravel; it looked as if the area had been bombed. It was quite a while before we could get him to grade the big holes, put topsoil over the grounds, and dredge the lake. Meanwhile, David insisted on exploring. We repeatedly warned him never to go too close to the lake or the road and not to play near the holes. He loved to put on his holster with his gun inside, mount his horse (a broomstick), and ride all over the territory where, of course, bad guys and hostile "Injuns" lurked. One day he disappeared for a nerve-racking length of time. When he was finally found, he was sitting, with quiet patience, on the corner of a stone wall, watching for Sharon and Jackie to come home in the school bus. In spite of his warlike equipment, David was a thoughtful, sensible youngster who loved to wander in the woods. He reveled in the grandeur of nature, and he found endless fascination in the mystery of the lake. He would spend hours fishing and swimming. He was always more outgoing than Jackie and we sensed, somehow, that he would not suffer the same identity crisis that had bedeviled his brother from babyhood.

It's possible that by the time David came along, we had found some magic way to blunt the impact of the mixed blessing in my being a celebrity. Or maybe David was different. At any rate, with David's arrival things began to change. Little Jackie, then six years old, and his sister Sharon, three, were as close as they could be. After David made his appearance, everything was still fine. However, when David was big enough to walk and Sharon was big enough to take care of him, she began to love mothering him. She took David over and the two of them would go off to play, ignoring Jackie totally. Jackie's sense of rejection became so obvious that I remember Rachel suggesting to Sharon that she invite her older brother along when she took the baby off to play. This didn't help much. Sharon passionately loved her baby brother and to Jackie, Jr., it must have seemed that David had taken both his parents and Sharon away from him. Jackie retaliated by criticizing the way little David was being raised. He came in the house one day and saw David playing with Sharon and her dolls.

"Humph," Jackie sneered, "you in here playing with dolls when you ought to be out on the front lawn playing football with the boys."

David didn't say a word. He put on his hat and snowsuit and marched outside. He had been out there only a few minutes when he came back inside, blood smeared all over his face. Rae didn't know where he had been hurt or how. If he was in pain, he was doing a terrific job of hiding it and he wasn't making the slightest attempt to wipe off the blood. But he announced to Jackie with tremendous triumph, "Well, I guess you're satisfied now."

The nursery school David was attending was all-white, giving rise to his first questions about the differences between people of different color and concern with inferiority. He wasn't happy about going to school because at first he had no playmates and he missed the freedom of roaming the grounds.

At first David refused to dance in the rhythms class. David's teacher was perplexed. We knew he did enjoy dancing barefoot at home. What we learned from him, however, was that when he did this at school, some of the kids accused him of having dirty feet. Rae and I had an emergency conference with him and explained that there was nothing wrong with his feet. We were brown people, we explained. We reminded him that we couldn't be dirty because we took regular baths. We wouldn't wash our precious color away if we could. He was happy and reassured by this.

He rejoiced in one of those precious childhood friendships with his classmate, Matthew Jamieson. Matt and David were best friends. They liked being together, doing things together. One day someone gave them a dollar. They tore it in half because they liked to share everything.

David and Sharon had remained very close until Dave went to a private elementary school. Sharon was afraid David was becoming a social and intellectual snob and beginning to look down on her. She didn't like the friends he had acquired. Two of his closest friends came from wealthy families in the neighborhood, people who had horses and huge estates. Dave dismissed Sharon's condemnation of him as an indication that she was stupid. When they tried to be friendly together, playing games at the table, he would point out how stupid she was and brag that he was much smarter and caught on to things faster. Inevitably, as in every household with children, there were tensions—and sometimes quarrels—but Rae and I can look back at this period of our lives as an essentially happy one.

Chapter IX

The Ninth Inning

Two years had gone by since my stormy meeting with Walter O'Malley in 1952. Although he persisted in making irritating anti-Rickey cracks, we didn't have any trouble until we played a game in Milwaukee and our team was infuriated by a decision the umpires made. Back in our locker room, we discussed the decision which had caused Pee Wee Reese to be thrown out of the game. The umpires could hear our conversation since their dressing room was next to ours and the walls in between were not up to the ceiling. Most of the Dodgers were complaining, but the next day I was the only one who received a telegram from Warren Giles, the president of the National League. I was fined $75 for making anti-umpire gestures in the dugout (which most of us had done) and for the things I had said in the locker room. I went to O'Malley and protested. He said he didn't want the matter to get out to the press and gave me the impression that he would look into it. The story did show up in the papers, however, and although I was not responsible for it, O'Malley promptly blamed me. He stayed on my back about that.

Trouble between the Dodger management and me seemed

to snowball. Charlie Dressen had been manager of the Dodgers from 1951, and I had the utmost respect for him as a manager. During those three seasons we had been in two world series. However the Dodger front office had a policy of giving contracts to managers only on a year-by-year basis. After the '53 season Dressen tried to get an extended contract, but the front office would not go along with this and he was fired. Dressen's replacement as I said earlier was Walter Alston. Alston and I started off on an awkward footing because he had a gut conviction that I resented his having taken Dressen's job. In fact, Alston came to me to say he hoped I'd work as hard for him as I had for Dressen. I told him I didn't see any reason why I couldn't, but it was obvious that Alston could not bring himself to believe this. I tried to cooperate with Walter, who was a pretty good guy, but felt, as did others on the team, that he had a tendency to lose his cool under pressure and make some boneheaded judgments during the games. Things went along fairly well until the end of the 1954 season when we began to get into minor hassles and exchange impulsive ill-tempered words. The tension between O'Malley and me, the uncomfortable situation with Alston, the tendency of the press to always hang the rap on me whenever there was dissension in the Dodger ranks—plus, worst of all, the fact that during 1954, the team was doing very badly—meant there was bound to be an explosion. The worst incident occurred at Wrigley Field in Chicago.

Duke Snider had hit a ball into the left-field seats which bounced back onto the field. I thought that the ball had hit one of the fans. The book says that a ball like this is an automatic home run if it clears the wall. The umpire, Bill Stewart, called it a double, apparently assuming the ball had bounced off the wall. I was sure that the whole Dodger team would react as I did. I jumped up and ran from the dugout to protest. Unfortunately, none of my teammates followed me. I became suddenly and angrily aware that Walter Alston was standing at third base, his hands on his hips, staring at me sardonically. His stare seemed to say, "OK, Robinson. You've managed to let all the fans see you. Cut out the grandstand tactics and get back to the dugout." It was a humiliating moment. I realized instantly that the hothead, umpire-baiting label that had been applied to me so often in recent months would be brought out again. I said a few quiet words to the umpire and walked back to the dugout, feeling like a fool even though I knew my action had been justified.

Later, I became even angrier when someone said, "You should have heard what Walt said when you were out on the field, Jack."

"If that guy hadn't stood standing out there at third base like a wooden Indian," I retorted, "this club might go somewhere. Here's a play that meant a run in a tight ball game, so whether I was right or wrong, the play was close enough for him to protest to the umpire. But not Alston. What kind of a manager is that?"

The "wooden Indian" crack got around and Alston heard about it. Naturally, it made matters worse. I suppose it made him even angrier the next day when the newspapers carried pictures of the fan who had been hit by the ball. This proved I had been right and the umpire wrong.

By the end of the 1954 season I was getting fed up and I began to make preparations to leave baseball. I loved the game but my experience had not been typical—I was tired of fighting the press, the front office—and I knew that I was reaching the end of my peak years as an athlete. I felt that any chance I might have had of moving up to an administrative job with the Dodgers or any other team was mighty slim. Had I been easygoing, willing to be meek and humble, I might have had a chance. But in fact this has not changed much even today. There are many capable black athletes in the game who could contribute greatly as managers or in other positions of responsibility but it just isn't happening.

My only hope of finding a job which would be fulfilling as well as financially rewarding seemed to be in private industry.

I like to work, and I don't want a dollar I don't earn, so I had to be certain I didn't get sucked in to one of those showcase jobs where you are a token black man with no real responsibility other than window-dressing.

My good friend Martin Stone, a lawyer, put out feelers, and during the 1955 and 1956 seasons I was constantly on the lookout for a solid opportunity. However, I'm glad in a way that I at least stayed through the 1955 season because with all the problems I was to have, one of my greatest thrills was in store. But before that, there were troubles.

During exhibition games Alston started making me spend a lot of time on the bench. One day I would play and the next I would sit on the sidelines. There is nothing so unnerving to a player used to steady involvement than sitting on the bench. He loses confidence and his timing becomes unreliable. Being benched disturbed me to the point where I made the colossal mistake of asking Dick Young, the sportswriter, if he had heard anything about my playing that season. Word got out that I had asked Dick the question, and Walter hit the ceiling. He called a team meeting and angrily singled out the players who run to newspapermen with their problems. Alston and I got into a shouting match that seemed destined to end in a physical fight. Gil Hodges kept tapping me on the arm, advising me, "Jack, don't say anything else. Cool down, Jack."

I listened to Gil because I had a tremendous amount of respect for him.

During the 1955 season I played in approximately two-thirds of the games. My batting average was down. I was doing a poor job in comparison to past seasons. The newspapers began subtly—and some not so subtly—to refer to me as a has-been.

However, despite this the team made it into the world series. It was the fifth series we had been in during my 9 seasons with the Dodgers. (We had been in only a total of 7 since 1905 and we had never won one.)

There was a saying in Brooklyn which everyone has heard

about the Dodgers ("the bums"): "Wait 'til next year." Well, here we were in our seventh world series in fifty years and there was hope that this would be the year, but our fans were also ready to shrug their shoulders and say "Wait 'til next year" if we lost. The way we were playing in that first game—down 6-4 in the eighth inning—it looked like we might have to wait. I was on third base and I knew I might not be playing next year. There were two men out, and I suddenly decided to shake things up. It was not the best baseball strategy to steal home with our team two runs behind, but I just took off and did it. I really didn't care whether I made it or not—I was just tired of waiting. I did make it and we came close to winning that first game. Whether it was because of my stealing home or not, the team had new fire. We fought back against our old rivals, the powerful "Bronx Bombers," and the series came down to the wire in the seventh game. Podres pitched a brilliant shut-out, and in the sixth inning with men on first and second and only one out Sandy Amoros saved the game with a spectacular running catch of Yogi Berra's fly ball down the left field line. It was one of the greatest thrills of my life to be finally on a world series winner.

The next year my troubles continued. I was benched a lot, my average was down and it was obviously time to leave the game. Two things happened that year which clinched the decision. I met Bill Black of Chock Full 'O Nuts. We took to each other and negotiations began for me to become a vice-president in the company when I retired from baseball. Also I was approached by *Look* magazine with a very generous offer if I would give it an exclusive on my retirement story. The time was ripe. However, I was faced with a dilemma. I wanted to be fair to the Dodgers and give them notice of my plans. However, I couldn't talk to anyone about my plans because negotiations with *Look* and Chock were not concluded. If the story leaked to the press, I would lose out on the *Look* story, and if the Chock negotiations broke down, I would face an insecure future with the Dodgers. It was touch and go.

In the end everything happened at once. The day before my signing date with Chock Full O' Nuts and the meeting with the *Look* editors, Buzzy Bavasi left a telephone message that he wanted to see me the next day. I sensed that something was up so I told Buzzy's public relations man, who made the call, that I would be tied up the next day. I didn't want to get into a conference with Buzzy before I had sewn something up for myself. I contacted Bavasi immediately after signing the Chock Full O' Nuts contract to tell him about it. Before I could say anything, he broke the news that he'd been wanting to tell me. The Brooklyn Dodgers had traded me for $30,000 and a pitcher, Dick Littlefield, to the Giants. I was surprised and stunned.

This kind of trade happens all the time in baseball, and it hurts players to realize they can be shunted off to another club without their prior knowledge or consent. My impulse was to tell Bavasi that Jackie Robinson was no longer the Dodgers' property to be traded. But I had to hold out on that because my agreement was to allow *Look* to be the one to break the story. I tried to persuade the Giants front office not to announce the trade for a few days, but since I couldn't explain why, they went ahead and did it. The press practically overran our house in Connecticut, but they got very little out of me. Notes came in the mail from Bavasi and O'Malley. They contained the good old "regrets" business. I appreciated Buzzy's note, but I didn't believe O'Malley meant the nice things he wrote. I took my family to Los Angeles to visit and to keep the press off our backs until the *Look* piece could be printed. Three days before the magazine hit the newsstands, however, the story was out in the press owing to the fact that a few *Look* subscribers had received their copies early. *Look* frantically called us to get back into New York to face the press.

The Giants offered me $60,000 in salary to reconsider. There was so much pressure from fans and youngsters for me to remain in the game that I did have some vague second thoughts. But when Bavasi told the press that I was doing this to get more money out of them, I wouldn't give them a chance to tell me I told you so, and my baseball career was over.

Some of the writers damned me for having held out on the story. Others felt it was my right. Personally, I felt that Bavasi and some of the writers resented the fact that I had outsmarted baseball before baseball had outsmarted me.

The way I figured it, I was even with baseball and baseball with me. The game had done much for me, and I had done much for it.

After the
Ball Game

Chapter X

New Horizons

William Black, a white businessman who was the founder-owner of the Chock Full O' Nuts Corporation, had started off in business selling nuts of various kinds. Business was so good that he moved to a larger location, one which had room for people to come in and stand at the counter. Soon Bill Black was in the restaurant business offering a limited number of rapidly prepared items at reasonable prices and with swift and polite service. The next step was to open chains of shops all over New York City and then to offer franchises and to sell his coffee and some of his other products in retail grocery stores. Bill Black became a millionaire with a flourishing business that eventually became a publicly owned company.

I was amused to learn that, in the minds of some bigoted people, Mr. Black was considered guilty of racial discrimination in hiring. The majority of his employees were blacks. A few racists referred to his company as, "Chock Full O'Niggers." Mr. Black once faced the charge that he was discriminating against whites. He took out a full-page ad in some newspapers explaining in the ad that when he was organizing his business, he had serious problems hiring countergirls and other people necessary to a restaurant. Black men and women who were so severely discriminated against in employment areas were easier for him to get than whites. Since he didn't give a damn about skin color if a person could do the job, he had hired black people. The ad went on to assure whites that if they applied, they would not be mistreated.

At the time I joined Bill Black, Roy Wilkins, who was even then executive secretary of the NAACP, had asked if I would chair the organization's Freedom Fund Drive. This was a national drive to raise major funds for the organization's activities. Membership recruitment and other activities around the country were coordinated from the national office. I have a feeling that when Mr. Wilkins asked me to head the drive, he did so in the same spirit that many organization heads ask public personalities to participate in their work. Get these personalities to agree to the use of their names on the letterheads, attend press conferences and a couple of ceremonial events, take a few publicity pictures, but let the real work be done by others. I was determined it wasn't going to be that way with me. If my name was going to be involved, then I wanted to be involved as much as possible.

One issue that Bill Black and I saw eye to eye on right away was the NAACP Freedom Fund Drive. Mr. Black told me that if he were in my place there wouldn't be enough he could do for the cause of freedom for black people. He said he approved wholeheartedly of my participation and if it didn't interfere with my work at Chock, I was free to use company time to travel, work, and speak for the NAACP. In a gesture that put meaning behind his words, Mr. Black then gave me a check made out to the NAACP that was in five figures. I felt I had a debt to my people and I wanted to volunteer my services at the same time to the organization I believed was helping them the most.

I let Roy know how I felt and said that I would be available to be the national chairman but not just in name only. I was committed to the principles of the NAACP, but I didn't know much about the organization's history and its goals. I would need some guidance and I said so. I had never been the spokesman for a big fund drive either. I would do my part, but I would need a professional teammate. Roy asked Franklin Williams to take a couple of weeks out from his West Coast work to attend the NAACP's annual dinner and accompany me on the speaking tour.

Franklin Williams was a brilliant young lawyer who, in later years, became ambassador to Ghana and now serves as executive director of the Phelps-Stokes Fund. From 1945 to 1950 Frank had been Thurgood Marshall's assistant, handling all the NAACP's criminal cases. In 1950 he had been sent to the West Coast to take over that region for the organization. Frank and I met for the first time at the NAACP's annual dinner, the night before we were to begin our swing through several cities to speak at major fund rallies. The morning after the dinner, we met at Penn Station to take a train for Pittsburgh where the first rally was to be held the following night. Frank and I shared a bedroom with upper and lower berths, and during the first few moments of the trip, there was a great silence between us. Frank tells me now that I was kind of withdrawn, not talkative at all, and that he was riding along, overwhelmed by being with me because he had been a long-time fan. He says he kept asking himself, "How am I going to prepare this famous baseball star to become a civil rights spokesman?"

Finally, I broke the ice and asked Frank to tell me all he could about the NAACP. Frank came up with one of the most amazing performances I'd ever heard. He talked and talked and talked. He talked about the NAACP's beginnings. How it had been founded and by whom. He spoke of all the cases and decisions the organization had won in courts all over the nation and in the Supreme Court. He talked about NAACP personalities like Walter White, Dr. William E. B. DuBois, the Spingarn Brothers, Mary Ovington White and Thurgood

Marshall. It was slightly after eleven o'clock that night when I glanced at my watch. I had become utterly fascinated by Frank's knowledge and by the clear and fluent way he had of communicating.

Frank and I worked out a format for the meetings we were going to address. He would be introduced by a local official. He would present me. I would talk about the NAACP, making a kind of general presentation about why people should support its work. Then Frank would move in again and make the professional money pitch. Anyone who knows anything about fund raising realizes that this is an art, and Frank was a master of it. Frank introduced me, referring to one of the recent cases which had a real emotional appeal. He praised me for being willing to participate in the drive. He said that many people who had achieved success didn't feel it necessary to help in the civil rights struggle. I began to speak, and Frank told me later that he was surprised at the many specific references I made. He was amazed that I was able to use so much of the material which he had given me for background—material he himself intended to use in the clinching fund-raising talk. This forced him to shift gears at the last minute.

Frank and I were greatly exhilarated at that meeting because we were proving that we were a team, that we had a good working spirit, and, between us, we evoked unusual audience response. After Frank's followup, people started literally marching from their seats to give whatever they could—ones and fives and ten-dollar bills. I got so excited that I forgot all about the script, forgot I was finished with my part of the program, and jumped up to stand beside Frank and urged those people on.

I started out talking for five or ten minutes at these meetings, and when I got going well I was doing half-hour speeches. Frank likes to tease me by telling people that I left nothing for him. Going back over it in my mind now, I remember the warmth and enthusiasm of those rallies. It was a thrill to learn that it is not true that black people are not willing to pay for their freedom.

Working with Frank was responsible for a lasting friendship between us. Frank later confessed to me that he had been pretty nervous about the outcome of our working together. He had worked with national chairmen before, he said, but this was the first time a national chairman had come out on the front lines with him and served as the central personality in the rallies. He had shuddered when he thought about how I could have blown the whole deal. Suppose a newsman had asked me in public what the NAACP's attitude was on this or that issue and I stood there with my mouth open. But it hadn't been like that and we were a great team. To this day, Frank likes to kid me because after we had run out of all the gimmicks we could think of, Frank was shamelessly selling kisses—not his, mind you, but mine—to coax ladies to come down the aisle and give some money. What a painless way to sacrifice for the cause.

Our NAACP fund-raising tour was only the beginning of a protracted drive for the organization. We were gratified to learn that the year of our tour was the first year the NAACP had ever raised a million dollars, and we were determined to continue working as a team. We had gone to Detroit together to speak at a $100-a-plate dinner spearheaded by a socially prominent and wealthy black physician, Dr. Alf Thomas, the head of the Detroit organization. During that era, $100-a-plate dinners held by blacks were virtually unheard of.

One morning afterward, I said to Frank, "Why can't the national office sponsor an annual hundred-dollar-a-plate dinner? Do you believe it could be done?" Frank agreed that it was a good idea and we planned a dinner honoring one black and one white person who had made an unusual contribution to the civil rights movement or to racial progress. The $100 admission could be applied—most of it—toward a down payment on a $500 life membership for those who attended. Roy Wilkins listened to our proposition and promptly said it wouldn't work. It would fail because it was too expensive. The reason the dinner in Detroit had worked was that the rich black doctors there had pressured their affluent friends into making it a success. We persisted with strong arguments. Working on it together, Frank and I were sure we could make it a success. Finally Roy reluctantly agreed to let us try it. At the first dinner we honored Marian Anderson and Rudolph Bing, who had given Marian her chance as the first black diva at the Metropolitan Opera. Frank worked like a demon. I put in the maximum time I could, but it was limited because I was heavily involved with my work at Chock. We were very proud when the first national office $100-a-plate dinner brought in a profit of $75,000. That dinner, inspired by the Detroit affair, was the start of the yearly national and branch $100-a-plate dinners around the country which have brought in millions of dollars to the NAACP. Through these dinners, NAACP President Kivie Kaplan received tremendous impetus for his pet idea, the life membership drive.

In January, 1967, I made a decision that I wouldn't have considered possible in 1960. A New York *Times* story stated that Mr. Wilkins' Old Guard had once again crushed the young turks in national board elections. After a great deal of soul searching, I sorrowfully announced that I could no longer be silent and appear to condone what I viewed as the dictatorial administration of Executive Director Wilkins.

I had traveled thousands of miles and made dozens of talks and speeches and raised important quantities of money for the NAACP. I regret none of this, for it remains today the oldest and the strongest civil rights organization we have. It has a proud history of achievement in the protestation of the rights of black people, and it has fought strongly for those principles on which America was supposed to have been founded. In spite of this, in 1967, I had reached a climax of disappointment with the NAACP. My deep doubts about its future, which my associates and my family shared, led me to resign from the national board. I still have my doubts about the NAACP. However I now believe I made a grave error in resigning rather than remaining on the inside to try to fight for reform.

My disenchantment stemmed mainly from my realization that Roy Wilkins and a clique of the Old Guard under his domination had become a reactionary and undemocratic political group. Up until the most recent conventions, Roy and the Old Guard had stifled the efforts of the younger, more progressive forces within the organization to become meaningfully involved. I am not referring to hotheads who want to come in and take over. I am speaking of qualified, thoughtful insurgents already in the ranks, who want to inject new blood and new life into the association.

Realistically, I recognize that the NAACP is so structured constitutionally that the executive director is given tremendous control and power and I feel that during the Wilkins' years, the administration has been insensitive to the trends of our times, unresponsive to the needs and aims of the black masses—especially the young—and more and more they seem to reflect a refined, sophisticated "Yassuh-Mr.-Charlie" point of view.

The determination to keep things as they have been instead of the way they ought to be may help to gain more Ford Foundation money, but it is not going to gain respect from the younger people of our race, many of whom feel the NAACP is archaic and who reject its rigid posture completely.

One of the conditions then existing that many believe has hampered the progress of NAACP was its inflexible position on constitutional provisions which made it impossible to bring younger members onto the board. The age issue has caused much polarization within the rank and file of the organization, on the board itself, and among young black people throughout the nation and within the organization. This state of affairs has improved little over the years.

At the time of its 1971 convention, there were only seven youths on the sixty-four-member board. Ten members were under forty years old. Two-thirds of the board members are over sixty—including ten members who, like Mr. Wilkins, are over seventy.

I do not think age should be held against anyone. I am not opposed to Roy Wilkins because he is over seventy. I am opposed to him because I believe he can no longer relate as effectively to the current problems of black people and black-white relations. I do believe he still has much to give—in terms of experience and wisdom—but that he should become senior statesman, perhaps at board chairman level. He would be able to become more mellow and speak and think with greater effect if he were not forced, by his ego and personality, to remain constantly on guard, an insecure man, despite his great talent and prestige.

Twenty years ago, if someone had suggested to me that Roy Wilkins should move out of the front ranks of civil rights and black leadership, I would never have agreed. For me and, I suppose, for many, many black people of all ages, Roy Wilkins was an idol, a hero, a truly great man. Roy earned the admiration and respect that he was given. He earned it long before black leaders and black youth were putting their bodies on the line for the cause. Roy Wilkins exposed himself to dangerous missions in the South at a time when the South was noted for lynchings and mob brutality against anyone who even thought about opposing its repressive system.

However, Roy's magnificent record is no excuse for enshrining him for life at the helm of the NAACP. Through the years he has demonstrated his inability to administer democratically. A classic example of Roy's manner of operation is the history of his relationship with Frank Williams.

Frank was thirty-nine years old when I met him, and he had been, for some years, one of the young turks of the NAACP hierarchy. He had come from a very angry experience in the American segregated Army, had completed law school in Brooklyn in two years and passed the bar. When Walter White was still in command of the NAACP, White and Thurgood Marshall had hired Frank and recognized that he was a proud and driving man. Marshall gloried in his spunk and gave him important assignments. Roy feared having strong men around him lest they become a threat to his hold over the national board of directors.

Although it has not been too well publicized, there have really been two NAACP's for a number of years. One of them is the Wilkins-controlled organization, which for many years was at 20 West Fortieth Street. The other, the Legal Defense and Educational Fund, which was then at Columbus Circle, was formed when Walter White died and Roy became acting executive director. Thurgood Marshall was boss of legal activities, and everyone who knew anything at all about the internal setup of the national office knew that there was not room enough there for these two giants. Some people thought Thurgood should have been made top man after White's death. But Thurgood Marshall could never have been confined to a glorified desk job, no matter how many speaking engagements were involved.

Roy and Thurgood were both so valuable that the board permitted the establishment of the Legal Defense Fund as an autonomous entity with its own board of directors and staff setup. The two organizations coexisted and cooperated whenever necessary. That's one thing you have to say about Roy. He could always cooperate when the chips were down, even if he didn't like you. However for a number of years, Roy regarded Frank Williams as a mixed blessing to the organization. Roy was aware that there were people around the country, members of the board, and some staff people who regarded Frank as a very good potential candidate for the top spot if Roy ever decided to retire. The laws governing the organization are written so that it doesn't matter if the majority of the paid membership around the country wants a change of command. There can be no change of command unless the national board members so elect. The majority of the national board members are under Roy Wilkins' control. I know. I have been a member of that board and I have seen at first hand how Wilkins is able to fight off any onslaught against his leadership and resist change. Some years after my fund-raising tour with Frank, a national committee was formed to push Frank as a candidate as a member of the board. Wilkins must have seen this as a threat and used his influence to defeat him. Frank Williams lost—a great loss to the NAACP. Frank, however, has gone on to do very well for himself.

Chapter XI

Campaigning for Nixon

I do not consider my decision to back Richard Nixon over John F. Kennedy for the Presidency in 1960 one of my finer ones. It was a sincere one, however, at the time.

The Richard Nixon I met back in 1960 bore no resemblance to the Richard Nixon as President. As Vice President and as Presiding Officer of the Senate he had a fairly good track record on civil rights. When I first met him, he had just returned from a trip around the world, and he came back saying that America would lose the confidence and trust of the darker nations if she didn't clear her own backyard of racial prejudice. Mr. Nixon made these statements for the television cameras and other media for all the world to hear.

Richard Nixon is capable of deep personal goodwill and grace in one-to-one relationships and particularly if he believes you can be useful to his goals. His instincts are flawless when he bends himself to win you to his cause. He can meet you today, be introduced, learn through casual conversation that you have a three-year-old daughter with the mumps and—three months later—approach you, call you by your first name, and ask about the state of health of your little girl—the one who had the mumps. This man has the most fantastic photographic memory for newsmen, politicians, or other humans useful to the art of vote getting, and he has always had a superb briefing staff. Whatever you think of the man personally, he is a consummate political animal.

I met the Vice President and several others, including Senator Hugh Scott, in his office in the White House following the 1960 primary elections of both parties. My trip to see him had resulted from some spirited discussions I had with friends, some of whom were for Nixon and others who were for Senator John Kennedy. I had found that there was a great deal of suspicion in the black community about Nixon, primarily because so many black people were disenchanted with the Eisenhower Administration. They felt that Mr. Eisenhower had a nice grin and little or no concern for rapport with blacks. I had campaigned for Senator Hubert Humphrey in the Democratic primaries because I had a strong admiration for his civil rights background as mayor of Minneapolis and as a Senator. I had heard that he was constantly being warned that his outspoken comments on civil rights would curtail his political progress. I had heard him publicly vow that he was pledged to be the living example of a man who would rather be right morally than achieve the Presidency. But since Mr. Humphrey had not been able to defeat Senator Kennedy in the primaries, I found myself faced with a choice between Nixon and Kennedy. Frankly, I didn't think it was much of a choice but I was impressed with the Nixon record on rights, and when I sat with him in his office in Washington, he certainly said all the right things.

There was one thing that bothered me during that talk, however. The telephone rang on his desk and I heard him telling, I suppose, his secretary, "No, well I can't do that. I'm tired of pulling his chestnuts out of the fire. He'll have to work his own way out of this one."

When he hung up, he turned and smiled at us confiding

that he had just been talking about the President. I couldn't help feeling that he was trying to impress me with the fact that he was really very different from his boss, the President. It sounded as if the Vice President wanted me to disassociate him from Eisenhower since he knew that blacks, in the main, didn't like Ike. It had the feel of a cheap trick. After all, even if it were true that Nixon held this view of the President, it didn't seem respectful that he would let me, whom he didn't know well, in on the secret.

The same day, after leaving the White House, I went to a private home in Washington to talk with Senator Kennedy. Chester Bowles, the former governor of Connecticut and a man I highly respect, had arranged this meeting, hoping I could be persuaded to campaign for Mr. Kennedy.

I found Mr. Kennedy a courteous man, obviously striving to please, but, just as obviously, uncomfortable as he sought to get a conversation going with me. It is remarkable how seemingly minor factors can influence a decision. My very first reaction to the Senator was one of doubt because he couldn't or wouldn't look me straight in the eye. Every time he answered a question or made a statement, he would avoid looking at me and look directly at Governor Bowles, as though he were seeking strength. My mother had taught me to be wary of anyone who talked to you with head bowed or shifty eyes. My second reaction, much more substantial, was that this was a man who had served in the Senate and wanted to be President but who knew little or nothing about black problems and sensibilities. He himself admitted a lack of any depth of understanding about black people. When I said politely that I didn't see anything too encouraging in his Senate record, his manner indicated he was willing and anxious to learn, and I suppose I was being invited to be one of his teachers. Although I appreciated his truthfulness in the matter, I was appalled that he could be so ignorant of our situation and be bidding for the highest office in the land. I was certain Mr. Kennedy was well-versed in foreign affairs, farm problems, urban crises, and so on. Why was he so uneducated about the number-one domestic issue of our time? I knew also that he had a very bleak record on civil rights. It was said that during some of the most vital roll calls on this issue, he had often been missing.

My meeting with the Senator had almost ground to a standstill when my instinct told me what was coming next. How much would it take to get me on board the bandwagon?

"Look, Senator," I said, "I don't want any of your money. I'm just interested in helping the candidate who I think will be best for the black American because I am convinced that the black struggle and its solution are fundamental to the struggle to make America what it is supposed to be." The meeting ended on that embarrassing note.

I came away feeling I could not support John Kennedy. I did write him a note advising him to look people in the eye. I was amused subsequently when a black friend of mine, Frank Montero, who visited the Senator said that Mr. Kennedy didn't take his eyes off him for a minute.

I ended up campaigning for Nixon despite my reservations. Whatever kind of rally we had—even when they were in all-white communities, the Vice President insisted on spotlighting me as one of his supporters. I had a staff and we set up rallies that did not include Nixon. When rallies were held in black communities, we drew such large crowds that the Democrats began sending one of their most potent political stars— Congressman Adam Clayton Powell—to conduct rallies before or after our rallies.

In political appearances, I have never tried to make what is formally accepted as a speech. I find it much more effective to talk to the people and express simply exactly how I feel. Sometimes some of the statements I made were embarrassing to the candidate I was supporting. For instance, I made the point that I was not beholden to any political party, that I was black first, and that, while I believed the candidate I was

On the track team at UCLA, 1940. NATIONAL BASEBALL LIBRARY

Throwing a pass for the UCLA football team, 1939. BETTMANN

Robinson, former lieutenant in the U.S. Army, signs with the Montreal Royals, 1945. BETTMANN

Robinson exhibits his slugging form while trying out for the Montreal club at the Florida training camp. BETTMANN

Robinson signs his contract with the Brooklyn Dodgers, January 24, 1950 with team president Branch Rickey looking on. BETTMANN

Robinson leaps to spear a line drive off the bat of Pittsburgh Pirates' Danny O'Connell in the fifth inning of a game at Ebbets Field, September 22, 1953. Brooklyn won, 5-4.
BETTMANN

OPPOSITE (*Above*): Jackie Robinson is the middle man in executing a double play. NATIONAL BASEBALL LIBRARY

OPPOSITE (*Below*): Jackie Robinson steals home against the Chicago Cubs in 1952. WORLD WIDE

Arguing with umpire Al Barlick during a game against the Giants in September 1952. (Robinson was called out at second.) BETTMANN

Caught by Braves' first baseman Frank McCormack, September 7, 1948. BETTMANN

Johnny Jorgensen, Pee Wee Reese, Eddie Stanky, and Jackie Robinson. NATIONAL
BASEBALL LIBRARY

Jackie Robinson. BETTMANN

At his home in Stamford, Connecticut, with Governor Nelson Rockefeller.

The Rev. Dr. Martin Luther King chats with Robinson before a press conference in
New York, September 19, 1962. BETTMANN

Robinson momentarily joins picketers outside the construction site of Downstate Medical Center, August 2, 1963. Workers were protesting against alleged anti-Negro discrimination in hiring at the site. BETTMANN

Robinson argues for "some progress toward equal rights in housing" before the Federal Civil Rights Commission, February 3, 1959. The chart behind Robinson shows a breakdown of where whites and African-Americans live based on rent and income.

Above: Edd Roush, Jackie Robinson, Bob Feller, and Bill McKechnie being inducted into the Hall of Fame, 1962. NATIONAL BASEBALL LIBRARY

Below: Branch Rickey, Jackie Robinson, Rachel Robinson, and Mallie Robinson (Jackie's mother) at the Hall of Fame induction ceremony. NATIONAL BASEBALL LIBRARY

backing was sincere, if I discovered he wasn't after he got in, I'd be right back to give him hell.

I began to have serious doubts about Nixon when two incidents occurred. In the first, Nixon spoke up, and in the second, he remained silent. Henry Cabot Lodge, the candidate for Vice President on the Nixon ticket, created headlines with a statement that he believed Mr. Nixon, if elected, would name a black man to his Cabinet. The press pursued Mr. Nixon for comment on Mr. Lodge's speculation, and after evading the issue as best he could, Mr. Nixon allowed an official statement to be made that Mr. Lodge was speaking for himself. This did not sit well with me. The second incident involved Mr. Nixon's refusal to speak out in behalf of Dr. Martin Luther King, Jr., who, during the campaign, was confined in a full-security prison in Georgia as the result of a minor motor vehicle infraction. John Kennedy and his campaign-manager brother, Robert, picked up this one and ran with it. The Senator telephoned Mrs. Martin Luther King, Jr., in Atlanta to express his concern, and Bobby Kennedy applied pressure, influence, and political muscle to bring about Dr. King's release. Dr. Martin King, Sr., trumpeted from his pulpit that he was going to gather up a bag of black votes and deliver them to Senator Kennedy to demonstrate his gratitude. I was in the behind-the-scene struggle to persuade Dick Nixon to express his concern for Dr. King, but apparently his most trusted advisers were counseling him not to rock the racial boat. Add to this the fact that Mr. Nixon refused to campaign in Harlem as his opponent did, and it is easy to understand why blacks overwhelmingly voted for Kennedy.

Several times during the Nixon campaign, I was on the verge of quitting and denouncing the Vice President. Rachel did not agree with my support of Nixon. However, she did not press me to quit until he failed to assist Dr. King. Then she and friends urged me to reconsider my stance. Mail and phone calls were coming in. People couldn't understand how I could continue to go along with the program. I kept my silence—certainly not for money. I wasn't getting paid a dime except for expenses and, in fact, never recovered some of my own out-of-pocket expenses. Furthermore, I wasn't staying in because I wanted a job from Nixon if he got elected.

It's hard to explain why I stuck, disillusioned as I was. It has something to do with stubbornness about continuing to want to believe in people even when everything indicates they are no longer worthy of support. It has something to do with the reason I went into politics in the first place and why I worked for the NAACP.

My motives were both selfish and unselfish. I wanted—and still desire—a better world, a bigger break, a fairer chance for my family. I have been very fortunate personally, but my children might not be as fortunate as their father. I don't want them to have to pay the dues I've paid, to experience the tensions and trials I have undergone. Rachel tried to understand, I'm sure, but I sensed puzzlement. I clung to the hope that Nixon would follow through on the things he had indicated were important to him in that first meeting after the pressures of the campaign were over. It was not only my own family I was concerned about but all black families and especially other black children growing into maturity. I admit that the Kennedy ticket had begun to look much more attractive. But I have always felt that blacks must be represented in both parties. I was fighting a last-ditch battle to keep the Republicans from becoming completely white. Nixon lost his campaign, and four years later I lost my battle when Goldwater was nominated.

Chapter XII

The Hall of Fame Award

In 1962 there was a great deal of conjecture about whether I'd be elected to the baseball Hall of Fame. Hall of Fame winners are determined by the Baseball Writers of America, an extremely powerful organization, and since I was a controversial personality in the eyes of the press, I steeled myself for rejection.

To qualify for the Hall of Fame, a player must have been out of the game five years and must receive 75 percent of the ballots. He must have played ten years in the major leagues and made a significant contribution to the game. This award is to the baseball player what the Pulitzer is to a writer or other creative artist; what being named to the Supreme Court bench is to a lawyer. It is the ultimate in recognition, the highest honor in baseball. All the greats of the past have been elected to the Hall of Fame, that is, all the white greats. For, of course, before I got my chance in baseball, black players weren't even admitted into competition. That meant that election to the Hall of Fame would not be as important to me as individual recognition, as it would be terribly significant in symbolizing one of the final full acceptances of blacks in the baseball world.

I would be lying if I pretended that I wouldn't have been thrilled to become a member of the Hall of Fame. On the other hand, I did not want to win election simply because I was the first black man to be considered. Equally, I did not feel that I deserved rejection simply because I had directed what was called "my fiery temper" against violations of my personal dignity and the civil rights of my people. If I got into the Hall, I wanted to get in because I had made it by the standards. The standards are clearly defined. They include ability, integrity, sportsmanship, character, contribution to your team and to baseball in general.

Ironically enough, the one sportswriter who had constantly used me for a target in his column wrote a strong article upholding my right to be elected to the Hall. He was the same man—Dick Young of the New York *Daily News*—who had warned me back in the early days that I would lose awards. A few days before the Hall of Fame results were announced Dick Young wrote:

> Jackie Robinson and I have a bet. We made the bet because he is a rockhead and I am a rockhead. We didn't bet anything. We did it the way kids do it; he said, "I'll betcha," and I said "Bet" and it was a bet. I bet he would be elected to the Hall of Fame at Cooperstown as soon as he was eligible and Jackie bet he wouldn't. Five seasons have passed since Jackie Robinson deprived baseball of his flashing feet and fiery temperament. I am certain that more than 75% pulled for Jackie and for what he represented back in those trying days of 1947 and 1948 when he endured, with a tight-lipped mouth, all the physical and mental abuse that it is possible for men to inflict on other men. I am also certain (though Jackie will dispute this) that, through the years, he received a generally fine and prudent press.

Dick went on to describe the reasons why I was doubtful that I would be elected—prejudice against me and the fact that I had antognized some of the very writers who would be casting ballots. Dick said:

He made enemies. He has a talent for it. He has the tact of a child because he has the moral purity of a child. When you are tactless, you make enemies. Perhaps "enemies" is a harsh word. I rather think that Robinson displeased people and offended them. He made few friends among the newsmen. There is a distinct and obvious difference between not making friends and making enemies. An enemy feels strongly and plots revenge. A non-friend feels indifference. I am confident Jackie's non-friends will sweep him into the Hall of Fame. . . . On ability alone, a strong case can be made for Jackie Robinson: for his .311 batting average through a 10-year career with the Dodgers, for his ability to beat you with his bat, with his glove, with his waddling speed. Jackie Robinson made baseball history and that's what the Hall of Fame is, baseball history.

Several days before the winners were announced, before leaving for my office at Chock Full O'Nuts, as I kissed Rachel good-bye, she told me to "be very careful what you say today."

Rachel has almost always agreed with my basic intentions when I sounded off. I could tell she was concerned that I might unnecessarily say something which would hurt my chances of being chosen.

On the evening of Tuesday, January 23, I learned that the baseball writers had given me 124 out of 160 ballots cast. Appropriately, I was with Rachel in Stamford when the word came.

The phones began ringing. The newsmen and cameramen began arriving. Everybody wanted to hear my reaction. Truthfully, after having steeled myself to be passed over and not to let it hurt me a lot, I was almost inarticulate.

Another honor came my way immediately after the Hall of Fame announcement: A couple of days before my official induction into the Hall of Fame at Cooperstown, Dr. Martin Luther King's Southern Christian Leadership Conference sponsored a testimonial dinner in my honor at the Waldorf-Astoria Hotel. The SCLC had created a special SCLC Hall of Fame award both to congratulate me and to express thanks for the work I had done on behalf of the organization. I really didn't need any thanks for that. I believed so fervently in Dr. Martin Luther King and his courageous aides that nothing I could do for them was too good. At the banquet telegrams were read from the President, the Vice President, and the Attorney General. Dr. Ralph Bunche, Governor Rockefeller, Floyd Patterson (who was honorary chairman of the committee)—oh, so many fine people—spoke and brought a glow to us. Ed Sullivan and Roy Wilkins paid their tributes, and, most fabulous of all, both my mother and Mr. Branch Rickey himself lived to see this day.

Chapter XIII

Conflict at the Apollo

The Apollo Theater, today the only New York City theater that still features live entertainment on a weekly, year-round basis, is an institution in Harlem. Important stars, even those who didn't start their careers there, play the Apollo for less money than they command in a score of other places. They do it because it gets them back to soul. The James Browns, the Ella Fitzgeralds, the Aretha Franklins, the Pearl Baileys, the Stevie Wonders—the stars who are in demand at the top nightclubs—delight in playing the Apollo. Over the years, many things have changed on 125th Street. The block on which the Apollo stands is a part of a main artery. Blumstein's Department Store, where a black woman stabbed Dr. Martin King, is there. Jay Lester's, the famed men's shop, flourishes. On the corner of the block where the Apollo is located is the Freedom National Bank, largest soul bank in the nation. The race wars ravaged Harlem and the street. Many businesses have been burned out or bombed or boarded up, their owners having given up in frustration and disgust. The Apollo seems to be marked with a special magic. During riots, when store windows were shattered, and looting, bombing, and rock hurling became the thing of the day or night, no one touched the Apollo. The angry mobs passed it by as though it were some sort of a temple exempt from destruction. There was a time, however, during a few tense days, when the Apollo faced the greatest threat of destruction in all its fabled history.

Frank Schiffman is the owner of the Apollo, and he either owned or had an interest in additional 125th Street real estate. Mr. Schiffman became involved in a squabble between a downtown steak house owner who had leased a Schiffman property and a group of black nationalists who wanted to prevent the downtown man from opening a steak house in Harlem. The proposed new store was a chain restaurant where, for less than two dollars, customers on a cafeteria line are served steak, salad, a baked potato, a roll, and coffee. The nationalists did not want the white merchant to come to the street with his low-priced steaks because it would hurt a black restaurateur who was selling steaks for a higher price. From what I understood, they would not have objected if the newcomer was willing to up his price to that of the black restaurant. I cannot tell you, to this day, who was right or wrong about the business issue. I know, however, that the tactics employed by the black nationalists were tactics that would have brought disaster to the community. The nationalists set up picket lines in front of the Apollo, and they resorted to blatant appeals to anti-Semitism. Their signs and posters referred to Schiffman as "a Shylock" who was trying constantly to get his pound of flesh from the community. The tone of the literature and the signs was racial and anti-Jewish and not based on the central issue in the controversy. A picket line in front of a white-owned business in the black community is a serious threat to the life of that business, especially when racial and religious undertones are brought in. Ghettos smolder even when circumstances appear serene.

Always, under the surface, are the boiling resentments of people who are underpaid, underemployed, overcharged by landlords, and exploited by merchants who sell them substandard goods. Chain stores and supermarkets from white upper-class communities bring the rotting foods they can no longer sell to their customers into the ghetto. These conditions make the ghetto a virtual tinderbox, ready to explode at the slightest provocation.

Aware of all this, Frank Schiffman and his son Robert, then his executive aide, made a number of phone calls to ministers, civic leaders, and other community people. For years these people had come to the Schiffmans for contributions and free use of the theater for charitable events. Suddenly they were not available to help. Apparently, they didn't want to tangle with the black pickets marching in front of the theater. They weren't about to stick their necks out. One day a newsman friend of mine learned of the Schiffmans' plight and phoned me to say he thought I should look into it with an eye to dealing with it in my column. My friend knew I'd be interested in the anti-Semitic picket signs, one of which said the equivalent of "blacks must stay, Jews must go." I have resented bigotry in any form, and I couldn't understand when no one came to Schiffman's aid. I was ashamed to see community leaders who should have known better afraid to speak out when blacks were guilty of blatant anti-Semitism—even if they were only a handful of blacks. How could we stand against anti-black prejudice if we were willing to practice or condone a similar intolerance?

I did not know Schiffman well personally and, before doing anything, inquired carefully about him. There were some people who said he had exploited the black community for years. Others told me about the stars, orchestras, and singing groups that might never have made it without the Apollo. The Apollo Theater gave weekly employment to hundreds, but since Frank Schiffman had made a fortune—and had made it because of black talent and black patronage—some black critics suggested he give money back to the community. On the other hand, I discovered some unknown facts about Schiffman; he had given, unasked, to civil rights causes *not* in the community, and for every tale I heard of "exploitation" by Schiffman, I heard a story about his help to black show business people who were down on their luck. I didn't feel that Schiffman was some kind of selfless saint or philanthropist, but I did decide he was not a Shylock and that he was a decent man who had given something of value to the community.

I wrote a vigorous column condemning anti-Semitism, branding it as thoroughly venal when it came from a race of people who had felt the sting of bigotry for so many years. When the column appeared, the black nationalist group's leaders were enraged. They struck back by throwing another picket line in front of the Chock Full O'Nuts store down the street from the Apollo, on the corner of 125th Street and Seventh Avenue. The nationalists also announced that they would picket a dinner to be given in my honor a few days later. It was the dinner, sponsored by the SCLC, to feature that organization's Hall of Fame award to me a few days before I was to go to Cooperstown to receive the award.

The nationalists' acts made headlines, and immediately a number of Harlem leaders as well as some national leaders began to express their support of Frank Schiffman and me. A. Philip Randolph and Roy Wilkins weighed in immediately on the side of decency and they didn't do it for publicity. Roy Wilkins wired us:

> THE NAACP SUPPORTS YOU 100%. IN THEIR FIGHT FOR EQUAL OPPORTUNITY, NEGROES CANNOT USE THE SLIMY TOOLS OF ANTI-SEMITISM OR INDULGE IN RACISM, THE VERY TACTICS AGAINST WHICH WE CRY OUT. WE JOIN YOU IN YOUR STRAIGHT STATEMENT THAT THIS IS A MATTER OF PRINCIPLE FROM WHICH THERE CAN BE NO RETREAT.

Mr. Randolph assured us in his wire that our stand was "timely, sound and constructive."

Among other supporters were Percy Sutton, now Manhattan Borough President, Leigh Whipper, the grand old man of black theater, and the late Dr. E. Washington Rhodes, publisher of the influential Philadelphia *Tribune.*

There were also a number of black church leaders who came through beautifully. The Reverend George Lawrence, the courageous and witty pastor of Antioch Baptist Church in Brooklyn, reminding people that Chock had products in neighborhood grocery stores, added, "You know they got a jingle—a singing commercial—that Chock Full O'Nuts is a heavenly coffee. And if it's a heavenly coffee, Christians ought to drink it anyhow."

William Black, the president of Chock Full O'Nuts Company, gave me complete backing. He told the press: "Jackie Robinson is right. The pickets can march until they can't walk anymore. They can close down the store but I am with Robinson."

Leon Lewis, the radio commentator, at the time with Radio Station WWRL, a black-oriented outlet, decided he could create a good radio program and perhaps ease the situation if he persuaded both sides to meet on his program and debate. He asked Lewis Micheaux and me to do a show that he would moderate. Lewis Micheaux was the proprietor of the National Memorial African Book Store, internationally famous for its publications by and about black people. It was then on Seventh Avenue and is now located on 125th Street and Lenox Avenue. Hundreds of Harlem's street corner rallies took place in front of the former location. From this corner Malcolm X spoke, Adam Clayton Powell campaigned, housing leader Jesse Gray cursed out slum landlords, and every major national and local political candidate who wanted black votes visited. Fiery anti-white-man speeches, "buy-black" speeches, and protest speeches were constantly heard. Mr. Micheaux, if he was not directly allied with the nationalists who had picketed the Apollo and Chock, was in very deep sympathy with their campaign.

I've been in a number of heavy debates on radio and television but never one as free-swinging and brutally frank as the one with Micheaux. He accused me of taking the white man's side in a black argument. I retorted that it was wrong for any group, of whatever color, to agitate hatred, to use religious prejudice to resolve a dispute. Mr. Micheaux labeled me a flunky for whites, and I responded by calling him a bigot, a demagogue, and on top of that—stupid. He said that I didn't even have sense enough to write my own column, and I replied that I was not ashamed of the fact that I am not a professional writer. I told him that I never hid the fact that Al Duckett ghosted my column, but I added that it was a joint effort, that the column never reflected anything that wasn't sincerely my conviction. I told him he was pretty dumb if he didn't know that lots of people in public life have ghost-writers. The exchange got hot but was managed well by the soothing influence of Leon Lewis. He is a fabulous moderator. He handled us so skillfully that, after a solid hour of knock-down, drag-out quarreling, Mr. Micheaux and I suddenly began to listen to each other. The rare quality of reasonableness stole into our minds. As the broadcast ended, we agreed that anti-Semitism was despicable and the black man should never resort to it. The press reported that the fight had been settled on the Leon Lewis *Controversy* show. Mr. Micheaux came to Chock Full O'Nuts and made a speech going all out for us. The pickets withdrew from the Apollo and from Chock. Mr. Micheaux and I have had a hearty respect for each other from that day on.

I believe our debate had a healthy effect on the community and on black thinking. It was a clear example of two people who were at terrible odds with each other resolving their problem through reason.

Chapter XIV

Crises at Home

After Jackie's very early years in school, it became obvious that his problems were becoming serious. He began to dislike school intensely, and in time he earned the reputation of being a troublemaker. Rachel had endless and seemingly fruitless conferences with the teachers, and her efforts to help Jackie with his homework were untiring. Jackie and Rachel were close to each other, and Rachel often felt that she had helped and that some progress had been made.

Sharon was also in public school, working conscientiously and doing well. When it was time to send David to school, our awareness of Jackie's miseries made us decide not to risk public school again, and we sent David to a private school nearby. Not long after David was enrolled, we asked Jackie if he would like to change to his brother's school. We felt that the smaller classes and better attention from teachers would help stimulate his interest in schoolwork. Jackie's feelings about school in general were plainly negative, and he made it clear that he really wasn't interested in any school under any circumstances.

As time went on, we tried everything we knew or had ever

heard about. When Jackie was twelve, we were advised to try psychological testing. The results showed that he was a normal boy and that we had little to worry about in that area. The test itself was a bad idea. It was composed of stock questions not at all related to Jackie, and we felt that subjecting him to it had undoubtedly heightened the pressures he was already feeling. We had conscientiously tried not to submit Jackie to the pressures a lot of parents put on their children; we didn't demand high marks or a super performance. He saw a therapist for several months until he decided it was of little value. However, there was very little we could do about the outside pressures that seemed to begin crowding in on Jackie more and more as he approached his teen-age years. He did display an interest in little league baseball and went all the way through to finish the Babe Ruth League. He enjoyed playing and he was good at it, but he was exposed to cruel experiences not so much by the youngsters as by their parents who made loudly vocal comparisons between the way Jackie played and the way I played.

During his years in junior high and high school, Jackie's record of failures and poor grades was becoming a real disaster. A friend suggested we send him away from home to a school in the Berkshires. We did send him away, but this turned out badly for Jackie. Jackie seemed to need more freedom, but at the time he probably needed more guidance and structure. He was uninterested in the academic work, but he was fascinated by the school plays, the art activities, and the work chores. One of the highpoints of his brief stay was getting to drive a garbage wagon. He didn't care what he was driving as long as he had a chance to drive. His stay at the school ended abruptly when he was suspended for breaking too many of the school rules. This meant coming home to Stamford and another try at public high school. He stayed at home for a year, but he seemed lost. A psychiatrist advised us not to try to force him to stay in school. It was felt this was a decision Jackie should be able to make on his own. Once we told Jackie the decision was his, he tried with commendable effort to stick it out.

For several years before Jackie reached adolescence, I had been painfully aware of the widening gap between us. My relationship with him was a very difficult one. I loved him deeply and he knew it. He loved me deeply and I knew it. But the peculiar chemistry that is responsible for free communication between two individuals was absent. I couldn't get through to him and he couldn't get through to me. We didn't seem to know how, although we both tried hard to reach out to each other. We often rubbed each other the wrong way and anger would start rising. Rachel, looking back, often blames herself, remembering that her mother, Mrs. Isum, who was living with us, had told her that she sometimes stepped in too quickly when Jackie and I seemed headed toward an angry argument. Grandmother Isum seemed to feel that perhaps my son and I needed a good, knock-down, all-out fight to unleash our inhibitions and clear the air.

Undoubtedly Jackie was hurt by his awareness of the tremendous rapport I had with his younger brother David. We talked together easily and naturally and we did things together. We played ball. When Jackie was growing up, there were many times when I was reluctant to play ball with him. I wanted to, but I had a gut feeling I shouldn't make him think that I was pushing him into baseball or that I was desperate to have him follow in my footsteps. In retrospect I realize it was a mistake. I know now that Jackie felt rejected by me and naturally became closer and closer to his mother. He spent most of his time with her. And, unfortunately, much of the time I wasn't available to him, particularly after my baseball career when I became deeply involved in the civil rights movement and politics and traveled constantly. Ironically, a lot of my time was taken up at meetings and sports events sponsored by organizations that were in the business of helping youngsters. When the roof caved in, when Jackie got into deep trouble, I realized that I had been so busy trying to help other youngsters that I had neglected my own. I felt that Rae and I had protected and loved our children and buttressed them with enough basic principles to the point that it never occurred to me that they could get involved in any serious trouble. When it happened, we were totally unprepared. Ugly things couldn't be happening to our child. We believed we could always depend on our children to tell us the absolute truth. The things that happened to other families couldn't happen in ours.

I've spent many hours trying to understand the reasons for the difficulties between Jackie and me. Maybe we were too much alike. We were both rather introverted, reserved, and conservative in personal relationships, and the kind of people who didn't openly express emotion. Rachel thinks I was not as aware as she was of Jackie's competitive feelings toward me. She remembers my discussions about my daily—and, to me, vital—experiences; they left the children with little to say and made them feel that their activities would seem insignificant in comparison with mine. She felt that David identified with my reports about "how the day had gone," but that Jackie felt it would be demeaning if he bragged about the fifty cents he had earned doing a chore for someone when his father had made $500.

Rachel blames herself for not telling me until it was too late that "some of the things you talk about at the table keep the kids from bringing up their own little successes." By the same token she feels my guilt feelings are much too excessive and that I never have given myself enough credit for how hard I tried to reach Jackie. I can only believe that I really did not understand the depth of the problem.

The communication problem became so overwhelming between Jackie and me that we often found ourselves resorting to a convenient copout; we used Rachel. I'd say to Rachel, "You tell Jackie that . . . " And Jackie would tell Rachel, "Will you ask Dad if . . . ?" We developed a wariness of each other; we were afraid of getting angry and we tried to talk to each other as little as possible.

In his teens Jackie ran away from home with a buddy of his. There had been no quarrel to trigger this, and later we discovered that Jackie had felt that if he could be on his own for a while, he would be able to come to grips with himself. He had been sinking further and further into depression about his school failures. Believing that any able-bodied young man could get a job, Jackie and his friend decided to hitchhike to the West Coast. They couldn't get jobs as they had planned all along the way, and when they finally reached California, where they had counted on getting hired as migrant farm workers, they found they had arrived during the wrong season.

The day Jackie left I had just been released from the hospital. I had had a major operation and I had been badly scared. I was profoundly thankful to come home.

But Jackie had disappeared. Mother Isum said the last time she had seen Jackie he was carrying a brown bag, and she thought he had gone to the bank. We called the bank and learned that he had taken the money out of his savings account.

Normally we never invaded our children's privacy. We didn't believe in entering their rooms without knocking or rummaging through their things without permission. But when Jackie disappeared, I felt justified in searching his room to try to find out where he had gone. The search wasn't fruitful in that sense, but in the course of it I came across an old wallet of Jackie's. It was jammed with typical teen-age possessions. Among them was a pocket-sized picture of me. It meant that Jackie had cared a lot more for his old man than his old man had guessed.

I couldn't hold back the tears. I broke down and cried in the terrible way a man cries when he's someone who never cries. Through all the bad times Rachel had never seen me

155

cry, and it made a bad experience that much more painful to her.

A few days later Jackie called and said that he had reached California and that he couldn't get a job. He wanted to come home, and he made it clear that his running away was not a sign of rejection of us and it didn't mean he didn't love us; he had to get away and see if he could get by on his own.

Shortly after he ran away, in the spring of 1964, Jackie volunteered for the Army. He told us that he hoped to pull himself together, get the discipline he knew he needed badly, and establish his own identity. He was seventeen and he believed all the stories he heard about the opportunity the Army gave enlistees to travel. Jackie got to travel all right. Within less than a year of training, he was shipped to Vietnam and straight into combat. However, before he was sent overseas, Jackie had taken high school equivalency exams and passed, and he was proud that he had taken his future into his own hands. His letters encouraged us to believe some of his problems would be solved.

When he was in Vietnam Jackie was bothered by the antiwar demonstrations at home. I didn't like them either, and I had disagreed with the stand Dr. Martin Luther King took on the war. Reverend Jesse Jackson has pointed out that Dr. King was against the war but not against the soldiers; that his fight was with those who set the policy that created the war. Disagreement about the war has created much bitterness and division in the country, and I felt strongly that those who opposed the war had no right to call the black kids who served in it willing dupes of imperialism and to ridicule and denigrate our men.

As for the blacks who joined the Army, often it was not solely for reasons of patriotism that they did so. Many of them sought opportunities in the Armed Forces that were denied them in civilian life. Many of them came to wonder, as Jackie finally did while he was in the hospital in Vietnam, about the contradiction of having fought for freedom for people on foreign soil only to come home to be denied equal rights. Jackie supported the war, but he didn't buy a system of government that preached democracy in Vietnam but had neither homes for blacks in certain neighborhoods nor jobs for the black veteran in certain areas like the construction industry.

While Jackie was in the hospital in Vietnam, newspaper articles about him portrayed him as a hero, but he shrugged that off by saying, "It wasn't all that much. I just got shrapnel in the ass." The reports we got, however, indicated that he had gone through a pretty traumatic experience. He got a sample of the horror of killing first hand when—on one side of him at the front lines—one of his best buddies was killed and another died in his arms. This happened as Jackie was trying to drag his own wounded body back behind the lines in search of the medics.

Sharon and David read and shared every letter Jack sent to the family. Quietly, Sharon was going through her own traumatic problems becoming a teen-ager. She went through a heart-wrenching experience in her friendship with Christy, a daughter of one of our neighbors. Christy was white, but her whiteness and Sharon's blackness had been irrelevant to both of them ever since they became friends at five. They were best friends and Christy's parents were as delighted with the friendship as we were. If Sharon wasn't spending the night at Christy's house, Christy spent the night at ours. When their friendship hit the rocks, it was a replay of an old and tragic story. It illustrates what society does to youngsters whose color blindness in their love for each other fades into a sad color consciousness during teen-age years. Young romance, date making, the whole social situation enters the picture. In the South and in many parts of the North, it would have been the white girl withdrawing, being warned perhaps by family or friends, that social contact with a black friend could create problems. It didn't happen that way with Christy and Sharon. Christy wasn't the one who withdrew. Sharon was the one, and

157

Christy was terribly hurt by it. But Sharon did it because something in her anticipated a rejection by Christy which could ultimately hurt her deeply.

Sharon, perhaps for the first time, began to wish we had never moved from St. Albans. She loved the country atmosphere and she loved our house, but she dreamed how wonderful it would have been to have these elements and still be within a black community where she could have black companionship. Sharon, I believe, is one of those young women who would have a hard time ever marrying across the color line because of the depth of her pride in being black.

Looking back to her teen-age days, Sharon thinks we were overprotective of our children, that we shielded Jackie and David and her too much. At home Rae and I had always been careful not to raise angry voices when the children were around. Maybe Sharon was right. At any rate, when she came out of her quiet little shell briefly and began to rebel, Sharon decided to go off with a crowd we didn't particularly approve of. She wanted to see life more realistically. She felt that Rae, even though she never overtly pushed it, hoped she would go into nursing. As a result, when Sharon decided to be independent, she vehemently declared she didn't want to be a nurse. Today Sharon is a nurse and admits she rejected the idea because she was looking for things to reject.

Rae and I have never had a deeply serious conflict. We do not have a storybook marriage full of sweetness and light. But we are both very grateful that our love for each other has been strong enough for us to give each other comfort through good and bad times. One of the factors that could have threatened our marriage if we hadn't applied patience and understanding to its solution had to do with Rae's professional career. When Jackie was twelve years old and David was in school full time, Rachel enrolled in New York University and began working for her masters degree in psychiatric nursing. She earned it in 1960. Rae says that one of her motivations in preparing to reenter professional life was crystallized one day when the children were going off to camp. She realized as they left that the day would be coming when they wouldn't be kids anymore. Probably all of them would go their separate ways. She would need something to do to occupy her mind, but, even more important, she did not want to go through her life being known only as Mrs. Jackie Robinson. She has a strong, independent spirit, and she wanted to be accepted as an individual in her own right. To be very honest, if I had my way, Rachel would not have a job. But having my way would constitute selfishness as well as insensitivity to her needs as a person.

Rachel says that I was proud as long as she was going to school. I was working for Chock Full O'Nuts then. We would get up very early in the morning, drive into the city from our Connecticut place, and in the evening I would go to the school and pick her up to drive her home. She studied into the wee hours and on weekends. She frequently went to bed with the kids but would then get up later to do her work. She says I was proud and pleased—and I was—when she was graduated but that when she actually began to go to work every day, my annoyance and resentment began to show. We had discussed the problem and made our agreement, but I know she is right. I really didn't want her to work, even though I knew she was entitled to aspire to her own personal goals. Now I am proud that my wife has had a successful career. Her first job was as staff nurse and supervisor on the administrative staff of the Albert Einstein College of Medicine of Yeshiva University. She didn't have to work late in the day and was generally at home when the children came home from school.

In 1965 Rachel went to Yale University as assistant professor in the School of Nursing. She was also director of nursing in the Connecticut Medical Health Center in New Haven. Holding down both jobs simultaneously meant that she was involved in teaching, clinical work, and administration at the same time. She loved the work. She found it challenging and she particularly liked the contact with students. On her job Rae was known as Rachel Robinson, not Mrs. Jackie Robinson. We still laugh about one experience she had when she first went to work. An article had come out about our family in *Life* magazine. One of her co-workers was looking over the magazine and turned to look at Rachel, then back at the magazine.

"Aren't you Jackie Robinson's wife?" was the inevitable question.

Without even giving it a second thought, Rachel promptly said, "No."

The denial just slipped out. She was so horrified when she realized what she had done that she promptly went to look for a fellow psychologist at the school. They sat down and discussed the incident. Rachel realized that she didn't really want to deny that I was part of her life but that she wanted to be known and respected as an individual in her own right.

For a while Rae told herself that it was necessary to conceal her married identity because it might make a difference to her patients who were usually accustomed to having those who took care of them remain fairly anonymous. Now she knows that this rationalization was a copout and that what she actually wanted was the assurance of her own identity. After she realized that, she didn't go around announcing that she was Mrs. Jackie Robinson, but neither did she do anything unnatural to hide it. People would discover her private identity when I went to staff parties with her. She told me once, "Now that I am established as an individual, I'm pleased to have people link me with you." Some of her patients or co-workers often ask about me and she likes to talk about me. She kids me about a habit I have had for years—of constantly saying "we" when I am referring to myself. I hardly ever say "I." I'm apt to say that "we caught a plane to Cincinnati" even when Rachel hasn't gone along. It's an integral part of my speech pattern.

Rachel has told me, "You don't think of me as separate,

and sometimes you have a hard time allowing me to be separate." She's right about that, and she has reminded me several times in a teasing way of what I said when mail started coming to the house addressed to Professor Rachel Robinson. I asked if that was the proper way to address her.

"Yes, honey," Rachel answered. "I have a name, too, and there's nothing wrong with people using it."

Sometimes I think that just about everyone in our immediate family has had an unusual struggle to gain acceptance as an individual. Although our problems were somewhat unique because of my position as a celebrity, we were really going through the crises common to any family— and particularly any black family growing up in today's society. It was the universal conflict of father and son, of growing brothers and sisters, of a man and his wife when she is trying to establish an identity and worth beyond her role as a wife—and it was the problem of an upward mobile black family in a subtly discriminatory affluent northern white society.

Chapter XV

On Being Black
Among the Republicans

My first meeting with Nelson Rockefeller occurred in 1962 during a public event at which we were both speakers. The Nelson Rockefeller personal charm and charisma had now become legendary. It is almost impossible not to like the man. He gives two distinct impressions: that he is sincere in whatever he is saying and that, in spite of his fantastic schedule, power, and influence—at that specific moment of your contact—he has shut everything else out and is focusing his complete and concentrated attention on you.

While I admired his down-to-earth maner and outgoing ways instantly, I was anything but overwhelmed at our initial meeting. I am aware that the enormously wealthy have time to spread charm as they like. They have their worries, but survival is not one of them, as it is with us. I wasn't about to be taken in instantly by the Nelson Rockefeller charm. After all, Richard Nixon had turned the charm on me too (although his is a bit brittle compared with Rockefeller's) and look how that had turned out.

I knew that Rockefeller's family had given enormous sums

to black education and other philanthropic causes for black people and that at that time (nearly twenty years ago) a significant number of black college presidents, black professionals, and a significant number of leaders of national stature had received a college education, financed by Rockefeller gifts. While I have no need to detract from the contributions of the family to black education, I felt it certainly must be weighed in terms of what went into the amassing of one of the world's greatest fortunes.

As for Nelson Rockefeller himself, I knew little or nothing about his politics. As far as I was concerned, he was just another rich guy with politics as a toy. Our first chat had nothing to do with politics. In fact, the governor took advantage of the occasion to tell me about a private problem. Since I was an officer of the Chock Full O'Nuts Restaurant chain at that time, he thought I might be able to help him. It seemed the Rockefeller family was unhappy about one of our advertising jingles which assured the public that our coffee was as good as any "Rockefeller's money can buy." Representations about the family's feeling in the matter had been made through legal and diplomatic channels, but the offensive jingle was still being aired on radio and television commercials. I promised to mention the matter to Bill Black, Chock's president. I was surprised at Mr. Black's reaction. When I reported the Rockefeller concern, he snapped, "Good! Let them sue. We can use the publicity."

As far as I was concerned, that was the end of that. As far as I knew, I'd probably never be in contact with the governor again. However, I began to change my mind about Rockefeller when I learned the extent of his support for a man I admired deeply, Martin Luther King.

When student sit-ins began in the South and many so-called liberals criticized them, Governor Rockefeller told the press that he believed the protesting youngsters were morally justified. I also learned that, unlike Richard Nixon who failed to speak out about the Georgia jailing of Dr. King, the governor had promptly wired the President asking for his protection.

I also learned of some of the governor's unpublicized actions. Before Rockefeller became governor, the world was stunned by the attempted assassination of Dr. King by a black woman in a Harlem department store. Rushed to Harlem Hospital, Dr. King who had been wounded by a letter opener plunged into a spot just below the tip of his aorta immediately was put under the care of a team of crack surgeons headed by Dr. Louis Wright. The newspapers gave intensive publicity to the fact that the then-Governor Harriman had sped to the hospital escorted by police convoy with shrieking sirens. Harriman ordered every available facility utilized to save Dr. King. Then he stayed at the hospital for several hours, keeping vigil and awaiting word of the civil rights leader's condition. Governor Harriman deservedly got credit for his concern about a beloved black leader. But it was Nelson Rockefeller who quietly issued orders to have the hospital bill sent to him.

I learned that the governor had made frequent gifts to Dr. King's Southern Christian Leadership Conference. I was on the scene a few hours after hate-crazed bigots burned Georgia churches to the ground. Dr. King asked me to head a national fund-raising drive to restore the churches. Two of the first substantial donations were made by my then-boss Mr. William Black and by Governor Rockefeller. We did rebuild those churches.

Yet with all his goodwill gestures and philanthropies, there was one fact which bothered me deeply about the Rockefeller Administration in 1962. Although New York has, for many years, enjoyed a reputation as a liberal state, the higher echelons of the state government were all white. There were no blacks at top-level, policy-making positions. There was not even one black man or woman who had a direct line to the governor and who could alert him to the concerns and grievances of black people. I wondered if Nelson Rockefeller's generosity to black causes was a compartmentalized activity of his private life, and I was sufficiently curious to write him a letter.

My letter to the governor was a harshly honest letter. I said I felt no self-respecting black man could respect an administration that had no blacks in significant jobs. Governor Rockefeller met my honesty head on. He telephoned me personally and told me how much he appreciated my truthfulness. He admitted that things were not as they should be for blacks in state government and that he wanted to take steps to correct this; he suggested we meet and talk things over within the next few days.

In the course of that telephone call, I bluntly said, "If you don't want to hear the down-to-earth truth about how you are thought of in the black community, let's just forget about it."

He assured me that he wanted and needed unbiased advice. The meeting, unadvertised in the press and unreported after it took place, was held in a private room at the top of Radio City Music Hall. About a dozen to fifteen people whom I had invited attended. For some three hours we told the governor our grievances about the failure of his administration to include blacks in the political and government action. The people there didn't hesitate to recite harsh facts. He was aware of some of the facts we gave him; other facts seemed to shock him. He accepted our criticism, our recommendations for change, and he acted to bring about reforms. He did not bring any apologists or token black leaders into the meeting to justify himself. He brought an open mind and someone to take notes.

Within a few months after that meeting, the governor had implemented virtually all the recommendations that the *ad hoc* committee had made. Out of that one meeting came some sweeping and drastic changes, some unprecedented appointments of blacks to high positions, ensuring influence by blacks in the governor's day-to-day policy decisions. Some of the governor's top-level people were very unhappy about these changes.

In 1964 Governor Rockefeller asked me to become one of six deputy national directors of his campaign. I had spent seven years at Chock Full O'Nuts. I decided to resign from my job rather than ask for leave. The knowledge I had acquired about the business world, I considered invaluable. I had been criticized by some of my fellow officers in the company who genuinely felt I took the part of the employees too often, that I was too soft on them. Even so I had been given generous raises and benefits, allowed to purchase a healthy bundle of stock, and been elected to the board. I was becoming restless; I wanted to involve myself in politics as a means of helping black people and I wanted my own business enterprises. I had been increasingly convinced of the need for blacks to become more integrated into the mainstream of the economy. I was not thinking merely of job integration. A statement Malcolm X made was most impressive. Referring to some college students who were fighting to be served in Jim Crow restaurants, Malcolm said he wanted not only the cup of coffee but also the cup and saucer, the counter, the store, and the land on which the restaurant stood.

I believed blacks ought to become producers, manufacturers, developers, and creators of businesses, providers of jobs. For too long we had been spending much too much money on liquor while we owned too few liquor stores and were not even manufacturing it. If you found a black man making shoes or candy or ice cream, he was a rarity. We talked about not having capital, but we needed to learn to take a chance, to be daring, to pool capital, to organize our buying power so that the millions we spent did not leave our communities to be stacked up in downtown banks. In addition to the economic security we could build with green power, we could use economic means to reinforce black power. How much more effective our demands for a piece of the action would be if we were negotiating from the strength of our own self-reliance rather than stating our case in the role of a beggar or someone crying out for charity. We live in a materialistic society in which money doesn't only talk—it screams. I could not forget that some of the very ballplayers who swore the most fervently that they wouldn't play with me because I was black were the first to begin helping me, giving me tips and advice, as soon as they became aware that I could be helpful to them in winning the few thousand more dollars players receive as world series champs. The most prejudiced of the club owners were not as upset about the game being contaminated by black players as they were by fearing that integration would hurt them in their pocketbooks. Once they found out that more—not fewer—customers, black and white, were coming through those turnstiles, their prejudices were suppressed.

When Governor Rockefeller invited me on board his campaign ship, I had no idea of any long-term relationship in politics. I saw this as a sign that now was the time for me to enter into a new world of political involvement with a man I respected. At the same time I could be free to pursue some business endeavors that had been proposed to me. I had been approached about becoming a key organizer in a projected, new insurance company, an integrated firm that, I hoped, could be a force in correcting some of the unjust practices of some insurance firms that treat blacks unfairly. At this time the group organizing a new bank in Harlem—Freedom National—had asked me to help put it together and to become chairman of the board, and there were other business ventures in which I felt I might be able to play a vital role. When I submitted my resignation to Bill Black, he understood my aspirations. He didn't want me to leave, and he was genuinely concerned as to whether I was making the wisest move. He tried to persuade me to stay. I appreciated his attitude, but my mind was made up. I joined the Rockefeller campaign headquarters.

One of the first things that became clear to me was that I had not been called on to be the black adviser to the campaign. Often white politicians secure the services of a black man and slot him only for appearances and activities within the black community. Sometimes they do this to avoid letting whites know that they are making a strong pitch for black support. During the Rockefeller campaign I met with groups and made appearances before audiences which were sometimes integrated, sometimes predominantly black, and other times mainly white. On several occasions, when the governor came into town for a meeting with politicians or community people, I would accompany him. At some of the larger meetings, I would be asked to introduce the governor.

I was not as sold on the Republican party as I was on the governor. Every chance I got, while I was campaigning, I said plainly what I thought of the right-wing Republicans and the harm they were doing. I felt the GOP was a minority party in terms of numbers of registered voters and could not win unless they updated their social philosophy and sponsored candidates and principles to attract the young, the black, and the independent voter. I said this often from public, and frequently Republican, platforms. By and large Republicans had ignored blacks and sometimes handpicked a few servile leaders in the black community to be their token "niggers." How would I sound trying to go all out to sell Republicans to black people? They're not buying. They know better.

I admit freely that I think, live, and breathe black first and foremost. That is one of the reasons I was so committed to the governor and so opposed to Senator Barry Goldwater. Early in 1964 I wrote a *Speaking Out* piece for *The Saturday Evening Post*. A Barry Goldwater victory would insure that the GOP's would become completely the white man's party. What happened at San Francisco when Senator Goldwater became the Republican standard-bearer confirmed my prediction.

I wasn't altogether caught off guard by the victory of the reactionary forces in the Republican party, but I was appalled by the tactics they used to stifle their liberal opposition. I was a special delegate to the convention through an arrangement made by the Rockefeller office. That convention was one of the most unforgettable and frightening experiences of my life. The hatred I saw was unique to me because it was hatred directed against a white man. It embodied a revulsion for all he stood for, including his enlightened attitude toward black people.

A new breed of Republicans had taken over the GOP. As I watched this steamroller operation in San Francisco, I had a better understanding of how it must have felt to be a Jew in Hitler's Germany.

The same high-handed methods had been there.

The same belief in the superiority of one religious or racial group over another was here. Liberals who fought so hard and so vainly were afraid not only of what would happen to the GOP but what would happen to America. The Goldwaterites were afraid—afraid not to hew strictly to the line they had been spoon-fed, afraid to listen to logic and reason if it was not in their script.

I will never forget the fantastic scene of Governor Rockefeller's ordeal as he endured what must have been three minutes of hysterical abuse and booing which interrupted his fighting statement which the convention managers had managed to delay until the wee hours of the morning. Since the telecast was coming from the West Coast, that meant that many people in other sections of the country, because of the time differential, would be in their beds. I don't think he has ever stood taller than that night when he refused to be silenced until he had had his say.

It was a terrible hour for the relatively few black delegates who were present. Distinguished in their communities, identified with the cause of Republicanism, an extremely unpopular cause among blacks, they had been served notice that the party they had fought for considered them just another bunch of "niggers." They had no real standing in the convention, no clout. They were unimportant and ignored. One bigot from one of the Deep South states actually threw acid on a black delegate's suit jacket and burned it. Another one, from the Alabama delegation where I was standing at the time of the Rockefeller speech, turned on me menacingly while I was shouting "C'mon Rocky" as the governor stood his ground. He started up in his seat as if to come after me. His wife grabbed his arm and pulled him back.

"Turn him loose, lady, turn him loose," I shouted.

I was ready for him. I wanted him badly, but luckily for him he obeyed his wife.

I had been very active on that convention floor. I was one of those trying to help bring about a united front among the black delegates in the hope of thwarting the Goldwater drive. George Parker had courageously challenged Goldwater in vain and Edward Brooke had lent his uncompromising sincerity to the convention. I sat in with them after the nomination as they agonized about what they should do. Some were for walking out of the convention and even out of the party. Others felt that, as gloomy as things looked, the wisest idea was to remain within the party and fight. Throughout the convention, I had been interviewed several times on network television. When I was asked my opinion of Barry Goldwater, I gave it. I said I thought he was a bigot. I added that he was not as important as the forces behind him. I was genuinely concerned, for instance, about Republican National Committee Chairman William Miller, slated to become the Vice Presidential candidate. Bill Miller could have become the Agnew of his day if he had been elected. He was a man who apparently believed you never said a decent thing in political campaigning if you could think of a way to be nasty, insinuating, and abrasive. What with the columns I had written about Goldwater, *The Saturday Evening Post* article, and the television and radio interview, I had achieved a great deal of publicity about the way I felt about Goldwater.

Although I know it is the way of politicians to forget their differences and unify around the victor, it disgusted me to see how quickly the various anti-Goldwater GOP kingpins got converted. Richard Nixon, who hadn't really fought Goldwater and had in fact been an ally, naturally became one of his most staunch supporters. You could expect that. Governor Romney who had fought the Goldwater concept so vigorously, got religion. The convert who aroused the most cynical feelings in my mind was Governor William Scranton. When Governor Rockefeller had withdrawn from the race, during the primaries, Rockefeller supporters turned to Scranton because he had become the governor's choice. At the request of the governor I had a meeting with Scranton in his beautiful home in Pennsylvania.

Governor Scranton welcomed me graciously, introduced me to his family, and conducted me to a veranda where we sat and sipped iced tea. The governor pledged that he was going to put up a terrific fight against Goldwater. He expressed his gratitude for Governor Rockefeller's support and for my agreeing to come to see him. For at least ten minutes he orated about Barry Goldwater, what a threat Goldwaterism was to the country and the party. I didn't ask him for it, but he gave his solemn oath that even if Goldwater won the nomination, he, Bill Scranton, could never conceivably, under any circumstances, support him. Even if he wanted to, which he said he didn't—it would be political suicide in his state for him to join a Goldwater bandwagon. He was unequivocal about this and months later, when I saw on television how quickly Governor Scranton pledged his loyalty to nominee Goldwater, how eagerly he engaged in some of the most revolting high-level white Uncle Tomism I've ever seen—fawning on Goldwater and vigorously campaigning for him around the country—I had to wonder if this was, indeed, the same man who had very nearly sworn on a Bible that he never could do what he was doing.

In marked contrast to the Scranton flip-flop, there were some Republicans who proved themselves true to their principles, party loyalty not withstanding. Senator Jacob Javits stated flatly that he could not support Goldwater; Senator Hugh Scott of Pennsylvania, who had sounded off early about the Goldwater threat, announced that he would be running his own campaign in the same state where Bill Scranton had had a change of heart. Scott, whom I had admired for years because of his liberal words and legislation, took his chance of letting it be known he was snubbing the head of his party's national ticket. As for Governor Rockefeller, while he did not publicly reject Goldwater, it was no secret that he didn't break his back to try to help elect him. No doubt, the Senator and his campaign manager, Bill Miller, made things more comfortable for the governor symbolically to go fishing by not going down on their hands and knees to beg for his participation. There was a great business of calling unity meetings of *all* prominent Republicans. Unity, it appeared, meant to Goldwater and Miller, "Let's cooperate. You do it my way."

Apparently, I was one of the preconvention opposition who Senator Goldwater thought he could unify into his campaign. Although I had let it be widely known that I intended to do all I could for LBJ, Candidate Goldwater sent me an invitation early in August to come to Washington to have breakfast with him. He suggested that I really didn't know him well enough to condemn him and that he felt we might be able to learn something from each other.

Some people will say I should have accepted that invitation. I did not reject it in hasty anger. My instinct simply told me immediately that the only way the Senator could sell me on his candidacy was if he repudiated the John Birchers, the dirty campaign tactics of Bill Miller who was his running mate, and some of the basic standards he and his crowd had set. I knew he wasn't about to do all that simply to get my support.

I resolved that I should not allow myself to get boxed into the image of being a hothead, unwilling, for no good reason, to talk things over. Consequently, I released the text of my reply to the Goldwater invitation to the press. In that letter I told the Senator I was releasing my reply to the national press. The letter said in part:

> You say to me that you are interested in breaking bread with me and discussing your views on civil rights. Senator, on pain of appearing facetious, I must relate to you a rather well-known story regarding the noted musician, Louis Armstrong, who was once asked to explain jazz. "If you have to ask," Mr. Armstrong replied, "you wouldn't understand."
>
> What are you going to tell me, Senator Goldwater, which you cannot or do not choose to tell the country—or which you could not have told the convention which you controlled so rigidly that it booed Nelson Rockefeller, a distinguished fellow-Republican?
>
> What are you going to say about extremism now? You called for it and the answer came in the thudding feet and the crashing store windows and the Molotov cocktails and the crack of police bullets and the clubbing of heads and the hate and the violence and the fear which electrified Harlem and Rochester and Jersey. I am solidly committed to the peaceful, non-violent mass action of the Negro people in pursuit of long-overdue justice. But I am just as much opposed to the extremism of Negro rioters and Negro hoodlums as I am to the sheeted Klan, to the sinister Birchers, to the insidious citizens' Councils.
>
> If, in view of these questions, which I raise in absolute sincerity and conviction, you still think a meeting between us would be fruitful, I am available at your convenience.

*   *   *

My letter to the Senator did not receive any response from him. It did get a response from many people who read it in the newspapers. The fan mail ran about half and half, with some people giving me a hard time for not accepting Senator Goldwater's invitation and others declaring that I had told him off.

I joined the national headquarters of Republicans for Johnson, based in New York, and accepted speaking assignments whenever I could to tell black and white and mixed audiences how deeply I felt that Goldwater must be overwhelmingly repudiated. It was during the Johnson-Goldwater campaign that I had one of my confrontations with the articulate, eyebrow-raising William Buckley, owner of *National Review* magazine and star of the controversial *Firing Line* television show.

I was booked on a television Conservatism panel which included Bill Buckley, Shelley Winters, and myself. When my friends and family learned I had consented to participate, they were aghast.

"Send a telegram and say you can't make it," one friend told me. "Bill Buckley will destroy you. He really knows how to make people look foolish."

I was glad to receive these warnings. I didn't have the slightest intention of backing out, although I already had a healthy respect for Buckley's craft as a debater. The apprehensions of my friends made me create an advance strategy which I otherwise might not have employed. I lifted it strictly out of my sports background. When you know that you are going to face a tough, tricky opponent, you don't let him get the first lick. Jump him before he can do anything and stay on him, keeping him on the defensive. Never let up and you rattle him effectively. When the show opened up—before Buckley could get into his devastating act of using snide remarks, big words, and the superior manner—I lit right into him with the charge that many influential Goldwaterites were racists.

Shelley Winters piled in behind me, and Buckley scarcely got a chance to collect his considerable wit. A man who prides himself on coming out of verbal battle cool smiling, and victorious, he lost his calm, became snappish and irritated, and, when the show was over and everyone else was shaking hands, got up and strode angrily out of the studio.

It was a small victory, but an important one for me. There didn't seem to be much to win in those days on the political scene but I have always believed in fighting, even if only to keep the negative forces back. That is why I had some measure of satisfaction in helping Johnson win in '64.

Chapter XVI

Differences with Malcolm X

Although I had disagreed with Malcolm intensely on many issues before he fell from grace within Elijah Muhammad's official family, I rated him as articulate, incredibly sharp, and intelligent. Despite our differences, I realized that he projected a great image for young black kids who needed virile black males to emulate. Because he had been in prison, had associated with whores and dope addicts, and had come out of it to prove that people can rise from the depths, Malcolm had a strong appeal for youngsters that lasted far beyond his death.

Malcolm attacked so-called moderate blacks as well as "the white man devil." Late in 1963 both Malcolm and Adam Clayton Powell blasted Dr. Ralph Bunche, the dedicated Undersecretary to the United Nations. Adam sneered publicly that Dr. Bunche had failed to speak out on racial issues, and Malcolm accused the distinguished black international diplomat of making statements to please whites. He described Dr. Bunche as a man who was not free to talk "because of the job the white man gave him."

I was outraged. I considered Ralph Bunche one of the finest men in this country. I was fed up with people who did not really understand or appreciate him and who insinuated that he was an "Uncle Tom." I wrote in my syndicated column that Malcolm and Adam were leaders who talked one hell of a civil rights fight, but who, in recent years, had done very little to back up their statements. I accused them of making speeches and taking positions to gain sensational headlines.

I expressed my deep respect for Dr. Bunche and said that in spite of holding a job that obligated him to remain aloof from the internal problems of the United States, Dr. Bunche had— on a number of occasions—let the world know his intense personal feelings about racial prejudice in the United States.

I pointed out that it had been a long time since blacks had heard from Congressman Powell in a real crisis. "When we have heard from him, it has usually been in the form of some grandstand publicity—a conscious barrage of wild promises that the Congressman failed to keep."

The column ended by saying that Dr. Bunche, notwithstanding his diplomatic ties, had made forthright statements during the Martin Luther King-Birmingham crisis and we had heard nothing about that from Adam or Malcolm. Dr. Bunche attended the Medgar Evers funeral in Jackson, Mississippi, and joined other leaders in that tense and dangerous city in a statement of denunciation of the murder. Adam and Malcolm were not there.

Malcolm responded to the column by letter. Below are excerpts from it:

DEAR GOOD FRIEND JACKIE ROOSEVELT ROBINSON:
You became a great baseball player after your white boss (Mr. Rickey) lifted you to the major leagues. You proved that your white boss had chosen the "right" Negro by getting plenty of hits, stealing plenty of bases, winning many games and bringing much money through the gates and into the pockets of your white boss.

You let yourself be used by the whites even in those days against your own kind. You let them sic you on Paul Robeson.

You let them use you to destroy Paul Robeson. You let your white boss send you before a congressional hearing in Washington D.C. (the capital of Segregationville) to dispute and condemn Paul Robeson, because he had these guilty American whites frightened silly.

In your recent column you also accused me and Dr. Powell of misleading our people. Aren't you the same ex-baseball player who tried to "mislead" Negroes into Nixon's camp during the last presidential election?

You stay as far away from the Negro community as you can get, and you never take an interest in anything in the Negro community until the white man himself takes an interest in it. You, yourself, would never shake my hand until you saw some of your white friends shaking it.

If whites were to murder me for the religious philosophy that I represent and stand for, I would die KNOWING that it was at the hands of OPEN ENEMIES OF TRUTH AND JUSTICE!

I replied to Malcolm, saying I would cherish his reply and that I was honored to be placed in the distinguished company of Dr. Bunche whom he had also attacked. I wrote, in part:

I am proud of my associations with the men you chose to call my "white bosses." I am also proud that so many others whom you would undoubtedly label as "white bosses," marched with us to Washington and have been and are now working with our leaders to help achieve equality in America.

I will not dignify your attempted slur against my appearance before the House Un-American Activities Committee some years back. All I can say is that if I were called upon to defend my country today, I would gladly do so. Nor do I hide behind any coat-tails as you do when caught in one of your numerous outlandish statements.

Your usual "out" is to duck responsibility by stating: "The Honorable Elijah Muhammad says. . . ."

Personally, I reject your racist views. I reject your dream of a separate state.

I do not do things to please "white bosses" or "black agitators" unless they are the things which please me. You say I have never shown my appreciation to the Negro masses. I assume that is why NAACP branches all over the country constantly invite me to address them and this is the reason the NAACP gave me its highest award, the Springarn Medal.

You mouth a big and bitter battle, Malcolm, but it is noticeable that your militancy is mainly expressed in Harlem where it is safe. I have always contended for your right—as for that of every American—to say and think and believe what you choose. I just happen to believe you are supporting and advocating policies which could not possibly interest the masses. Thank God for our Dr. Bunche, our Roy Wilkins, our Dr. King and Mr. Randolph.

The column and letter-writing duel was only one of several encounters between Malcolm and me. Even when I sharply disagreed with what I thought was his philosophy of hatred and his taunting of other leaders who disagreed with him, I consistently gave him credit as a man who said what he believed. When we clashed, Malcolm stuck to his guns and I to mine. Many of the statements he made about the problems faced by our people and the immorality of the white power structure were naked truth. It was in our approach to solutions that we differed radically.

The 1965 assassination of Malcolm was a tragedy of the first order. Word that he had been killed by a hail of bullets came to me while we were vacationing and playing golf in Miami. A lot of blue went out of the sky and some warmth from the sun when the sinister news came. Death had not taken Malcolm unaware. As Dr. King later predicted his own slaying, Malcolm, in his last days, had warned the country that his days were numbered.

Minister Elijah Muhammad had "suspended" Malcolm for saying that white America's "Chickens had come home to roost" in the slaying of President Kennedy. For months after his suspension Malcolm worked to organize his own movement. He was disillusioned with the Muslim hierarchy and openly stated that he had been misled by the man to whom he had so consistently pledged allegiance, Elijah Muhammad. His death was deeply tragic because Malcolm, toward the close of his life, had seemed to be groping for and stumbling into a new religion, a different point of view. His travels in Africa convinced him that the chart to freedom for black America lay not in the setting up of a segregated state within America's borders, not in an approach of hate and violence, but in a grand, international coalition with African brothers. His travels in Mecca turned him sharply from the narrow view that all nonblacks were enemies. He had begun to see that it was possible to make strong alliances around the globe—white alliances as well as black—in order to solve common problems.

Malcolm made his hajj, which is what the historic pilgrimage to Mecca is called, after his banishment from the world of Elijah Muhammad. In a remarkable letter from that part of the world, the man who had so often been accused of hating all whites and who had consistently castigated people of pale skin in harsh language revealed an astounding change. He says in his book:

> I knew that when my letter became public knowledge back in America, many would be astounded—loved ones, friends and enemies alike. And no less astounded would be millions whom I did not know—who had gained during my twelve years with Elijah Muhammad a "hate" image of Malcolm X.

Even I was myself astounded. But there was precedent in my life for this letter. My whole life had been a chronology of changes. Here is what I wrote . . . from my heart:

Never have I witnessed such sincere hospitality and the overwhelming spirit of true brotherhood as is practiced by people of all colors and races here in this Ancient Holy Land, the home of Abraham, Muhammad and all the other prophets of the Holy Scriptures. For the past week, I have been utterly speechless and spellbound by the graciousness I see displayed all around me by people of all colors.

I have been blessed to visit the Holy City of Mecca. There were tens of thousands of pilgrims, from all over the world. They were of all colors, from blue-eyed blonde to black-skinned Africans. But we were all participating in the same ritual, displaying a spirit of unity and brotherhood that my experiences in America had led me to believe never could exist between the white and the non-white.

America needs to understand Islam because this is the one religion that erases the race problem from its society. During the past eleven days here in the Muslim world, I have eaten from the same plate, drunk from the same glass and slept in the same bed (or on the same rug)— while praying to the same God—with fellow Muslims whose eyes were the bluest of blue, whose hair was the blondest of blond and whose skin was the whitest of white. And in the words and in the actions and in the deeds of the "white" Muslims, I felt the same sincerity that I felt among the black African Muslims of Nigeria, Sudan and Ghana. We were truly all the brothers. If white Americans could accept the Oneness of God, then perhaps, too, they could accept in reality the Oneness of Man. . . .

This was a powerful tribute and testimony to the power of the practice of brotherhood for real brotherhood in action.

And a revealing spiritual close-up of a man who had grown to such bigness that he could feel the healing and cleansing power of a new vision. He had the strength to confess himself mistaken and misguided. It was ironic that, just as he seemed rising to the crest of a new and inspired leadership, Malcolm was struck down, ostensibly by the hands of blacks. His murderers quieted his voice but clothed him in martyrdom and deepened his influence. In death Malcolm became larger than he had been in life.

Chapter XVII

The Freedom Bank

Aside from my fund-raising efforts with the NAACP, the seven rewarding years I spent as vice-president of Chock Full O'Nuts taught me much of the inner workings of the world of finance. I became fascinated with the way big business was conducted, with the operation of the stock market and the power which exists in the board rooms of banks and corporations. Black people were coming to the point where they would be crying out in behalf of Black Power, but it was pathetic to realize how little we knew of money. The financial establishment of America was as much of a mystery to us as we were to the establishment. I recall that when I first joined Chock, after leaving baseball, my picture was used on the financial pages of the New York *Times*, and a very knowledgeable newsman told me that it was the first time a black man's picture had been featured in that section.

During the post-baseball years, I became increasingly persuaded that there were two keys to the advancement of blacks in America—the ballot and the buck. If we organized our political and economic strength, we would have a much easier fight on our hands.

For some months, prior to 1964, Dunbar McLaurin, a businessman prominent in the Harlem community, had been trying to convince me that I should associate with him in his dream of creating a bank in the black community which would be owned and operated predominantly by black people. I knew McLaurin to be a brilliant man in the field of economics and finance.

At first I resisted McLaurin's suggestion that I become involved with his project. After all, what did I know about banking? But Rachel and I felt that my decision to join the business world put me into the center of the black business community and I had to go all the way. Also, McLaurin was a very persuasive man. He convinced me that there was a great need for the kind of bank he envisioned if for no other reason than to set up a competition with the white owned and operated banks. The white-owned banks were not doing very much to fulfill the needs of Harlem people. By and large, in the banking business, blacks were considered bad credit risks, not only because of their median low income as compared to that of whites, but because of the stereotype which had existed for many years that they were not to be trusted.

George W. Goodman, a Harlem leader, was quoted in a newspaper interview in the early sixties as saying that he remembered listening to a white bank president in Connecticut who said, in his presence, that "he had never known a Negro in whom he had confidence for more than a $300 loan."

This was an attitude that was widespread in the financial community. When it came to mortgages to buy homes, business loans to enable blacks to become entrepreneurs, blacks were discriminated against. Yet they faithfully and religiously deposited their savings in white banks.

Dunbar worked on me persistently, and when I realized what effort he was putting into the project and the distinguished people he had involved, I reluctantly agreed to serve on the organizing committee. Reluctantly—because something in my personal radar told me to be cautious about my involvement with McLaurin.

The concept under which we planned to organize was a fine one. We were to capitalize at $1.5 million. In a letter that went out over my signature as chairman of the board, I emphasized that Freedom National Bank would be "a community enterprise which will in every way belong to the people it is to serve. . . . Moreover, it is intended that these people shall be represented in the formation and administration of the policies of this bank to assure its role in helping to eradicate those financing practices that restrict the economic growth of the community and erode the money power of its members."

The letter also said that 60,000 shares of capital stock would be offered and that no controlling block would be permitted to emerge from the sale. Priority of purchase was to go to Harlem residents. The organizing committee was limited to 20 percent of the offering. To prevent any individual from gaining control, we limited the sale of shares to 1,000 for any single person. We had a really difficult job getting blacks to purchase stock. One reason was that we, as blacks, have had so little experience with investing and some of us have had bad experiences. Many of us are afraid to trust each other. To increase the skepticism in the black community, there were negative memories of an instance in the past when there had been an attempt to establish what Harlem people believed to be an interracial bank. This was the Dunbar National Bank organized by John D. Rockefeller on West 150th Street and Eighth Avenue in 1928. Dunbar closed after ten years of operation. What the public did not recognize was that the ":nterracial" character of this bank was that blacks were hired and black money was solicited. But the bank was controlled by Mr. Rockefeller, and the top five executives, including the president and the cashier, were white.

It was ironic that during the early years of Freedom, because I was politically involved with Governor Rockefeller, the rumor, in many different parts of the country where I campaigned for him for the Republican Presidential nomination, was that Freedom was really my bank and that the governor had given it to me as a present. Maybe I should have wished that was true. It wasn't.

As we got further into the organizing stages of Freedom National Bank, I began to feel very uncomfortable with the way Dunbar McLaurin was performing his duties. There wasn't really anything I could put my finger on except that he began making a number of trips and submitting bills for them, which, I suspected, had nothing to do with the bank's operation.

There was an interracial organizing committee; included were Judge Samuel Pierce, a black attorney now General Counsel for the United States Treasury Department; Herb Evans; Irv Altman; Alva Hudgins; myself; Frank Schiffman, the astute owner of the Apollo Theater on 125th Street; Jack Blumstein, a veteran businessman from 125th Street who heads Blumstein's Department Store; and Dunbar McLaurin.

The plan was that McLaurin would be president of the bank. I told some of my fellow-organizers about my uneasiness about McLaurin. In my opinion, unless the bank was to be operated with absolute dedication and integrity, it would fail. I had no basis, except for personal qualms, to doubt that McLaurin would supply those qualities. Yet something told me that I would be wisest to withdraw if he was going to be allowed to be president. I brought this up at a committee meeting of several members of the organizing committee in McLaurin's presence. I had hardly got my words out of my mouth when McLaurin produced resignation papers for me, already drawn up, indicating my withdrawal from the organizing committee and the proposed board of the bank. I was about to sign the papers when someone—I think it was

Alva Hudgins—advised that I wait. He said that no one person controlled the whole organizing committee and that the whole committee should discuss whether I should resign. I agreed. We held a few more meetings and the majority of the committee members finally voted that Mr. McLaurin could not be president of the bank. He took his case to the newspapers, accusing me of stealing his idea for the bank, then having him ousted. Not long after we had rejected him as president, we all went to Washington, McLaurin included, and met with the United States Comptroller of the Currency. He told us that under no circumstances would his office allow Mr. McLaurin to be president. Having no other alternative, McLaurin resigned and the rest of us carried on.

Our next problem was the selection of a black president, and, of course, the history of black expertise within the financial community being such a sparse one, we had a difficult time finding a capable man. But we were determined that the president be a black man.

Looking over the field, we settled on a very successful real estate executive and businessman, William R. Hudgins. Mr. Hudgins had been connected, for some years, with the black owned and operated Carver Federal Savings and Loan Association, which had been established in 1949 on East 125th Street. In 1964 Bill was chairman of the board of Carver. The Carver operation was a sound one. Under the dogged leadership of its late president, Joseph E. Davis, by 1964 the organization had made close to $50 million in loans and had extended many mortgages to people in the black community, most of whom could not have received them elsewhere. Bill Hudgins, for whom I had real respect in terms of his business acumen and who was also a personal friend, agreed to resign from Carver to run Freedom National Bank. Like the other organizers of Freedom I had great confidence that, under Hudgins, Freedom could enjoy a highly successful career.

I can recall now that several people whom I respected highly questioned the judgment of our board in selecting Mr. Hudgins, but I dismissed these comments as having no basis except possible personal prejudice against the man. As the bank opened with great acceptance initially from the community, I felt even better about the situation. Because of the publicity about disagreement with McLaurin, there were those who had doubted that we would ever open and that, if we did, our career would be short-lived. I felt very proud to be associated with the only interracially owned and operated bank in the Harlem community and also the only bank in Harlem which was black controlled. The attendance at the opening was heartening not only in terms of numbers but also because of the pride that so many Harlemites, young and old, seemed to take in the bank. Throughout the ceremonies, as people passed through, I heard several references to "our bank."

Bill Hudgins really took hold. He delighted in saying that Freedom was a bank which is "color blind." It was, for him and for all of us, a bank which would not discriminate against anyone because of color, but also it would make a real difference in the economic health of Harlem. And since Harlem is regarded as the black capital of the black national community, its success could become a very influential factor in this country.

Bill pledged that Freedom would also be a bank to which anyone could come to discuss a problem directly with the president.

I would find it hard to describe how hard Bill Hudgins worked at building our new bank. There were times when we directors feared he was seriously jeopardizing his health with the energy and industry which he applied.

Naturally, the growth of Freedom also did much to ease the problem New York City blacks have had for years in getting mortgage credit. As Carver president Joe Davis once said,

"Where there is a lack of mortgage credit, there is no money to improve the ghetto, no money to get out of the ghetto."

Bill Hudgins voiced well the philosophy of our bank when he said that we did not subscribe to the idea of chasing the white merchant out of Harlem. He felt that as Freedom became more competitive in quality, knowledge, and service, we would automatically move to the forefront and render a more competitive service. He felt that this would motivate the white banks to become more competitive, to hire more blacks, and to expand the services to the community which they had withheld while accepting the community's deposits.

A typical reaction about Freedom National Bank on the part of aware Harlemites was voiced by Clarence Funnye, a CORE leader. He said, "Before Freedom National, you went into the white bank with the distinct impression you went with what you had in your hand, begging the powers that be and generally you were turned down. With Freedom the community looks less like a colony, less of an area for exploitation."

In February, 1966, Mayor Lindsay participated in our first anniversary, unveiling a plaque of the bank which honored more than two hundred "charter depositors" who opened major accounts with us. The list included institutions, corporations, individuals, agencies, and labor unions which had deposited with us a minimum of $10,000. When we marked that anniversary, we had gone from the initial $1.5-million capitalization to a volume of more than $9,000,000. We had loaned more than $300,000 to small businessmen. We could feel justifiably that the future of Freedom was assured.

During the years since its founding in 1964, Freedom National Bank had really become a source of pride for black people. It had grown in status to the largest of the black banks in the nation.

I was happy about that, but I had mixed emotions, which I had entertained for a couple of years. I finally began to feel convinced that, although we had made tremendous strides, we were approaching the brink of disaster.

Among those closest to me—family, friends, and close business associates—there are two schools of thought as to whether I should be talking about the behind-the-scenes story of how we at Freedom Bank narrowly averted a major crisis which could have wrecked the institution. Today, since we have successfully weathered the storm, some people think that it will do damage to public confidence in us to talk about the danger we confronted and overcame. I have given a great deal of thought to that point of view because I love the bank and what it has achieved and would not want to hurt it. But I think there are vital lessons to be learned by telling frankly what happened to us and why. I think that my own ego or that of any other individual is not as important as the need for maturity and stability in black business.

In the first place, I want to declare honestly that I, as chairman of the board of directors, and some other members of the board were guilty of a very serious mistake. I don't choose to confess for anyone else so I will focus upon my own shortcomings. I think that if I had taken more time to probe into the daily administration of the bank, I could have helped to avoid trouble long before we had to confront it the hard way. Even to me, a novice in banking and financial matters, it was becoming obvious in the latter part of the sixties that we were not being cautious enough with the processing of loan applications—auto loans and otherwise—that we were not doing enough research on applicants, and that we had a tendency to favor friends on the basis that one can trust one's friends in business—an utterly risky philosophy. I also began to get worried about the large amounts of money we were writing off in bad loans.

My worries were constantly lulled whenever these questions came up in board meetings, and Bill Hudgins and Irv Altman, our white executive vice-president who had a thorough banking background, would reassure us with what seemed to be perfectly logical explanations. At the same time, I was hearing warnings coming from respected friends and business associates who were telling me that I would have terrible regrets if I didn't check out what was going on at the bank. People who were knowledgeable in the financial community were persistently telling me that the word was around that the bank was headed for serious problems.

I couldn't help feeling uncomfortable at constantly hearing all these warnings. But I had a lot of confidence in Bill Hudgins and his administration of the bank.

One day in 1968, one of the most powerful men in Wall Street circles bluntly said to me: "If you want to save Freedom National Bank, the only way you are going to be able to do it is to take it over and clean house. You are in serious trouble."

Shortly thereafter, I was leaving the bank one afternoon and met Bob Murray, our in-house attorney, and a former employee of the bank, Hector Williams.

We began talking and they said that they hated to bring up a negative subject but I had better check out the administration at Freedom. I smiled and told them that I thought everything was going well even if there might be a few problems.

"Jack, all we're asking you to do is to take a look at five specific loans. We'll call them for you and you just look into them, and if you are still satisfied that conditions are fine, we'll forget about it."

I couldn't ignore a challenge like that.

From that day forward, I began to seek out sincerely concerned staffers and to ask questions. I soon realized that my informal investigations could prove very distressing for some of the employees who wanted to cooperate but who were afraid that if they went too far, they might get caught in a cross fire between me, as chairman of the board, and their day-to-day boss, Mr. Hudgins, the president of the bank. It was late in February, 1971, when I began really digging in. Never having been a banker and having had no experience with such matters, I began talking with Madeline Walburg who was in charge of the mortgage department. I have to say that this lady played a heroic role in what turned out to be a dramatic behind-the-scenes struggle to literally save the bank. When I first began to talk with Madeline, I found her eager to help, and surprised that I was interested. It was valuable to me to learn that she had been deeply concerned about conditions for some time. Though she was a key employee, she was still an employee, and she had decided not to stick her neck out by calling attention to certain problems since she didn't think the directors were really interested anyway. I learned that there were several times when she had sat in on meetings and heard questions raised by us with management. She said she shuddered to hear the answers which were given to soothe us. That was when I began to realize how much more fully informed directors of a corporation should make themselves.

There was one other factor involved in the false sense of security I experienced toward management. As is their duty with all banks, various representatives and examiners from the office of the Comptroller of Currency in New York would come around to the bank periodically and check out our situation. I had made it my business to question some of these examiners, raising the question whether our operations were sound. I kept getting the reply that "Things are not as bad as you think they are," or something equivalent. Yet I knew that we were writing off thousands of dollars in bad loans at each examination.

One day, one of the examiners came to visit us. Someone told me he was the best they had in the state. I took him aside and really laid it on the line. I said that I had a growing suspicion that the Comptroller's office was patting us on the back when they should be hitting us over the head with a club.

I told him that I thought we were not being judged by the same standards that would have been applied if ours were a white bank. I said that they were doing us no favor if they were telling us everything was all right when things were not right. The response from him was amazing. He never admitted it, of course, but it became apparent that my suspicions had validity. We were being handled with kid gloves because certain officials did not want to get themselves accused or suspected of persecuting a black institution. From that day on the Comptroller's office began to focus in on what we were doing right and what we were doing wrong, and it became absolutely clear to me that we were in trouble.

By this time my concern about the bank had become a major preoccupation. I found myself losing sleep nights and involved in a great deal of activity at the bank trying to make certain that I had a strong basis for making a move. It happened that during this period I was having a very serious health crisis. My breathing had become constricted at times to the extent that I could not bear the pressure. I was having trouble with my legs and my doctors were unable to pinpoint the problem, unable to tell whether there was a direct relationship to my diabetes. The more involved I got with the bank problems, the sicker I became.

My personal health wasn't my sole concern. I had to give serious attention to the position in which my one-man investigation was placing Madeline Walburg. The fact that I was checking out the situation in the mortgage department and that she was spending a great deal of time assisting me had to have come to the attention of Mr. Hudgins to whom she was directly responsible. Madeline didn't complain to me, but it was obvious that the situation was far from comfortable for her. She knew quite well that she could have lost her job and that, even if I went to bat for her as I would have, the whole affair could become messy. As for me, I had decided that I could no longer go it alone in my investigation. I decided there were two steps I must take. I had to confront Bill Hudgins frankly and confirm what I was certain he already knew—that I had serious questions in my mind about the administration of the bank and intended to get to the bottom of matters. Also, I had to advise some of my fellow directors about the probing I had done, the information I had gained, and get them involved.

I phoned Bill Hudgins at his home one Saturday. Our New York apartment is in the same neighborhood as the Hudgins' home. I told Bill I had to talk with him. When I arrived at his place, I asked him if he wanted Mrs. Hudgins in on the conversation. I did this because we had been longtime friends. Bill said that it would not be necessary to involve his wife. I told him all of my concerns and how I had been investigating. Bill assured me that the bank was in great shape, that I had been grossly misinformed, and he told me that everything about the operation was on the up and up.

I've said that my fellow board members didn't know about my probe of the bank. There was one exception, and I have to give this lady credit because she was a tower of strength to me. Mrs. Rose Morgan is the founder and owner of the Rose-Meta System of Beauty which operates on a national level. Rose, a dear friend of many years, is an amazingly gifted woman. She has an inborn talent for good business operation. Rose can cut straight through the niceties to the heart of the matter, and she does this because she doesn't believe in wasting time or sentiment. I had not asked her to do anything to help me in my investigation, but I certainly am glad that I chose her early as a confidante.

Having talked with Bill Hudgins, I now felt it appropriate to bring in the total board for consideration of the state of the bank. Here, of course, I was to become more aware of what I had always known—that there are cliques on boards of directors. Of course, there were some members who were still very much committed to Bill, and, unfortunately, he began to get out the word that I was out to get him and that I was being vindictive about it. That really bothered me because my only concern was the welfare of the bank and how awful it would be for so many people all over the country if the bank went under.

Marty Edelman, a lawyer friend of mine and member of the firm of Battle, Fowler, Stokes and Keel, and Charlie Jaffin, the senior partner of that firm, responded to my request for help and guidance during this period. Through them we were able to chart a proper course in getting to the basics of what was wrong with Freedom National Bank's operation.

Before the problems at the bank were resolved, a sad thing happened. Madeline Walburg, without whom I could not have got the probe going, had become increasingly ill, nervous and upset. She suffered from high blood pressure. I am sure she was worried about what might happen to her. A couple of times she had told me she wanted to quit. But Bob Murray, who himself was putting his job on the line, joined forces with me to persuade her that without her help, our efforts might be in vain. So she continued to help, and one day a blood vessel burst in her head. She died a few days later. Madeline's death hurt me as much as if she had been a member of my own family. I think her family and friends should be proud of the contribution Madeline made to a very important matter affecting black people.

Bob Murray also deserves a lot of gratitude. His attitude was that if he lost his job, so be it. He wanted to see the bank problems straightened out, and that was his main desire. People like Madeline and Bob only strengthen the conviction I've held over the years that the people who want to shut white people of goodwill and dedication out of black life and black affairs are so wrong.

As the board continued to check out my own investigation, Bill Hudgins and I really lost faith in each other. Our friendship became a thing of the past. I made it clear to him that, as far as I was concerned, there would have to be a drastic change in administration. Some of the board members still found it hard to believe that Bill could do any wrong. I can't blame them. I won't soon forget the utter faith I had in the man.

The concern we all had at the bank—even after a majority of the board agreed that there had to be a change in administration—was that if Bill was summarily dismissed there would be the strong hint of scandal which could badly hurt the bank. Furthermore, we could not, in fairness, say that he had done anything illegal or dishonest, and he had worked very hard over the years in the interest of the bank. He was respected by many in the community.

Furthermore, being a black bank we were in a delicate position in the business community. On the one hand, we did not want the white banking community to coddle us, to overlook mistakes we made because we were a black bank. The more they had patted us on the back where we were wrong, the deeper we had become involved in our problems. Our doors could have been closed because of this kind of paternalism. We wanted to mature and grow toward an equality of experience and ability. Otherwise we would always be subservient. Yet on the other hand, with regard to certain internal affairs, there are some ways that we had to be different because we were a black bank. Without being loose in policies, we had to be a lot less rigid than white banks have been under similar circumstances. A delicate balance had to be struck. This is what we had in mind when we settled the matter of the need for a new administration. Some people may criticize us for it or not understand it, but we believe we did the right thing. We accepted Bill Hudgins' resignation as president. We brought in a new president, Bob Boyd, formerly of the Los Angeles Rams, a brilliant football player in his athletic days and a businessman of proven ability.

The thing we did which might be called unorthodox is that

we refused to allow Bill Hudgins to resign completely from the bank. He became vice-chairman of the board. He had no jurisdiction in areas where some of us had questioned his judgment. But he could still contribute his very definite skills to our growth and development. The job Bob Boyd has done and is doing to turn Freedom around covers a wide range. For example, he has made a number of personnel changes and works closely with staff. He attends various outside meetings which are helpful to him in the administration of the bank, and he often invites members of the board to accompany him. But mainly he has tightened up procedures throughout the bank and raised the standards of our operation considerably.

As it is probably quite obvious, the telling of this episode in my personal and business life is painful to relate. I suppose I take the chance of being misunderstood for telling it. I have told it because I feel there are lessons to be learned from it by many people—black and white.

Chapter XVIII

Hope and Disillusionment in White Politics

The Democrats have traditionally been the party that blacks have given their allegiance to. Despite my reservations about John Kennedy, his brief administration turned into a period of hope. However, although I respected Kennedy for his articulate concern when he was forced to face issues, I felt that it was Robert Kennedy who was the driving force behind the advances made on civil rights issues. It seemed to me that Robert Kennedy had more integrity on racial issues and that he wanted to be more bold and forthright.

But at least there was progress during these years. The Kennedys pushed implementation of the rights of blacks established in the earlier Supreme Court decisions on bussing and schools. Eisenhower had said that it was his duty to recognize the Supreme Court ruling on school segregation but that he saw no necessity to go to any lengths to speak out for it or to move to enforce it. When he finally sent the troops to Little Rock, I believe he acted because his West Point mentality was angered by Faubus' defiance of orders rather than out of any deep moral conviction. But when John and Robert Kennedy took on Governor Wallace, I think they were acting on the belief that black rights had become top-priority national business.

The assassination of the President was a great shock. I did not idolize Kennedy as many did, but his death was a great loss. Later when Robert Kennedy was killed, I felt the same. The two men did much for the cause of black rights. Furthermore, when John Kennedy was assassinated, I was deeply concerned because of grave doubts about the future of blacks under Lyndon Johnson. His ties to the South and his closeness to men like Senator Russell made many of us fear that the gains made under Kennedy would be lost. Then, when Johnson began implementing pro-civil rights legislation, I suspected that this was political sleight-of-hand to disguise a subtle Southern strategy. However, when the 1964 campaign came, I worked to have Johnson reelected because of the dangers of the Goldwater politics, as I said before. But my uneasiness about Johnson continued.

The events in Selma, Alabama, found me at the height of my dissatisfaction. The atrocities against civil rights activists, the brutalization of peaceful marchers, the deaths of blacks over the years such as Evers, Till, Chaney, deeply angered me. I had spent a weekend in Mississippi making speeches in which I blasted the Johnson administration for its seeming don't-give-a-damn attitude toward these terrible events. I had pointed out at mass rallies in the North and South that it takes more than a big job, big talk, and big gestures to wipe out the bad taste of a thirty-year-old record of adamant opposition to civil rights. I mentioned that the same statesman who calls for Congressional allegiance to civil rights from the White House is the same politician who only last year voted to make it necessary for two-thirds of the Senate to curb the filibuster.

Finally there was the murder of the white minister, the Reverend James Reeb. I actually felt a swift rush of anger when I learned that the President had sent flowers to the hospital room of the dying Reverend Reeb and that when he received word of the young minister's death, he had sent a jet plane to be at the disposal of Mrs. Reeb. It was no time for flowers and public relations moves, I felt. It was time to send into Alabama the same kind of force we had dispatched to Vietnam.

However, my attitude toward Johnson underwent a drastic change when I heard his address to Congress following Reeb's death. I felt that he offered to the world the essence of the finest leadership which could come from the highest seat of power in the world. He was soft-spoken in his description of his personal goals for freedom. He was eloquent as he outlined personal views about the rights of all Americans. He was courageous and forthright as he dared to repeat the official chant of the movement: "We shall overcome." He was almost savagely strong when he let the Congress know that he was staking his leadership in the free world upon their response. I felt high praise for Mr. Johnson.

I wasn't always happy with President Johnson in the White House, of course, but I have to admit that he did a courageous job of translating into hard legislation some of the key issues of the civil rights movement. Many blacks remained suspicious of LBJ because he was a Texan and his early voting record was antiblack. But there's something really unusual about a Southerner who was once a dyed-in-the-wool states' righter and who, for whatever reason, changes his mind. Somehow it seems that those from below the Mason-Dixon Line who come over to the liberal cause bring with them a firmness and sincerity that Northern liberals don't have. Harry Truman displayed some of this and President Johnson even more. Some cynics go around saying, "Oh, well, you know, they just did it to get the black vote" or "Every move he makes is political." They seldom allow for the possibility that a man like Johnson, for years a bigtime clubhouse politician with his loyalties tied to a regional constituency, could grow into the consciousness that national responsibility has been suddenly thrust upon him. This meant that he must widen his views to attempt to be President of all the people and to do those things, no matter how foreign to his past instinct, which would serve the best interests of the whole country. I believe Lyndon Johnson made the leap to this kind of awareness. I believe that, with his tremendous sense of history, he truly wanted to leave a record of radical achievement as President.

LBJ's Southern background had something to do with the force he exerted when he became a civil rights President. This personal theory is grounded on my own experience in baseball. Some Southern-bred ballplayers who were initially appalled at the idea of having a black teammate, turned out to be allies when they realized the economic gains for baseball. When you strip away all the demagogic talk on both sides and get right down to the real nitty-gritty, the black and white Southerners have the basis for a much more genuine understanding of each other and realization of their absolute need for each other on a partnership level than Northern blacks and whites. There was a popular saying once that in the North the white man didn't care how close the black man came if he didn't climb too high, and in the South the white man didn't care how high the black man climbed if he didn't come too close. This attitude has been changing in recent years. One big factor, added to the Southern white man's awakening to the fact that blacks could use their combined purchasing power as a weapon, is the new respect in Dixie for black voting strength.

There is no doubt that President Johnson played a magnificent role in the political liberation of blacks. He was able to do this because black people started demonstrating that they were determined to vote. He was also peculiarly qualified to bring about change because, unlike his predecessor, he had a magic touch with the Senators and representatives with whom he had related so skillfully for so many years. They accepted him as one of them because he had become a giant among them, in terms of power and the ability to cajole, persuade, threaten, and negotiate.

But Johnson's contribution could only be backed up by the

people. I remember after the President's speech after the death of Reeb how strongly I realized that the final test rested with Congress. I felt it to be the duty of every person in our society to remain alert and vigilant to any threat to freedom. The freedom to vote could only be unleashed by the members of Congress. They were politicians. Politicians react to pressure. I know that we who were shocked over incidents like the brutal clubbing of Reverend Reeb on a dark street had to establish a counterpressure. I was certain that the President and the Congress had received many angry letters from people who were in favor of keeping blacks in their "place," who were resigned to the status quo. I have never been in favor of aggressive violence, but neither am I a turn-the-other-cheeker, so I called for letters and public statements. They came by the thousands.

But letters and statements were not enough. I began to sense the need for greater involvement. My opportunity came in 1966 when Governor Rockefeller asked me to become a member of his Executive Chamber as Special Assistant to the Governor for Community Affairs. Even though I had vowed many times that I would not accept a full-time political job, and although I would be making a financial sacrifice, I felt the position would hold an important challenge. The governor announced my appointment at a press conference in Albany in February, 1966.

I told the press that day that one of the reasons I wanted to join the governor's staff was that I deeply respected his personal and public record, his family background, and his determination to work for human dignity.

I found the day-to-day business of representing the governor in his Fifty-fifth Street, New York City, offices quite different from campaigning for him.

A campaign worker has to interpret the candidate to the people, sometimes justifying his views on minor issues even though he might not always thoroughly agree. But because, on an overall basis, he believes in the man and what he stands for, he goes along. In working for the governor, as a special assistant, there is more choice. It is not a question of stooging for him and endorsing his every word and deed or doing one's best to give him honest reports.

A man like Rockefeller is surrounded by people trying to please and soothe him and I think he appreciated my outspokenness. On several occasions, not always happily, the governor conceded that I was one of the few people close to him who usually spoke up when I thought I had to. No one should be brainwashed into believing Uncle-Tomming is a black habit. In the service, in my business associations, and in politics, I have seen some of the most creative kissing of behinds done by white people that one can imagine.

I was given the kind of easy access to the governor that very few people in the state government enjoyed. I had a direct line to the governor to wherever he was in the state. I didn't ask for this kind of communication and I didn't abuse it. I learned that only half a dozen people in the state had the same privilege.

Once when we were campaigning in Queens in a predominantly black community the governor, full of good humor, carelessly referred to a couple of local candidates as "boys." Instantly I knew this was a grave error. I know how black men feel about being called boy. I myself always react with instant resentment no matter how decent the person using this offensive word seems to be. The crowd, with angry protests, made it quite clear to Rockefeller that they were insulted.

The governor was genuinely shocked. Normally, he has perfect instincts in not making ethnic mistakes. I knew him well enough to know he hadn't meant the word in the way it was received. He was very upset to have given offense and said so. He explained forthrightly, without stuttering or faltering, that he and his brothers were used to referring to each other as the boys. He admitted that he should have been more sensitive than to use the word and he deeply regretted it. It was a straightforward and handsome apology, and the crowd seemed to accept it as sincere.

The next morning I sent him a brief interoffice note which said that I thought he had handled a tense situation rather well.

"But, Governor," I wrote in the last line, "don't let it happen again."

On another occasion, during the days of wheeling and dealing and all kinds of speculation about the upcoming 1968 Republican National Convention, the political columns and grapevines were filled with rumors. One of them was that California Governor Ronald Reagan might join Governor Rockefeller to stop Dick Nixon. I knew that a Rockefeller-Reagan ticket would be something I could never be associated with. However, I didn't even give credence to the possibility until I learned that the governor of California had met with the governor very very quietly at the Rockefeller Fifth Avenue apartment. I made it my business to confront Governor Rockefeller directly.

"You know," I told him, "I hope this talk about you and Reagan is just talk. I personally couldn't go along with such a hookup, and, furthermore, if I could, I'd never be able to justify or explain it." The governor laughed heartily, then told me why he was amused.

"You should have heard the hard time I had explaining *you* to Reagan," he said.

I laughed, too, but pointed out that I couldn't care less what Reagan thought of me.

I constantly told the governor that I didn't think he'd ever make a good Conservative. I believed that challenging actions—such as going to the mat with Nixon for a civil rights platform in 1960 and fighting back before a hostile Goldwater convention in 1964—were the kinds of untraditional conduct that he loved most and that suited him best. I felt that he had little to lose and a world to gain by continuing to refuse to conform to the mold of political accommodations and compromise.

The governor always listened to me thoughtfully and talked with me frankly. The acid test of his confidence in me came during the 1966 campaign for his reelection as governor. I heard a rumor that the governor was going to accept William Miller as campaign manager. The Conservatives had been warning Rockefeller that he must do some things to change his liberal image, that if he didn't, the growing Conservative numbers could weaken the GOP sufficiently to ensure a Democratic victory. I couldn't conceive of Nelson Rockefeller for one minute considering taking this man on his campaign staff, and I knew that if he did, I would have to quit. I knew that my quitting would give a dangerous weapon to the opposition, so I tried to put through a call to the governor to ask him if Bill Miller was going to be accepted by him. If he said yes, I would tell him I would be forced to resign. Normally, I had no problem getting through immediately even in spite of the governor's always hectic schedule. For whatever reason, my request for an appointment was not honored within the next day or two. I had, in accordance with protocol, routed it through top people in the campaign. Perhaps somebody there didn't want me to see the governor. Or maybe the governor himself was ducking me.

The Miller situation had become such a real possibility that a couple of newsmen, knowing how I had fought Goldwater, began asking me how I would feel about working with Miller. I knew that I would be forced to answer their questions very soon. One day, when I was scheduled to do an important radio interview show, I realized I had to do something drastic because I was certain the question about Miller would come up on the air. I telephoned Hugh Morrow, the governor's communications director, and left a message that I had to have assurance before going on the air that the Miller rumor was not true. If I didn't, I would have to state my frank opinion about any intended use of Miller in a key position in the campaign. I waited until the last minute for a return call. When it didn't come, I went on the air for my interview. The Miller question was raised, and I answered that the campaign staff would be too small for both Bill Miller and Jackie Robinson. The newspapermen had a Donnybrook. On front pages and all over radio and television, the news was blasted that I had threatened to quit. My phone began ringing furiously. Most of the calls and comments were encouraging, praising me for my stand and telling me, "I don't blame you."

There was no call or comment, however, that evening or all the next day from the governor. I had no way of telling what the governor's decision would be. The Conservative and right-wing influences were furiously at work and I knew it. Word came down that there would be a press conference one morning, and I was requested to meet the governor in his private office a few minutes before it took place. I happened to get to Fifty-fifth Street just as the governor arrived, tired and unsmiling. Well, I told myself as he greeted me with a casual air, I guess I'm on my way out of the political business. A few minutes later, the governor and I sat down in his private office for a brief chat and then we went downstairs together to face one of the most crowded press conferences ever held at the Fifty-fifth Street office.

That press conference turned out to be an unforgettable one. When I think about it, I still get a little emotional. Rockefeller supported me all the way and announced that he wanted me to stay on. Miller's offer was turned down. The conservatives were very upset, but Rockefeller had made his stand and I was proud and moved by his support.

One of the prominent Conservative big shots who was really disturbed by this incident was William Buckley. William Buckley, one of my favorite feuding partners, has never forgiven me for being against Goldwater. He sneered in his syndicated column that the governor, who originally had become governor on the issue of bossism in the Democratic party, is himself a boss, who gives orders virtually to everyone in the party and in the state government except Jackie Robinson. Criticism of this nature was high praise to me because, most of the time, if I can irritate Bill Buckley, I figure I'm doing something constructive.

Two years later, in 1968, Bill Buckley and the whole Conservative crowd had their turn to taste triumph when Richard Nixon made his remarkable political comeback at the Republican National Convention. Even though the odds seemed overwhelmingly against us, there were still some of us in New York State and around the country who believed the perpetuation of the two-party system depended on the party's nominating someone who could rebuild it from the shambles it had become during the Goldwater debacle. Our man was, of course, Governor Rockefeller. Rockefeller had been off again, on again, doing what some disgusted friends and foes called a hesitation walk about his intention to seek or not to seek the 1968 nomination. There were periods when he was convinced that he ought to make a fight for the nomination and other times when he seemed resigned to the fact that his party had completely turned its back on him. Unfortunately he finally decided not to run. This put me in a difficult position.

The Agnew nomination and the choice of Richard Nixon by the Republican party convinced me of something I had long suspected. The GOP didn't give a damn about my vote or the votes—or welfare—of my people. Consequently, I could no longer justify supporting them. I got word to the governor that I was resigning as his special assistant. I knew that political protocol would dictate that he go along with the party nominations. When I told Governor Rockefeller that I was resigning, I also told him that I would be campaigning for Hubert Humphrey and didn't want to place him in the embarrassing predicament of campaigning on one side of a street someday for Nixon-Agnew and having a member of his staff—me—campaigning on the other side of the street for the Democrats.

Proudly I have to say that the couple of years I put in working for Rockefeller did make a difference. Not enough of a difference, however, because we were up against the kind of neglect of blacks in the state of New York which had long preceded the Rockefeller administration. In the realm of high political and government activity, there are many instances in which prejudice against blacks is not a problem.• Blacks simply don't exist in the minds of the people in power.

I did what I could. I managed to get some things straightened out in state civil service. Maneuvering behind the scenes was responsible for some significant appointments that didn't benefit just one individual but also put that individual in a position to help many. When I went to the scenes of unrest and riot as the governor's representative, I went not to emphasize the "cool it" bit, but to listen and learn why things had become so hot. I didn't listen only to the law and order people or the black and white bourgeoisie. I got together the so-called militants and offered to do what I could to communicate their beefs to the governor, to housing people, and to industry. I felt the job was worthwhile and that I had made some progress for the black cause while I was in it.

There had been headlines about my leaving the Rockefeller administration, and many people had falsely concluded that I was angry with the governor. This was not true. Our warm personal relationship still exists, even though I have been dismayed by the welfare and education slashes, the one-year residency regulation to qualify for welfare, and a few other moves the governor has made in the last couple of years. He seems to have made a sharp right turn away from the stand of the man who once fought the Old Guard Republican Establishment so courageously. During the summer of 1971, I met with the governor and voiced my concerns; I told him I was beginning to wonder if he was the same Rockefeller. For the first time he became a little angry with me, but I had no intention of backing down and he wouldn't have expected me to do so. He assured me that he was the same Rockefeller, but he spent quite a while telling me about his problems and how he was convinced that some of the steps he had taken were the only possible ones to try to stop the wreckage of our economic system. I could clearly see some of the points he made and understand why he felt he had to take certain positions. However, I told him honestly that I could not in good conscience support some of his current political philosophy. Mr. Rockefeller seemed to respect this personal conviction just as I had respected his. He said his only ambition was to be the greatest governor New York State ever had. I told him I thought he had been well on his way but had got sidetracked.

Even though I can't agree with a lot of steps he has taken recently, I personally like the guy. I have been under constant fire from friends and even from members of my family who harshly condemn the governor's role in the terrible Attica situation. But I believe that he sincerely used his best judgment in a crucial situation and took the advice of people he really believed in. I think he should have gone to Attica in person, but others close to him said it would not help. The final results were disastrous, but if he was wrong in the Attica tragedy, I do not believe his decision or his actions reflect the full measure of the man.

Chapter XIX

The Influence of
Martin Luther King, Jr.

The Montgomery boycott against the buses, which led to the 1956 Supreme Court decision, is almost ancient history now. But the memory of the man responsible for the first real breakthrough in the civil rights movement lives on.

Dr. Martin Luther King, Jr., had led the black community in the boycott that caused almost unendurable hardship to his people for over a year before the Supreme Court decided segregation on buses should be eliminated. During this period Martin Luther King and his family were the constant target of threats. In fact, whites—afraid they were losing—condemned the use of car pools, sent the Ku Klux Klan out to burn and destroy Negro property, threatened the arrest of anyone who picked up a Negro pedestrian, and in the end bombed the King home.

At the time, Martin was at a regular mass meeting at Abernathy's church and Coretta was sitting in the living room at home talking with a visitor. She heard something that seemed to land on the porch and thought that she and her visitor should go back to the bedroom "just in case." Halfway down the hall, they heard the explosion and saw smoke. The telephone rang. Coretta answered it to hear a woman's voice say, "Yes, I did it. And I'm just sorry I didn't kill all you bastards."

Martin arrived home to find steadily increasing throngs of black men and women armed with anything they could get their hands on—sticks, bottles, rocks, and in some cases guns and knives—surrounding his house. Threats and curses filled the air.

Who can forget Martin Luther King's words spoken from the porch of his bombed home?

"Don't get panicky. . . . If you have weapons, take them home. . . . We cannot solve this problem through retaliatory violence. . . . We must love our white brothers no matter what they do to us. We must make them know that we love them. Jesus still cries out in words that echo across the centuries: 'Love your enemies; bless them that curse you; pray for them that despitefully use you.' This is what we must live by. We must meet hate with love."

I met Martin not long after the bombing. I had been extremely impressed by his calmness in the face of such terrible violence and threats to his family. When we met, through Al Duckett who was a close personal friend of Martin's, I was immediately struck by his dedication. I joined him whenever possible. I became a close friend and I began to understand the remarkable qualities that made him the leader he was. Godliness, strength, courage, and patience in the face of overwhelming odds were his chief characteristics.

As much as I loved him, I never would have made a good soldier in Martin's army. My reflexes aren't conditioned to accept nonviolence in the face of violence-provoking attacks. My immediate instinct under the threat of physical attack to me or those I love is instant defense and total retaliation.

Martin had designated me head of the fund-raising drive to rebuild the burned-out Georgia churches. I felt that if Martin

King could make the kind of sacrifices he was making, I had to do what little I could to support him. He was and is my idol, but we didn't always agree.

I was one of the many people who were convinced he was wrong in his stand on the Vietnam War. Early in May, 1967—reluctantly, though I felt I had to do it—I wrote him an open letter in my newspaper column asking him to use one of the succeeding columns for his reply.

I started out by saying that I considered him the greatest civil rights leader in the history of mankind. I said that, although I might be mistaken, it seemed to me he was utterly wrong in his stand on Vietnam. I was confused by this because I knew that he was a totally sincere and dedicated man and my respect for him was unbounded. I added that the children had started to ask us questions we were unable to answer.

"Isn't it unfair," I asked, "for you to place all the burden of the blame on America and none on the Communist forces we are fighting? You suggest that we stop the bombing. It strikes me that our President has made effort after effort to get both sides to the peace table. Why should we take the vital step of stopping the bombing without knowing whether the enemy will use that pause to prepare for greater destruction of our men in Vietnam? Won't you admit that, whenever there has been a lull or a cease-fire, our opponents have used this time to regroup and rebuild and to make themselves stronger in order to kill more of our soldiers? Yet, you have called the United States—and unfairly, I feel—the greatest purveyor of violence on earth. There was one 30 day period, you will recall, when we permitted a cease-fire and the Viet Cong used it to build roads and tunnels and to store food in order to further the murder of our men and their own fellow-countrymen. Why do you seem to ignore the blood that is on their hands and speak only of "the guilt of the United States"? Why do you not suggest that the Viet Cong cease, stop, withdraw also? I am firmly convinced that President Johnson wants an end to this war as much as anyone. If you want to be very cynical about it, you have to admit that the termination of the war would be in his best political interest in the coming elections.

"I am confused, Martin," I concluded. "I am confused because I respect you deeply. But I also love this imperfect country. I respectfully ask you to answer this open letter and give me your own point of view."

It was painful writing this letter. It was all the more painful for Al Duckett who had been writing the column with and for me for a few years. Al was also a writer for Martin Luther King, and, in fact, he did a major job on the famous "I Have a Dream" speech and on one of Martin's books—*Why We Can't Wait*—and some of his sermons. Al knew about my convictions in favor of the United States' position on the war. But he did not really agree. He was strictly on Martin's side on this one. It wasn't often that we didn't see things the same way about the column, but this was one of those times. Al thought I ought to talk to Martin directly before releasing the column and I agreed. But I was unable to contact Martin for several days, and since I felt we could no longer hold up the column, we went to press with it. Immediately after its publication, Martin telephoned me at home that night. I was terribly touched by the fact that Martin was not nearly as anxious to defend my attack publicly as he was to have me, as a friend, understand his philosophy and motivation. This was one more attribute of Martin's humanity. Criticism, especially from friends, wounded him deeply. He wasn't concerned about possible embarrassment in front of the public; he felt hurt when he was misunderstood by someone who he felt understood him.

We had a long and, for me, enligntening conversation that night, and in the end I understood Martin's inner compulsion to speak out against war and for peace. He would have been untrue to himself if he had not taken a stand for the principle in which he so deeply believed. He was one of the world's leading exponents of nonviolence, and it made as much sense to him to oppose wars throughout the world as it did to oppose violence in Montgomery, Selma, and Birmingham.

I felt he was calling for a mismatched marriage between the civil rights movement and the peace movement, and that such a marriage could be a disastrous alliance. We covered this point and others in our lengthy discussion. Contrary to public opinion, Martin's criticism of the U.S. policy in Vietnam was not coming out of a vacuum. He had done a fantastic amount of research and had brilliant arguments to support his position. Months later he made a major speech at New York's Riverside Church, explaining with great detail and eloquence his position against the war. Much of what he said on that occasion he had said to me on the phone that night.

I can't say that Martin convinced me that I was wrong and he was right on all counts. I am proud to say, however, that learning, first hand, his point of view only served to increase the deep admiration I held for him. No matter how much we disagreed, I had renewed faith in his sincerity, his capacity to make the hard, unpopular decision, and his willingness to accept the consequences. He had taken a magnificently brave and lonely stand. Within his own organization there was much concern about his views—enough to make him agree to emphasize that he was expressing his own personal viewpoint rather than that of his board and staff. The fund-raisers for the organization continued to warn him that many whites who had been substantial contributors were withdrawing their support and that the allegiance of many blacks was also in jeopardy. The war, however, was one issue on which Dr. King would not compromise. He took the position that, if all the sources of income for his organization dried up and he were left alone crying out against organized killing, that would have to be the route he had to take.

Today, in the early seventies, I cannot bitterly oppose, as I did in my open letter to Martin Luther King, the notion that

America leads the world in violence. I do not make these statements because the tide of public opinion has changed about the war. I originally felt strongly about our role in the war; that we had a commitment to honor and should not back down in the face of an aggressive enemy. I have not embraced nonviolence, but I have become more cynical about this country's role in Vietnam. I have become skeptical about the old domino theory; that the fall of Vietnam would bring Communist domination to Southeast Asia. I feel that the regime we are supporting in South Vietnam is corrupt and not representative of the people. I am personally upset by the plight of the American GI—and particularly the black soldier. The drug situation, which I learned about at great personal cost because of my son's addiction, angers me greatly. Finally, I cannot accept the idea of a black supposedly fighting for the principles of freedom and democracy in Vietnam when so little has been accomplished in this country. There was a time when I deeply believed in America. I have become bitterly disillusioned.

The tragic death of Martin Luther King, the short-lived national sorrow over that death, and the nation's speedy recovery and return to business as usual, causes one to wonder if this country will ever rise to the capacity to be true to itself, to be true to those lofty aims we say were our reason for coming into being.

At the funeral services, I was plunged into deep contemplation as I thought of the sadness of saying farewell to a man who died still clinging to a dream of integration and peace and nonviolence. I could only hope that perhaps his death was symbolically hopeful. Perhaps after the streets of American cities were no longer haunted by angry blacks seeking to avenge the assassination, we would find ourselves. Perhaps Dr. Martin Luther King's last full measure of devotion for the cause of brotherhood would not prove to have been in vain.

It is still too soon to assess the impact of his death, as it is too early to measure the meaning of the death of Malcolm X. There have been some hopeful and positive developments, and there has been evidence that hatred is still a brutal and vicious force. Martin Luther King accomplished much in his lifetime, but Americans still have a long way to go in terms of working toward the beloved society concept for which he lived and died.

Chapter XX

Jackie's Prison

In June, 1967, Jackie was discharged from the service. When he came back home, he was more confused than he had been when he went into the service. He didn't stay around home much. He said he just wasn't ready to decide what he was going to do and that he had to stay away from us to figure it all out. He kept trying to reassure us that we didn't have to worry about him, that he would be all right. And though we were concerned, we tried to believe him because we wanted to.

The last thought in our minds was addiction.

We knew that things weren't right, but there is nothing that can blind parents as much as loving hope. We talked with Jackie and we listened to him. I felt my communication with him was improved. We were relieved when he laughed off the idea of his ever becoming addicted. He was most persuasive when he frankly admitted using marijuana, warning us that there was no point in our forbidding him to use it, telling us that he liked grass, that he was not going to give it up. He gave us the familiar argument that marijuana is harmless, not addictive, that it only leads weak-minded people into the hard stuff. We didn't have a thing to worry about in terms of his sticking a needle in his arm. He was afraid to stick himself with needles. It would never get to that. Not with him. He was convincing. We found out later that there is something about drug addiction that imbues its victims with a terrible kind of craftiness and ingenuity. Jack sold us on his point of view. We looked around us. We read everything we could get our hands on. We went down the primrose path part of the way, though not all the way, with those goddamed experts that make young people and their parents believe that marijuana is harmless. Look at all the brilliant achievers who smoke it. It isn't any worse than alcohol.

As I look back, I become bitter about people like Dr. Margaret Mead. I am sure that she and many others who call for the legalization of marijuana are quite sincere, but I think they are doing an incalculable amount of damage. What we did—and what thousands of other parents are doing—is so terribly wrong. We depended on Jackie to have the ability and strength to restrict himself to marijuana—an ability and strength that he didn't have, that a lot of troubled people don't have.

The morning of the day the roof fell in on us, I had been interviewed by the Associated Press on the telephone. A few minutes later the reporter called back. I had expressed some strong and controversial views to him, and I assumed he was calling for some clarification. Instead he said, "What about Jackie?"

"What do you mean?" I demanded.

"Don't you know that your son was arrested about one o'clock this morning on charges of possession and carrying a concealed weapon?" the reporter asked.

I was stunned. Dully, I heard the information that Jackie was in jail at that moment. He was of age, and when he gave the police instructions not to contact us, they went along with it. That was why we had not heard.

I remember clearly my first gut reaction. If I could have put it into words then, I would have said, "The hell with you, Jack. We've tried to do our best. You've been getting into trouble every time we turn around. Now you've placed us in a terrible position. There's going to be a lot of bad publicity and grief for everyone in the family."

That was my first reaction, but it was wiped out in seconds. I immediately called Rachel. We had to let Jackie know we expected him to shoulder the consequences of his mistakes but that we were 100 percent behind him and would leave no stone unturned to do whatever was necessary to help him. Rachel and I went to the police station and posted the $5,000 bail required.

After a long talk with Jackie, we decided that the best thing to do was to put him in the New Haven hospital. It seemed logical because Rachel was working near there and could see that he got the proper attention. That was a mistake also and Jack told us so after he had been there a few days.

"This place is doing me absolutely no good," he said. "You're really just wasting your money. I'm the only addict here. The other people have mental problems. I need to be with some people who have the same kind of problems I have. That way we could learn from one another, help one another."

What Jackie was saying was sound. He admitted that he had become an artist at lying his way out of virtually any situation. He could simulate absolute sincerity.

"I can tell those doctors anything and they'll believe it," he said. He was convinced that he could persuade the people in the hospital that he was cured. He did—and he was discharged and went right back to his addiction.

When Jackie went to trial, he was given two alternatives—prison or enrollment in a rehabilitation program. That was when he joined the Daytop program. I don't have the words to pay tribute to what the Daytop experience did for him. The people who run the house at Seymour, Connecticut, are ex-addicts, and their dedication to helping others who have become seemingly hopelessly hooked is total. They have gone

219

through all the stages and phases and tricks of the junkie world, and it is impossible to pull the wool over their eyes as Jackie had done with the hospital doctors.

Jackie was put to stiff tests. He was taken into the Narco Pre-induction Center, and his first assignment was to clean some latrines. All kinds of filthy, revolting, and menial tasks were given him to see how much he was prepared to help himself. The first night he went through the Pre-induction Center, he came home terribly discouraged. He didn't think he could stand the trials. One of the things that hurt him the most was being told he would have to shave off his beloved beard and mustache. That's what they do at Daytop. They find out what you like best and then they take it away from you. It is known as making an investment in the program. They are testing you all the time to see if you have enough stamina to face the awful task of curing your illness mainly through your own self-reliance. There was one time when they had him sitting on a stool for hours just to see if he could observe the rigid discipline he was going to need. He convinced them that he was ready and they took him in. That was only the beginning of his ordeal—and ours.

Jackie was at first admitted to the Daytop installation on Staten Island. The people in charge there immediately warned us of a situation we would undoubtedly have to face. Within a few days or the first couple of weeks, they told us, Jackie would decide that he couldn't stand the confinement and the regimen and deprivation of dope any longer. He would decide he was going to leave. In all probability he would call us up and ask to come home.

"When he does," they instructed us, "here's the way we want you to handle it. This will be terribly difficult for you to do, but if you want to save your son, you will inform him that he cannot come home; that if he tries to, you will have him picked up by the police the minute he gets to Stamford. You will have his bail revoked and let him go to jail. You will have to say to him that if he refuses, at this point, to do what is necessary to help himself, he's had it, as far as you are concerned."

The advice was chilling. We listened and just hoped the situation would not arise. It did. One night, sometime between midnight and one in the morning, we received the call. The Daytop people were on the line, informing us that Jackie was threatening to leave. We asked to talk to him. The answer was that he wouldn't speak with us. We asked that the message be relayed that if he left, he would go to jail if he tried to come home. Can you imagine the anguish of being a parent and having to give that kind of a message to a son you love? Imagine the nagging fear that you might have made a terrible mistake—experts or no experts. After all, this was your son. Suppose he didn't have the strength for this supreme test—the slamming of the doors that had been open to him all his conscious life. Suppose a sense of rejection drove him back out into the streets to find retaliation or temporary relief from hurt with a needle.

There wasn't going to be much sleep for us that night. But about three hours later, the phone rang. It was the Daytop people again. They had just finished a long talk with Jackie, and he had been persuaded that it was the wisest thing for him not to leave. We were grateful for the advance advice we had received, which had prepared us to be strong. Otherwise, we would have been right there at the Stamford station, waiting for Jackie to run away from his own salvation.

Jackie told us much about the Daytop way of restoring life. It's pretty obvious that a junkie is an individual on a suicide trip. Daytop uses methods that make it impossible to play games. The individual who has collided with the law because he has broken it to support his habit and whose motive to get into Daytop is to avoid prison very seldom gets away with it. He finds he has to commit himself to self-redemption or lose his opportunity of becoming a part of the program. Daytop is centered in a philosophy of the effectiveness of people with common troubles pulling each other up. Daytop is strict—

terribly strict. While addicts are in that program they are constantly being taught to be thoughtful rather than thoughtless. They don't drop a cigarette ash on a floor. They don't leave lights on or forget to check out. And they don't get any drugs to help them withdraw. It's done the hard way—cold turkey. An addict can rant and rave and carry on and a Daytop man will tell him, "Come on, buddy, knock it off." He can't regard the man as a cynical, unfeeling person who doesn't know how he feels. He knows how the addicts feel. Back in the Daytop man's recent or distant past, when he was ranting and raving, somebody who had once ranted and raved, had told him the same thing. The Daytop theory is that the terrible agony associated with withdrawal is not nearly as excruciating as it is pictured on the screen or reported in novels. Within seventy-two hours, Daytop people say, an addict is withdrawn—physically. The body is detoxified and can function without heroin. After that period of time, there are psychosomatic reactions—the runny nose, the watery eyes, the self-pitying conviction that it's impossible to live without a fix. His weakness, his self-indulgence, no longer has free rein because he is in the presence of others who he knows know the score. In the past the addict, like a spoiled child, has been able to get others to do his will by persuading them that he is in a desperate state. The Daytop gospel is that much too often the roots of addiction are the result of receiving too little love—or too much—equally dangerous.

The Daytop philosophy states firmly that no one owes the addict a living. He owes a lot to life. And the task of recovering his life is his alone. Daytop avoids what is called horizontal therapy; the addict goes to a hospital, stretches out and gets shot with dextrose for a certain number of days, and is soon back in the streets and back into heroin. Or he lies on a psychiatrist's couch and equates his needle-sticking with his hatred for his grandmother. Daytop believes in the vertical theory. The addict's therapist is an ex-addict and he challenges his patients to invest in their own recovery. In a Daytop group anyone guilty of the tiniest bit of hypocrisy gets a merciless tongue-lashing. The entire company jumps in. If a little lie has been told, they magnify it all out of proportion. The addict is made to realize the stupidity of being phony and taught that behavior is not as important as the attitude behind behavior. Drugs are not the problem, the Daytop philosophy says. Drugs are the manifestation and the symptom of the problem.

All this Jackie learned. All this he absorbed.

And while he was learning, we were learning that the Daytop philosophy is perhaps the one viable approach to the narcotics addiction problem. It doesn't supply all the answers, but a check of the results it achieves would make any reasonable person wonder why this program receives so little support from government and private sources. Daytop is understaffed and underbudgeted; it has long waiting lists of people wanting to be helped.

I was appalled when I learned how little was being done in the state of Connecticut about the narcotics situation. I wrote to Governor John Dempsey and suggested that a massive program be initiated and that such organizations as Daytop be given more help. Given the extent of the problem, the answer was most inadequate. The governor bragged about all he was doing in the state to fight drugs. His solutions didn't begin to sound the depths of the problem.

I went to the baseball commissioner. I thought that, since the drug problem is a big problem among our youth and since baseball has many young fans, it would be a great idea for baseball to indulge in a creative and constructive program, at least an educational program. I thought that at times when games are not being televised—and even when they are—the baseball idols of young people could say a word about the perils of drugs. I was given great courtesy and attention by the commissioner's office, and I was told what a wonderful idea this was. Later, an educational campaign was launched, but again, given the scope of the problem and the resources of the business, the campaign had not been adequate.

Every moment of agony we had ever suffered, every fear we had ever experienced, seemed worthwhile on one special day—after Jackie had spent a year in the Daytop program. That was the day that Kenny Williams told us confidentially that he believed our son was out of danger, that he was cured. He didn't tell Jackie this and he cautioned us against false hopes. It was necessary that vigilance continue to be observed to insure that Jackie did not backslide, as so many do; the fear that an ex-addict will revert to his old habits is genuine. One or two or, sometimes, ten years cannot guarantee that an ex-addict will not be driven back to addiction by weakness or by circumstance. Experts have found, however, that one of the most successful ways a former addict can keep himself cured is through deep involvement in helping others who are fighting addiction. Knowledge of this fact, added to his tremendous gratitude to his Daytop associates, made Jackie decide to become a member of the Daytop staff. He worked at the same Daytop house where he had been helped and did group work on the outside. He gave talks at schools, to young people's groups, to social clubs, and to church groups. He also conducted a rehabilitation group. We attended some of his activities and felt extremely proud of his development. After Jackie's death we learned from others whose lives he touched how much of an impact he had been having. He had been clean for three years, and he spoke with authority about all that he had been through—about the way he had become an addict, the reasons for it, the hell into which he had been plunged as an addict—stealing, robbing, pushing dope, pimping—anything to get the money for dope. He had learned at Daytop that the core of the cure was in being absolutely and utterly honest with himself and with others. As a result, when he appeared before audiences, he didn't spare himself. He was merciless in laying his own soul bare, and because he was willing to be so open about it, he had a conviction and a sincerity which had a powerful effect on those who heard him talk. Jackie, who had learned to love himself properly, was now able to love others adequately. His capacity for loving had opened up.

Rachel and I had been trying to think of ways to show our appreciation to the Daytop staff. One day, on a holiday late in May, we invited all the members of the Daytop family, perhaps about fifty of them, to a picnic on the grounds surrounding our house in Stamford. They arrived about ten in the morning. Seldom have I seen a more organized group. They had a kitchen crew which went to work and prepared some great salads. They had brought along chickens, watermelons, and other fruits to add to the food we were providing. They had work squads assigned to take care of every detail. Some of those who didn't have an assignment for the moment were out on the grounds playing ball.

We were delighted seeing Jackie's pride in his friends and sensing how much our warmth toward them and their warmth toward us meant to him. He was like a mother hen, supervising the whole affair—the preparation of the food, the games, the cleaning up they did at the end of the day. About four thirty in the afternoon, they were ready to return to Daytop, and all of them came to Rachel and me saying what a fabulous time they had had, some of them declaring it was the greatest day of their lives. As that line of kids dwindled down, our son Jackie was the last. There was a proud look on his face that put a lump in my throat because I remembered. . . .

When Jackie had left home to go into the service. We drove him to the train and I suppose I had the thoughts any father has watching his son leave for service. I was proud of him and I was concerned because I knew quite well there was a chance he might never come back. I was worried because I knew that telling him good-bye was rough for Rachel. As he was about to leave us, Rachel reached out and took him in her arms in a loving hug. Impulsively, I wanted to do the same thing. But just as I raised my arms to embrace him, his hand shot up and stopped me, and he took my hand in his in a firm handclasp. In our unspoken language, I knew that the love was there but what he was telling me was that men don't embrace. And I understood. That had been several years ago. . . .

Now on the lawn of our home, on the evening of the picnic, our confused and lost kid who had gone off to war, who had experienced as much life in a few short and turbulent years as many never do in a lifetime, that same kid had now become a young man, growing in self-esteem, growing in confidence, learning about life, and learning about the massive power of love. He stood in front of us, the last on that line of thankful guests, and reached out and grabbed Rachel and hugged her to him. His gratitude and appreciation were a tremendous sight. I stuck out my hand to shake his hand, remembering the day of his departure for the service. He brushed my hand aside, pulled me to him, and embraced me in a tight hug.

That single moment paid for every bit of sacrifice, every bit of anguish, I had ever undergone.

I had my son back.

Immediately, after that picnic, began a new era of closeness for the family. Jackie was open in talking with us. He could talk about the shadows of the past because he had faced them and was walking away from them and because he knew who he was.

We had learned that we had done the right thing in closing ranks as a family. This is what families must do when crisis strikes. Forget about the whispers and stares of neighbors. I especially appeal to black parents because there is a special paranoia in the black communities when it comes to drugs. Most of the kids at Daytop with Jackie were white. Not because Daytop practices any kind of racial discrimination. But black kids are harder to reach because, in general, they grow bitter younger.

There is another phase of addiction that hits blacks the hardest. That is the addiction which either begins or accelerates while our GI's are in service. Blacks who volunteer are in proportion higher than their percentage of the population. This seems to mean that more of them proportionately are falling victims to addiction. Jackie appeared to testify before the United States Senate Sub-Committee to Investigate Juvenile Delinquency. The date of his testimony was October 30, 1970. Here is Jackie's statement:

STATEMENT BY JACK ROBINSON, JR.

I joined the United States Army for three years in March, 1964. My first duty station was at Fort Riley, Kansas. I was only seventeen years old, and because of my age I couldn't get into a lot of the military clubs or entertainment establishments the other fellows went into.

I really didn't like the types of recreation that were provided by the Army. I found myself very much alone and bored in my off-duty hours. So during these hours I found myself searching for something that would give my time and my life some kind of interest, some kind of meaning. In my searching for these things, I met other people who were pretty much in the same bag that I was in. They were also pretty much lost and looking for something. So we turned to the use of alcohol. We drank quite a bit and began to use drugs occasionally. I guess the only reason we only used them on occasion was because there weren't really that many drugs out in Kansas at that time, or at least that I knew of, so we didn't have that much contact with them.

When we did have contact with them we used them. It was mainly marijuana and a few different types of pills.

I had smoked marijuana infrequently before going into the Army and during the time just prior to that I didn't smoke at all. It was in the Army that I got most heavily into drug use, where it became an everyday thing with me.

I got to use marijuana and opium as well as various

227

different types of pills which I got from the medics as often as not.

In Vietnam we landed at a place called Camranh Bay, and there was no military action for the first couple of months. This is when we started smoking pot kind of slowly. We didn't really jump into it. We smoked like twice a week in the beginning. And then after a while our use picked up, and as our use picked up there were a lot more people that started using. A lot of people that had never smoked any pot or marijuana when we were in the States started to smoke it then. I guess this was because it was more prevalent over there. There was more marijuana growing wild, and in any village you could get as much as you wanted to. So besides the added tension and added fears that people have to deal with I think the fact that it was so readily available was another reason that started people using so heavily.

I was in the infantry the entire time I was in Vietnam. I was wounded in action and I saw quite a few different combat missions. Drugs were used on these missions.

At first when I got over there the drugs were much more powerful than those I had been used to in the United States. I thought at first that I wouldn't use them when I started pulling guard duty or when I was on combat missions. But as I got used to the more potent high that was created by these drugs I started taking them with me everywhere I went and after a while smoked marijuana or the opium-dipped marijuana regularly. Anyway, it didn't matter to me if I was on guard duty or going out on combat duty mission. And with me it kind of intensified all the feelings that I had. I was fairly aggressive when it came to fighting anyway.

I think that the use of marijuana made me want to get into it more. I found myself wanting something to happen, hoping the fighting would start. And I was always looking around, very anxious, very tense. It seemed from what I saw of it, everybody was using drugs.

It did basically the same thing to them. And when I say the

same thing I mean that it intensified their feelings. If they had a lot of fears about the combat action, they became really paranoid, and when they heard a gunshot it really scared them. You would see them dive behind bushes or fall to the ground really quickly. They were truly scared. I think it is because of the fact that your feelings are so much intensified and your fears are so great that you react differently to different situations than you would ordinarily. I don't think you can have someone out in the field who is smoking marijuana and expect rational actions from them at all times because their view of the world when they are high is not that orderly or that structured. A lot of things don't really make sense to you. You could find yourself out in the middle of a field and you have been smoking pot and all of a sudden you ask yourself a question like "What am I doing here?" It hits you. Like what am I really doing here? And this can go beyond just a moral conviction about not fighting. This can go to your head. "You know you can get killed doing this sort of thing" or "I don't want to do it." While other people just got carried away with it, I never did anything really crazy while I was using drugs. But I have ridden through villages with a .38 of my own and I put my arm over the side and just pointed it at different people and pretended in my mind that I was just shooting them down. I would have been smoking a lot of marijuana and I think that had I been agitated at the time or something happened which scared me it would have been a very easy thing to shoot instead of just pretending.

I think that everybody acts differently when they are really high, when they have smoked marijuana, and most GI's did after a while. Many smoked while sitting up at night alone pulling guard duty. This is mostly the heavier smokers I'm speaking about now. Just before going out on a patrol or to set up an ambush they might smoke some.

And I know personally now, that it was a very dangerous thing to do. In difficult situations, say at night, if anyone moved near me I might have taken a shot at him.

We had a number of accidental deaths while I was over there and it wouldn't surprise me if some of those "accidental" deaths were possibly caused by some GI's being scared under combat conditions because of marijuana.

When I said the heavy marijuana users, I said that because it was mostly the heavy users that smoked marijuana when we were out on missions. The guys who smoke it only occasionally generally wouldn't smoke it when we were out on a mission. When I said heavy user I meant somebody who used it like every day, pretty much all day, as I did. And I would say about 25 percent of my outfit fell into this category. And then, perhaps, from 50 to 75 percent of my outfit smoked pot irregularly.

Why was there so much drug use?

I think it had to do with the extraordinary amount of fear, the harsh realities, they had to deal with. They weren't accustomed to the pressure and sought some relief. Facing reality is easier when you are high. Reality is altered, made more comfortable by drugs, and I think this is basically what causes the drug abuse.

That is particularly true about the idle, bored GI's not in combat. You don't want to just lie around and think about what you are involved in. It would be much more comfortable to lie around and just be high and not have to deal with the fact that the next hour or the next day you are going to be going back out and facing the people who are hostile and want to kill you.

I think another big thing was the apathy that smoking marijuana created. Once we got into marijuana we weren't really interested in the war thing; you know, it just didn't seem relevant to what we wanted to do. You know the thing of serving your country, and any other reason that somebody might have there, kind of went right out of the window because our whole thing was we wanted to be high. There was no purpose to too much of anything else that wasn't directly related to us getting high.

After I arrived in Vietnam I used drugs constantly for the remaining two years of my tour of duty, including pills and opium as I became familiar with them. I think the environment came into play, had something to do with it. I know now that I have to take the responsibility for my own actions because there were guys around me who didn't use drugs, but I think that the environment played a big part in it.

The military code on drugs was never really enforced. I was in the stockade for going AWOL after I came back from Vietnam, and there was one member of the Army CID that knew I was using drugs. I think he learned this from people in town somehow or possibly from one of his investigations. But as far as the officers or any of the people in my units are concerned, they didn't know, and nothing ever happened to me because of drug use. I was never treated for any drug use, obviously, because they didn't know, and I was never punished for it. The Army isn't a very personal place, it isn't a very sensitive place, and most of the people who are in charge of the Army don't seem to me to be very sensitive people. They seem indifferent to a lot of the personal problems that a person has. They really weren't concerned with anything except your doing your function as a soldier, and as long as you did that they really didn't care about anything else that might be going on with you.

I was court-martialed only once for going AWOL, but it had nothing to do with drugs. When I returned to Colorado from Vietnam I brought some marijuana back with me. At the time we weren't really being searched very thoroughly so I brought back enough to last me a couple of months. I had eighty opium-treated marijuana cigarettes. I even had a bag with a broken zipper that nobody bothered to open. I tried to open it. The zipper was broken. They told me, that's all right, go ahead through. I had the cigarettes right on me in cigarette packs which were packed over there.

Quite a few of my friends smuggled drugs into the United

States but none got caught. I knew one man who brought back $10,000 worth of opium to New York City.

In Colorado I started getting involved with a lot of the camp followers. These are people that are prostitutes, gamblers, thieves, drug users, and pushers that kind of follow Army towns. In Colorado I mostly used marijuana and pills and cough syrup on an everyday basis. I left Colorado and came to New York City where I started using cocaine, heroin, occasionally LSD, the amphetamines—I was using all types of drugs at this point. After a few months back in New York and Connecticut I went back to Colorado where I was using heroin, cocaine, and drinking a lot of cough syrup, and smoking marijuana—just heavily involved in all types of drugs. I was into about every type of crime that you could get into, in order to support my habit at this point.

I would steal from other soldiers, civilians; I would sell marijuana on the post. But I was never arrested and never got into any trouble for it. I was breaking into houses, and after a while I was selling heroin and cocaine. And just doing a lot of stealing. These are basically the things I did while I was in the Army. When I was honorably discharged after three years I got into some other things.

My commitment to Daytop was for two counts of carrying a dangerous weapon, aggravated assault, possession of narcotics, and using a female for immoral purposes. From the time I came back from Vietnam to the time I was arrested I continued carrying guns. I think it was something I got obsessed with over there and fit very well into the image of what I thought was a man I had gotten from the Army, the image of being tough and fighting and this whole thing being what manhood was all about. I carried a gun until I was arrested two different times here in Connecticut. The first time for possession of narcotics and possession of a dangerous weapon. I went into a hospital and I stayed about three months and I really didn't do anything for myself. I came back out, and in about four months I was arrested for the offenses I listed above and committed to Daytop.

I now have found some direction. I am presently a resident of Daytop, Inc., at Seymour, and I've been there for about two years now. I should be graduating shortly. Daytop is a self-help program staffed and run entirely by ex-addicts. It is an eighteen to twenty-four month program and deals with helping the individual grow up and get a good enough understanding of himself to deal with the realities that he finds around him without having the need for drugs.

I have been involved in other programs, but for me Daytop has been the only effective approach to my problem. I've seen it work for a lot of people around me as well.

When I leave Daytop I may do some community work. I have had a number of different job offers from people that I know in the community because I am interested in community work. I have learned to deal with people through being in Daytop and through running groups and being involved with getting an understanding of myself and others. I would like to continue working with people either in the community or possibly with the Daytop staff.

Since my discharge from the military I have not heard from them at all. I filed for a claim with the Veterans Administration. I was wounded when I was in Vietnam and I never got any compensation for that. I was also shot in the foot when I was on pass from the Army when I was in Colorado. I've been limping on my foot for the past three years, and I haven't gotten anything for that either. While I realized that I have to take most of the responsibility for my becoming a drug addict, I don't think that the Army has helped me at all in overcoming my problem, which started pretty much in the Army. I think that if, in that period of my life when I was as confused as I was and as messed up as I was, if I had gotten some good guidance at that point I might have been turned in the right direction. But instead I was given a lot of bad values I feel. I was helped by a very insensitive organization to get further and further down the road to destroying myself. I feel that since I did get heavily into drugs while in combat and

233

while fighting at eighteen years old, I feel the Army maybe should compensate me for this.

I talked to a lawyer about it and I filed a claim with the VA. We decided to wait and see what kind of action they would take. I'm not sure if the VA is really planning to do anything about this or not.

So I've been inactive for the last two years, and the Army hasn't done anything up to this point to help me with this thing at all, either financially or with my rehabilitation.

To sum it up, I was a pretty mixed-up kid when I went into the Army, but the type of guidance I received there didn't help. Things got worse. I became more confused about manhood, responsibility, and a lot of other things. Although I can't hold the Army entirely responsible for my being as messed up as I was, it didn't do me any good.

I think that drug-using servicemen are getting a real bad deal from the government and have been for a long time. They have been looking at the problem and treating these people as criminals. Addicts are not criminals. I feel we are people who are sick. I feel that drug addiction is the symptom of a problem. The problem, the sickness, must be treated. To look at this as a crime is really wrong, and it will not solve the problem. I think it is in part a reflection of a lot of the confusion we find around us in society today.

I think your military Drug Legislation S. 4393 is a good bill. I think it could be improved with stipulations in it for more money for drug programs. I think that a lot of people now who are being sent to jail really should not be and a lot of people who aren't being helped at all should be. I think that the government should allot more money to different drug programs so that we in the programs could handle a larger input of people who are using drugs. I think that Daytop could probably do a lot more if we had more funds, but it seems that the state of Connecticut hasn't really been meeting its responsibility in terms of dealing with drug addiction.

Chapter XXI

Politics Today

The political outlook at the approach of the 1968 elections had not been particularly encouraging. Robert F. Kennedy was dead. Martin Luther King had been taken away from us. Rockefeller had withdrawn from the Republican race, leaving us with the Nixon-Agnew ticket. I did feel quite strongly about the possibilities of positive leadership under Humphrey because of his past record on civil rights. However, despite a hard campaign in which I was given freedom to work completely on my own, we just didn't have enough time.

I was terribly disappointed in Nixon's 1968 victory. I feared that his Administration would cater to the conservative backlash that seemed then and now to be increasing in American politics.

Nevertheless, soon after his inauguration, I wrote Mr. Nixon, reminding him that in 1960 I had been solidly in his corner because I believed him to be sincere about wanting to see the hopes and aspirations of black Americans realized.

"I opposed you as vigorously in the last election," I wrote Mr. Nixon, "because I felt strongly that your position regarding the Old South, the rumors about Strom Thurmond, and the report from the convention would adversely affect the goals we as black people have set."

Since he had been elected, I continued, all of us—those who supported him and those who opposed him—would pray that his years in Washington would be most successful. I was afraid that unless the Administration took action indicating that it had some empathy with the problems of my people the bitterness between blacks and whites would inevitably grow to the point of explosion. A lack of understanding of the complexities of these problems seemed obvious to me in some of the statements made by some of Mr. Nixon's newly chosen Cabinet members. I warned him that young blacks were sincere and unafraid. I predicted that only sincerity and enormous effort on the part of both races could prevent a holocaust. I ended my letter with the hope that the President had the capacity to provide the necessary leadership. I received a reply that was characteristic of most political correspondence and said little except that my letter had been received.

The President's appointed Attorney General Mitchell went through motions of filing suits against abuses of voting rights, job discrimination, education and housing. However, Mitchell and the Administration demonstrated a marvelous sleight of hand, holding out the promise of progress in the one hand and appeasing the Silent Majority and the sullen South with the other. It was a game of one baby step forward and two giant steps back. The hostility to and "benign neglect" of the black man caused the few token blacks selected for high office to quit in disgust and others to run like hell if it appeared they were being approached with job offers. Only very brave or very insensitive blacks accepted Nixon Administration appointments. The tragic case of James Farmer—who learned the hard way that the Administration cared very little about the health, mis-education, and welfare of blacks—is a classic example of the kind of yawning credibility gap anyone hired by Mr. Nixon had to fight in the black community.

In January, 1970, as chairman of the board of Freedom National Bank in Harlem, I was one of several witnesses who appeared before the Senate Small Business Committee's Subcommittee on Urban and Rural Economic Development. Joe Namath, Willie Mays, Pat Boone, and Hilly Elkins, the New York producer, were some of the other witnesses.

I had a chance, then, to take a good swing at Mr. Nixon's obviously forgotten pledges of what he would do , if elected, to promote black capitalism. I testified that I believed the country's next real crisis would be in economics and politics because blacks, in spite of campaign oratory, were still being denied "a piece of the pie."

Actually, the hearings were called to discuss the franchise business which then represented $90 billion, or 10 percent, of the gross national product. I was at that time vice-president of a seafood outlet that was seeking to establish franchises all over the world. However, the committee chairman, Senator Harrison Williams, decided to broaden the subject to explore other economic questions.

The New York *Times* of January 21 reported as follows:

> Mr. Robinson said that, "The poor relations between black Americans and the present Administration are causing a serious rift in this country."
>
> Mr. Robinson, a Republican and long-time supporter of Governor Rockefeller, criticized the Administration's black capitalism program, which is administrated by the Department of Commerce. Under the program, the Federal Government matches 2 for 1 the investments of big companies to finance ghetto enterprises.
>
> He said the program was failing because of bureaucratic inefficiency, red tape and mistrust by Negroes.
>
> In a small, packed hearing room in the new Senate Office Building, Mr. Robinson contended that because of such problems, businessmen do not want to deal with the Commerce Department's Office of Minority Business Enterprise.

"Making more black millionaires is not as important as moving people from $6,000 a year, to $15,000," Mr. Robinson commented, adding that "Mr. Nixon and this Administration are the key to this program."

President Nixon failed to keep the promises he had made and he continued to bemoan the fact that blacks didn't trust him. On one occasion, with what I really regarded as counterfeit humility, the President said he hoped to gain the respect of blacks. After that I wrote him again. Below is an excerpt from my letter of February 9, 1970.

If you are sincere in wanting to win the respect of Black America, you must be willing to look at your own administration's attitude. There seem to be no key officials in your administration who have an understanding of what motivates black people. I find it difficult to believe there will be any, when it appears your most trusted advisors are Vice President Agnew, Attorney General Mitchell and Strom Thurmond. How can you expect trust from us when we feel that these men you have selected for high office are enemies? You would not support known anti-Semitics to placate Jewish feelings. Why appoint known segregationists to deal with black problems? If you could see a projection in terms of influence by others of your administration, men like Secretary of State Rogers, Secretary of Commerce Stans, HEW Secretary Finch and Housing Secretary Romney, many of our frustrations would dissipate. Confidence in and respect for you will be based upon the attitudes of those whom you trust.

I respectfully submit this, and hope that it is received in the same spirit as it is sent.

Sincerely,
JACKIE ROBINSON

A few days later, after sending that letter, I received the following reply:

DEAR JACKIE:

First, I want to thank you for having taken the time to write such a thoughtful letter. As I indicated in my press conference this past week, when asked about the attitude toward me of many Black Americans, all I can hope is that by my acts and those of the men who I have chosen to help set policies, I can earn the respect and then the friendship of Black America.

I want to express my desire for all of us to work for one America and I enlist your help in building together a country that has for too long now been divided.

We must rebuild respect for the institutions of this country and for the process of government; but at the same time that respect will not be rebuilt until government is truly serving the needs and aspirations of all Americans.

Sincerely,
DICK NIXON

This was vague and it sounded like double-talk, but perhaps I was being invited to help. Just in case, I promptly replied, offering to help in any specific way the President thought I could. This time the answer came, not from Mr. Nixon, but from a special assistant I'd never heard of who said the President had asked him to thank me for my kind letter and for the spirit of my offer to serve my country. I was to rest assured that I would be kept in mind and that Mr. Nixon appreciated both my interest and my offer. That was the end of that.

Mr. Nixon has done very little to "bring us together," and his handling of youthful dissent was a tragic example of the way to promote alienation. He pretended to be wrapped up in a televised sports event when thousands of youngsters came peacefully to the White House lawn to dramatize their feelings about the Vietnam War.

I have not heard from Mr. Nixon in any official capacity since our exchange of letters. However he recently made a statement about me in conjunction with a dinner given in my honor. Here is the statement:

> Jackie Robinson's place in baseball is already assured, not just because he broke the color barrier, but also because he was a superb ballplayer, a second baseman whose effortless grace around the bag was matched only by the powerful whip of his bat at the plate.
>
> However, Jackie Robinson continues to carve an even larger niche in our country's history for he has not been satisfied to rest on the laurels won at UCLA or with the Dodgers.
>
> Because he was the first black to crack the color line and because of his love for America, Jackie has felt a special obligation to other blacks and minorities that barriers to equal opportunity are taken down wherever found in our society. This is why he has worked so hard for black people, giving them counsel, support, and encouragement—and, in doing so, he has made America a better land for all.
>
> Much has happened since 1947 when the name of Jackie Robinson first made national headlines. Our country has done a great deal to right the wrongs of an earlier time, and this vital work goes forward precisely because Americans like Jackie Robinson are determined that it shall be so. I share this resolve and salute Jackie for the courage to see it through, for the joy and beauty he has given our national pastime and for the enrichment he continues to give our national life.

Naturally I could not ignore such a generous tribute. However in my reply to President Nixon I felt it necessary to bring up the disturbing implications of his politics.

THE HONORABLE RICHARD M. NIXON
President
United States of America
The White House
Washington, D.C.

DEAR MR. PRESIDENT:

Your understanding of the inadequacy of our present social structure to meet the needs of every citizen was well expressed. Truly, it is most important that we stand up like men, express ourselves, and, in the dictum of Mr. Cashen, realize that in our attempt to help others, our own image is observed and read by others.

This letter, these words, coming from you, are most important, and, I believe, they will help in the effort to get blacks to understand that it is totally unnecessary to get on their hands in order to be accepted or recognized.

Because I felt strongly that it is not good policy for any minority to put all of their eggs in one political basket, many of us had decided it may be best to support you and your candidacy in the coming election. However, your Vice President, Mr. Agnew, makes it impossible for me, once again, to do so. I feel so strongly about his being anti-black and anti-progressive in race relations that I dread the fact of anything happening to you and Mr. Agnew becoming President of the United States.

As always, I am available to discuss the forward movement of black and white relations.

Again, my sincere thanks for your kind sentiments.

Sincerely,
JACKIE ROBINSON

With the critical problems facing us today it is not enough for one man to admire another because of his past accomplishments. There is too much to be done today. In the face of being written off by Mr. Nixon's party and being taken for granted by the Democrats, we must develop an effective strategy and learn how to become enlightenedly selfish to protect black people when white people seem consolidated to destroy us.

Chapter XXII

"... And He Was Free"

Jackie Robinson, Jr., was killed in the small hours of the morning on Thursday, June 17, 1971. He was driving up the Merritt Parkway to our home in Connecticut. He was twenty-four years old, and when he died he was totally involved in a project that was going to be the most important one he had ever undertaken. He had fought his way back up out of the hell of drug addiction. His surrogate father, Kenny Williams, the director of the Seymour, Connecticut, Daytop, was proud to say that "he had been clean for three years." On that Thursday morning, Jackie was coming home in his brother David's 1969 MG Midget. The car spun out of control, slammed into an abutment, severing guard rail posts and crashing to a halt leaving Jackie pinned under the wreckage, his neck broken, his life swiftly fading when the state police arrived a little after two o'clock that tragic morning.

Rachel was out of town, in Massachusetts, attending a conference. Sharon was in from Washington, D.C., to spend the weekend. David, Sharon, and I had dinner out together, and I remember Sharon saying she had some things she wanted to talk over with Jackie. Jackie had been putting in long hours and intense work on his project. He was putting together a jazz benefit that was ten days away. Among the things he had been doing during that day he was killed was attending a meeting in New York where he had been lining up the musicians who were going to perform. All the family was helping him, but it was clearly understood that the benefit, to raise $15,000 for the Daytop program, was his baby. In recent years, we had opened up our home to give benefits—for Dr. Martin Luther King's SCLC, the Urban League, and the NAACP. We had been fortunate in getting top stars to help us raise something like $100,000 for these causes. The back-breaking job of making these events a success had been done mainly by Rachel and our close friends Marian Logan, George Simon, and Bea Baruch. This time, however, we respected the importance of letting Jackie take the entire responsibility on his shoulders—contacting the stars and making the one thousand and one arrangements such events call for.

Jackie had responded to the challenge like a champion. In fact, although we had been keeping it to ourselves, we were concerned as to whether he was putting too much of himself into the job. His desire to make the affair a success was so great he couldn't sleep. But we were happy that he was taking the benefit seriously and trying in a small way to repay what he saw as his great debt to Daytop.

We had turned in early that night. Sharon had an appointment to go to the graduation exercises of a friend at Radcliffe and her friend's father was to come by and pick her up at the crack of dawn.

Normally, I had been sleeping lightly. Jackie had been keeping some very late hours, and while I was trying not to be overprotective of a twenty-four-year-old son, I didn't sleep too well until I heard him come in. He was aware of this and often he would call softly, "It's me, Dad." I think he was a little amused and secretly pleased rather than irritated at my concern.

That Wednesday night, however, I fell into a very deep

sleep. When I heard the doorbell and woke up to realize that it was still dark outside, I had no sense of threat because I figured it was Dr. Allen calling to drive Sharon to Radcliffe. Sharon must have thought so too because she was already at the door. Looking over her shoulder, I saw a policeman—not Dr. Allen. I was instantly aware that something was terribly wrong. The uniform, the hour, but most of all the policeman's manner, told me his visit meant that something dreadful had happened. He didn't know how to break the news to us as gently as he wanted to. We heard him saying that we must come over to the Norwalk Hospital right away. It was Jackie. Jackie had been in an accident.

I had to ask the question. "Is he all right? Is it very serious?"

"I'm afraid so," the officer said, and from the way he said it, I knew. Jackie was dead. Someone would have to go and identify the body.

By this time David had joined us.

I had gone weak all over. I knew that I couldn't go to that hospital or morgue or whatever and look at my dead son's body. David wasn't about to allow me to take that awful responsibility. "I'll go," he said.

My next thought was Rachel. I had to get to her before someone heard the news over a radio or read it in a newspaper. Sharon and I got into my car and drove to Massachusetts. Rachel was in her hotel room, just getting ready for breakfast when we arrived. We knocked on her door, and she called out asking who it was.

"Sharon," our daughter said.

"Sharon?" Rachel repeated in a surprised tone.

She opened the door. One look at Sharon's face and a glance at me standing there with her caused Rae to cry out.

"What's wrong? Has something happened to Joe?" Joe is Sharon's husband, our son-in-law of whom we are all very fond.

Sharon couldn't hold out any longer. She couldn't answer and she began to cry.

"It's not Joe, Rae," I said huskily. "It's Jackie."

"Jackie?" Rae repeated dazedly. "What about Jackie?"

"He's gone, honey," I said.

"Gone? Gone where?" she demanded.

"He's dead, honey."

She collapsed. Sharon and I picked her up and carried her to the bed. When she was able to move, she got into the back of the car with Sharon and we drove home.

David had come back home. His strength was magnificent. I knew that the death, Sharon's and his mother's grief—and mine—were almost more than he could bear, but he has so much compassion, so much understanding love that he was able to put on a great front. He had gone through the ordeal of identifying his dead brother, seeing the twisted mass of rubble the car had become and taking care of the rest of the grim details.

I was spending my time trying to comfort Rachel who couldn't stop crying.

David switched on his radio and turned it up as loud as he could. It was playing soul music and David was cleaning the house. I knew that he had to do these things. Later he told me he looked out the window and saw the pastor of the local Congregational church coming up to our door. He knew the good reverend would never understand all that loud soul music at a time like this. So he turned it off.

Then the phone calls began to come in. People began to fill up the house. It's so difficult at a time like this. You appreciate the sympathy and concern, and you can't tell whether your need for the knowledge that these people care is greater than your need to be alone and bear your sorrow privately. People say they're sorry, but they feel miserable saying it and you feel miserable acknowledging it. Some people say they know how you feel and you know that they can't possibly, but

245

you are as gracious as you can be. Somehow sorrow gives you extra grace. Some people are awkward in what they say. Several days after the funeral, when the wound was still a very open one, I was engaged in conversation by a man I didn't know too well. He talked about a couple of subjects, then he said casually as if he were referring to news that I had lost a ball on the golf course, "By the way. I heard you lost your son the other day."

That grabbed me inside. Instinctively, I knew that he meant no wrong, but I replied. "It's true, and I don't want to hear another word about it."

He apologized and walked away.

Then there are the religious and sociological philosophers who either assure you that "he's in the arms of God" or that "he's better off." There are the nonbelievers who couldn't accept the fact that Jackie had been able to stay clean for three years. They murmured consolations that "what with the drugs and everything" perhaps it was all for the best. You couldn't hide the resentment sometimes and you had to retort that drugs had nothing to do with your son's death, but all the time you were aware that these were people clumsily trying to communicate an empathy with your sorrow.

Not all of them have that kind of goodwill, however. I still wince to hear Sharon tell about an experience she had at Howard University where she was recently capped as a nurse. She was in a small group one day when some slob shot off his mouth and introduced the subject of the death of "Jackie Robinson's addict son." He didn't know that Sharon was Jackie's sister.

The day of the accident I couldn't take all the people sitting around, being sorry and discussing Jackie anymore. I was terribly frustrated. I left the house alone, got into the car, and the next thing I knew, I was on my way to the hospital where Jackie's body was. There was one security guard on duty who began telling me the routine procedure one is supposed to follow in order to view the corpses there. When I explained how my son was killed and said I just wanted to come and sit with him for a little while, he told me to follow him. He was taking me to the morgue. He began moving down the corridor about two feet ahead of me at first, then I began to realize that I was slowing down until he was perhaps fifteen feet in front of me. I made myself follow him, however, but, as fate would have it, when we reached the dreaded place, I was relieved to find the body had been released to the funeral director.

I could go back to the house now. One of the reasons I had to leave was that I had begun to feel so helpless about Rachel. She couldn't believe, wouldn't accept Jackie's death. We just couldn't stop her from crying. When she wasn't engulfed by her grief, she was caught up in bitterness. She didn't want to hear about God "knowing best" or any of the other clichés that people use to make you feel better. God had taken her son just at a time when he had begun to help a lot of other youngsters less fortunate than he had been. I didn't know what to say to her, didn't know how to lift her up out of the deep emotional valley into which she had fallen. Once, during those few days, she began to run around, crying, and I almost couldn't stand it. But there was my tall nineteen-year-old ready to do anything he could to ease our pain.

"Go get her, David," I said.

And he did. And he took her hand and they went running off into the woods, running together like a couple of children, running off grief. I shall never get over the loss of Jackie, but at that moment I had a special prayer of thanks to God for David.

During those sad hours after Jackie's death, we learned about the kind of influence Jackie had had with others, most of them his peers, some of them older than he. The letters, telegrams, and phone calls came in; people came by, genuinely brokenhearted because he was gone. A great many famous people sent us sympathy, and although we appreciated that very much, we were more impressed with the response from ordinary people, the kids, and the young people

247

who testified to Jackie's great concern for others. He had let them know he cared, given them the benefit of his mistakes, and tried to keep them from making the same kind of mistakes.

There was Bootsie. That's the only way I'll identify him. Bootsie was like Jackie's blood brother. He had been Jackie's best friend for a number of years. They'd been in trouble together all their lives. When Jackie found himself, he tried to pull Bootsie up with him, up out of the shadows. The night before Jackie died, he had gone to Bootsie's home to visit his kids. He promised that the next time he came by he would bring a ball and glove and take them out to the park to play. Bootsie was in jail, but we hoped that we could talk to the parole people about letting him come home for the funeral. We called the Corrections Department and learned that it wouldn't be possible to arrange. We had a letter from Bootsie that touched us so that we just had to make some sort of contact. We finally got permission to speak with him on the phone. He broke down and cried right in front of the officers there, and he told us he didn't know what he would have done if he hadn't had the chance to talk with us. He told us, sobbing, that now that Jackie was gone, he would have something to strive for, to live for, for Jackie and for himself.

There was another one of Jackie's friends, the kind of young activist the papers call a militant. He had a fantastic following in New Haven at one time. He came all the way from Atlanta so he could talk to us and attend the memorial service. He came, not even knowing how he would get money to pay his way back.

The Daytop family was inconsolable. Kenny Williams summed it up. "He was tired," Kenny said. "He had helped people a lot."

One of the people Jackie had helped said, "I'm thirty-three and he was twenty-four. But, often, when we were having a dialogue, I got the feeling like he was thirty-three and I was twenty-four."

248

A forty-year-old member of the Daytop house wrote eloquently to say what it had meant to him in terms of being black to have Jackie working with the program.

After the memorial services, we learned that not only Daytop, Incorporated, but some other drug programs had received donations along with letters saying the gifts were being made in honor of Jackie. We were notified that a tree is being planted in Israel as a tribute to him. Some Catholic people held special masses.

All this made us realize how far Jackie had come, and it drew us together. Sharon, who not only loved Jackie as a big brother but also learned to respect him as a young black man, put it this way. She said that perhaps Jack's death was meant to bring us closer together. After being the shy, sweet, no-problem girl who chose to spend most of the time in her room when she was an adolescent, Sharon had grown into her phase of teen-age rebellion. When I say she was a no-problem youngster, what I mean is that she was no problem to us. She certainly had problems of her own, and in her own way she suffered from the same kind of identity crisis that had hurt Jackie. Sharon has the same kind of sweetness but the same kind of strength that is characteristic of Rachel. As a child, Sharon had been unselfish enough to keep her problems from us, but as she got into early teens, she began to feel as though she had been too sheltered, too protected. She wanted to establish her independence by doing what she thought we didn't want her to do and not doing what she felt we wanted. Her nature didn't allow her to get so carried away as to do anything really bad. Just foolish things. Just things to help her to break out of the parental cocoon.

If you ask Sharon today, she'll honestly admit that she felt closer to Jackie than to any of us. She attributes this, in part, to their having what she calls a "beautiful" relationship. Sharon wanted more discipline than we gave her when she was quite young. We never saw the need for it because we saw her as a model child. Sharon says that when arguments or misunderstandings arise in the Robinson household, people just clam up, unable or unwilling to express anger, disappointment, frustration. "I'm not speaking to you" is the attitude. It wasn't so with her and Jackie. When they got angry with each other, they'd go after each other verbally tooth and nail. Jackie was so harsh with Sharon sometimes that it hurt. But she liked that because she knew it was a gift of love. For her part, she didn't hesitate to tell him off when he came home for not having written after having been away for a long time. She would become so angry with him sometimes that she'd start swinging at him. Jackie would laugh at her while he held her off. Sharon's loss in Jackie's death was very profound, but she had the wisdom to sense that it could bind us closer and inspire us to carry on the work of helping others that Jackie had begun.

I too believed that there had to be a deep meaning to Jackie's being taken away from us at this particular time. Not so with Rachel. Rachel was a mother and she grieved as a mother.

On the Sunday morning preceding the Thursday of his death, Jackie had made what was fated to be his last public appearance. He gave a talk on the drug menace at the Nazarene Congregational Church in the Bedford-Stuyvesant section of Brooklyn. When the Reverend Sam Varner had first approached him, Jackie had been reluctant. He wasn't sure the congregation would appreciate the kind of blunt talk Jackie felt he had to give on the subject.

Reverend Varner and Jackie met in a bar in Harlem.

"I found him quite reserved at first," Reverend Varner told us. "I suggested that he could draw a parallel of his experiences with those of the prodigal son who landed in the gutter, broke and destitute. At first Jackie couldn't see the analogy. Then I told him that the prodigal son's father had instilled in him the belief that wherever he went, whatever he did, whether his father agreed with him or not, he would always be willing to receive him back home and do whatever he could to help him."

At this point Reverend Varner remembers that Jackie nodded his head and said, "Yes, that's like my father. I knew I could always go back to him. But I kept running from that, trying to escape because I was still haunted by the image of being the son of a father who was a great man. So when I found I couldn't deal with him as a man and found that my father couldn't identify with me as his son, I stopped trying to find a man who wasn't there. I tried to eliminate the desire that I thought would never be fulfilled.

"Daytop helped me through discipline to find the father I had lost."

He spared them nothing. He told them that he had lied, cheated, robbed, and dealt with prostitutes; that he had grown up with an identity crisis, in my shadow. He said that after he tried marijuana he had reached out for bigger and better thrills, egged on by his friends who called him a square for being afraid. He talked about Daytop and the love he had found there and how his family had closed ranks to help him in every way possible.

He said, "My father was always in my corner. I didn't always recognize that and I didn't always call on him, but he was always there." At the end of his talk, he appealed to kids not to be tempted by dope and to parents to keep their closeness with their children.

It wasn't until after Jackie's death that we realized the full impact of that sermon. It made us aware of how far Jackie had traveled and how solid his strength and courage had been.

David had written a poem for his brother's memorial services. We first heard it when he read it to us in the limousine that took us to Brooklyn for the services. We found it very moving because of what it said, but David was stumbling badly trying to read it, and I didn't know how he could get through it at the funeral. But Rachel asked him to read it and he agreed.

The whole block around Antioch Church was jammed and packed with people and cars. The church had been filled long before we arrived, and there were people all over the steps, crowding the sidewalk on both sides of the street. We could feel the vibrations of sympathy as we moved from the limousine up the steps. Later we were told that as we went up those steps, the crowd of people seeing our grief gave forth with a big soft "ahhhhh" of sympathy. I was so consumed with grief and with concern for Rachel, David, and Sharon that I didn't even hear it. This was the day, the day when Jackie's body would be laid to rest and with it any fantastic hope that it had all been a terrible mistake. There is nothing so final as the lowering of the body of the loved one into a grave.

The service was to be short. The honorary pallbearers were Daytop residents, buddies of Jackie's. Reverend Lacy Covington, the assistant pastor at Nazarene where Jackie had spoken a few days ago, assisted Pastor Lawrence in conducting the services. Singer Joyce Bryant sang two beautiful solos. When the Daytop choir sang "Bridge Over Troubled Waters" and "Still Water Runs Deep" I could hardly bear it. I knew how genuinely these young people were going to miss our son. One of the Daytop choir kids was so overcome that they had to carry him away. Pastor Lawrence did a remarkable job of trying to keep emotions under control with a simple and beautiful service. He said he was going to present two of Jackie's brothers—one not a blood brother. The first was Kenny Williams who spoke a few, heartfelt words. Then David came up front to read his poem. His voice was clear and resolute. There was none of the stumbling there had been in the limousine in his reading at the service. His voice grew and deepened in intensity and volume as he went along. He reached the climax, fighting back tears, and cried the words, "I am a man." Sharon was holding me. I heard Rachel scream a sharp scream that I suppose was only a pain for her dead son and joy in her living son. And she got up and left the pew to meet and embrace David as he came back down to his seat. Reverend Lawrence paid his tribute to Jackie. It wasn't a sermon or one of those "he only sleeps" orations people so often give. He spoke of Jackie as a hero—in Vietnam and in the larger war he had to fight when he came back home.

Michael Hinton, Antioch's organist, did a lot for that memorial service. Often the music at a funeral service is sad and depressed, but as we walked out of the church in the recessional, Michael was playing a joyous version of "We Shall Overcome," and the ladies in their white gowns were gathering the flowers to bring them out to the flower cars. As we sat in the limousine waiting for the rest of the cemetery-bound procession to be organized, we saw so many of the teen-agers who had been at the service, plucking flowers from the wreaths—plucking a single flower apiece—and as the procession moved off, they marched behind it in a single file, bearing these flowers. Some people later said they thought it was disrespectful of the youngsters to pluck flowers from the wreaths. I thought it was an act of love. As Rachel and I came out of the church and moved through the crowds to our funeral car, we saw, gathered at the car, a cluster of little kids in baseball uniforms. They belonged to a Jackie Robinson fan club. I stopped and talked with them before getting into the car. For me they signified that none of the suffering had been in vain. They were the bright hope of tomorrow. They were the age that Jackie had been when I dreamed that what I was doing in baseball might make things easier for the kids of the following generations.

Six days after Jackie's funeral we held the jazz festival he had dreamed of and for which he had been working so hard when he died. It was a great success and with far more people contributing to it than we had counted on. Billy Taylor and Peter Long produced an inspiring show.

One of the artists who appeared was Roberta Flack—

Jackie's idol. Jackie and Rachel used to spend hours together listening to Roberta's records, and when she had let him know that she would be present at the jazz festival, I really believed he thought he didn't have to get any other stars. Roberta gave her usual fantastic performance. But so much emotion and so many strong vibrations were in the air that she did one major piece and left the stage. Rachel followed her and asked her if she was going to sing some more, and Roberta said she didn't know whether she could or should because the emotions were getting to her and she was getting ready to really "get down" if she continued. She was concerned about our reaction to so much emotion so soon after Jackie's funeral. Rachel begged her to carry on.

"That's the kind of people we are," Rachel said. "We're down. We're with it. No phonying up. Just like it is."

When Roberta Flack went back on stage to continue her performance, a point came when it was too much for Rachel. The beauty of it all, mingled with the sadness of it, was more than she could bear. She was wearing one of her long, graceful African gowns and sitting near the front on the lawn. Suddenly I saw her jump up and start running up the hill toward the house. I was concerned. I wanted to run after her, but I know her so well that I knew she wanted to be alone. Then, suddenly, David running fast came from the top of the hill to meet her. Halfway up the hill he met her, took her hand, and they ran off together like a sister and a brother. I knew that Rachel would be all right.

David and Sharon were the central core of our strength during those haunting days. The practical things they did to help, combined with their sensitivity, pulled us through. The piece he had written in memory of his brother and had recited at the funeral was called "The Baptism." I would like to quote it here as an epitaph for Jackie:

> And he climbed high on the cliffs above the sea and stripped bare his shoulders and raised his arms to the

water, crying: "I am a man. I live and breathe and bleed as a man. Give me my freedom so that I might dance naked in the moonlight and laugh with the stars as they play amongst the darkness in the sky and roll in the grass and drink the warmth of the sun and feel it sweet within my body. Give me my freedom so that I might fly."

But the armies of the sea continued to war with the beach and the wind raced through the giants of stones which guard the coast and its howl mocked its cries and the man fell to his knees and wept. Then he rose and journeyed down the mountain to the valley and came upon a village. When the people saw him they scorned him for his naked shoulders and wild eyes and again he cried: "I am a man and I seek the means of my freedom." But the people laughed at him, saying, "We see no chains on your arms, no weight on your feet. Go! You are free. Fly! Fly! Fly!" And they called him mad and drove him from their village. His soul wept, for it knew the weight of chains, and tears fell like tiny stones into the well of his loneliness, and his heart was empty as a giant hall is empty after a feast. And the man journeyed on until he came to the banks of a stream, and his eyes, red as the gladiator's sword, strained, for he saw an image dance across the stillness of that water and he recognized the figure though his eyes were now sunken with hunger and skin drawn tight around his body and he stood fixed above the water's edge and began to weep, not from sorrow but from joy, for he saw beauty in the water and he removed his clothing and stood naked before the world and he rose to his full height and smiled as the sun kissed his body and he moved to meet with the figure in the water and the stream made love to his body, and his soul cried with the ecstasy of being one, and he sent the water flying up like a shower of diamonds to the sky, and he laughed for he felt the strength of the stream flowing through his veins, and he cried: "I am a man" and the majesty of his voice echoed off the mountaintops and was heard above the roar of the sea and the howl of the wind, and he was free.

Chapter XXIII

Aftermath

Some of the people who have criticized me have labeled me a black man who was made by white people. They justify this by stating that I have had three fabulous, white godfathers— Mr. Rickey in baseball, Bill Black in business, and Nelson Rockefeller in politics.

These critics overlook the fact that they are talking about three of the most hardheaded, practical man who ever lived. As capable as all three of these men may be of sentiment, no one of them did what they did out of misplaced emotionalism. Of the three, the closest to me was Mr. Rickey. But even though he was motivated by deep principle to break the barriers in baseball, Mr. Rickey was also a keen businessman. He knew that integrated baseball would be financially rewarding. His shrewd judgment was proven correct.

Bill Black is a highly principled human being, but he didn't hire me because he was a humanitarian. Bill Black had built an empire from a nut stand. He was a shrewd businessman, and he believed he could have a more efficient organization and more satisfied employees if I became an official of the

company. During my baseball career I had been both em-
barrassed and pleased to learn that people who hadn't seen
the game asked each other, "How'd Jackie do today?" After
Bill Black hired me I'd go into retail stores that sold Chock
Full O'Nuts products, to be told that people were coming in,
saying, "Give me a can of that Jackie Robinson coffee."

It's probably apocryphal, but one of the stories that has
gone around is one about a dear, very old black lady from a
rural community in the Deep South who listened religiously to
ball games on her radio. One day this little old lady, who was
somewhat naïve about baseball language, was aroused to
righteous indignation when the announcer said I had stolen a
base.

"They just lyin'," she is quoted as saying. "That Jackie
Robinson is a nice boy. Why, that boy wouldn't steal a thing.
They just lyin'."

Early in December, 1965, the message came. Mr. Rickey
was dead.

As I mourned for him, I realized how much our relationship
had deepened *after* I left baseball. It was that later
relationship that made me feel almost as if I had lost my own
father. Branch Rickey, especially after I was no longer in the
sports spotlight, treated me like a son.

Often, when you are useful to people, they give you all the
affection and respect you could possibly need. But after I left
the game, after I had nothing left to offer Mr. Rickey in his
business life, he continued to remain close to me, to be
concerned about how I was doing.

I will never forget two incidents.

One occurred when I was inducted into the Hall of Fame.
At the precise moment when the dream of all baseball players
came true for me, I said to the audience at Cooperstown that I
felt my induction should be shared with the three people in
that audience who had meant the most to me—my mother, my

wife, and Mr. Rickey. I asked them to come and stand by my side and they did. From Mr. Rickey's reaction, I knew it was a great moment for him.

The second was when I was in the hospital. It was not too long before his death. Doctors had assured me that my upcoming operation was important but not critical. Complications arose and I became critically ill with a staph infection. Mr. Rickey was sick himself. But he traveled to New York just to come to see me. He talked with me and made me feel better.

At Mr. Rickey's funeral I was deeply disturbed at the lack of recognition paid to him. A couple of black players were there, and one of them said that although he had not known Mr. Rickey, he felt he owed him tribute because Mr. Rickey had created the opportunity for him to play today. I could not understand why some of the other black superstars who earn so much money in the game today had not even sent flowers or telegrams.

Memories of Mr. Rickey remind me that for a couple of decades now, baseball has been increasingly the most democratic of sports—but only at the bottom level. The sickness of baseball—and it is being more and more openly discussed today—is that it exploits and uses up young, gifted black and brown talent on the playing field, then throws them away and forgets about them after they have given the best years and the best energies of their lives. Certainly handsome salaries are being paid to some of the superstars, but they are earning every penny of that money in drawing power. Baseball, like some other sports, poses as a sacred institution dedicated to the public good, but it is actually a big, selfish business with a ruthlessness that many big businesses would never think of displaying. Baseball moguls and their top advisers seem to earnestly believe that the bodies, the physical stamina, the easy reflexes of black stars, make them highly desirable but that, somehow, they are lacking in the gray matter that it supposedly takes to serve as managers, officials, and executives in policy-making positions. Some prominent personalities in the game have even said it out loud; that they do not believe the average black player has the skill to be in a command position on the field or from the dugout or in the up-front office.

New York *Post* writer Maury Allen once quoted Yankees' General Manager Lee MacPhail as declaring, "There are very few jobs in the front office of baseball. There is also a very small amount of turn-over. It is very difficult to find qualified Negroes with the right educational background for the front office job."

When Maury wrote his piece, neither of the New York clubs had a single black man working in the front office. In April, 1969, appearing on a radio interview, I took exception to the statement reportedly made that black players can make it as players but not in the front office. MacPhail had been quoted in the press as saying this and apparently had not demanded a retraction. A week later, when I referred to the statement on the air, however, he wrote me complaining that I had attacked him unfairly and misquoted him. I replied and asked why he had been so long in denying the statement, requested that he let me know what he had really said, and that if I had done him an injustice, I would apologize publicly. MacPhail sent me a long letter in which he denied the exact quote but went on to say something very similar. He said, "In my opinion there had not been a black league manager or many black coaches or executives because, until recently, there had not been a large number of black players qualified for such jobs, who were finishing their active careers."

He went on to say that it was his personal opinion that there were then (in 1969) many black players active in baseball who were qualified and that as these players finished their active careers, he felt sure many of them would stay in baseball in nonplaying positions. He said he had Bill White in mind, for instance, and he pointed out that the Yankees had recently signed Elston Howard as a coach. He added that Elston, the first black player hired by the Yankees, had been offered the choice of managing a minor club in the organization.

I wrote Lee a final note saying I had no desire to carry the exchange further. Later that year, I received MacPhail's traditional letter inviting Rachel and me to attend the club's twenty-third annual "Old Timers Day." I was informed that the fans had selected me as among the "Greatest Ever" in a national polling and that I would be an honored guest. There was to be a weekend celebration that sounded quite glamorous. I wrote MacPhail thanking him for the invitation but telling him that "my pride in my blackness and my disappointment in baseball's attitude requires that until I see genuine interest in breaking the barriers that deny black people access to managerial and front office positions, I will make my protest by saying no to such requests." I knew this would not have much effect on those who run the game, but this was my position.

I feel strongly about the hypocrisy of the moneyed club owners who try to cover up their bigotry. I am not the only one who feels that way. I quote from a feature by Associated Press sportswriter Mike Rathet who wrote from Fort Lauderdale:

> There are 24 major league baseball teams. And there are 24 major league managers.
> They are all white.
> Why?
> Eliminating the possibility that Negroes don't want to be managers, there are three possible answers to that sensitive question which rose to the surface again last week when Frank Robinson of the Baltimore Orioles discussed the subject.
> 1. No Negro has been qualified.
> 2. The time isn't right yet.

3. Discrimination.

To be the black athlete, particularly one with major league managerial aspirations in a world where no black athlete has ever attained that position, is to look at the color of your skin and wonder.

But no matter how much the black baseball player wonders he can't escape the one conclusion that has to be drawn:

All managers are white and have been hired by white owners: no white owner has yet hired a black man as a manager.

That inescapable conclusion was frankly stated by Frank Robinson:

"There's only one reason a Negro has never been a manager—his color," he said. "The reason there hasn't been a Negro manager is that no one has ever given a Negro a chance to be one."

I say that the answer is discrimination, bigotry, and racial prejudice on the part of the same kind of men who bitterly fought against Branch Rickey and who do not want to see black men in power.

I've always admired Bill White for refusing to cop out when asked what he thought about the situation. Bill has a fighting spirit, anyhow. He led the fight which brought about integration of housing and eating facilities for the Cardinals during spring training in St. Petersburg, Florida.

Bill wrote a courageous article in *Sport* magazine, entitled "A Man Must Say What He Thinks Is Right." He attacked the policies excluding blacks from administration in baseball and even pointed out that there were few bench warmers or second-string players in the game. The black man, he said, had to be first rate or doomed to the minors.

The day of the black manager is coming, but only because it is inevitable. It will get here when an owner finally realizes that the argument that white players will not accept advice and orders from a black is phony.

Bill Russell proved, in basketball with the Celtics, that the business about whites not being able to take orders from blacks was absurd. I was so proud of Bill after he first took command and a press guy asked him if he anticipated any trouble out of his men because he was a black boss now. Bill's answer was a quick and firm "No." That's all he said. "No."

I would have eagerly welcomed the challenge of a managerial job before I left the game. I know I could have been a good manager. I know that the average ballplayer then would have welcomed and accepted leadership from any fellow player who he sincerely felt could help produce a victorious team. This was proven to me during my closing years with the Dodgers. My associates in baseball over the years were men of broad and reasonable thinking. Managers don't make players. Players make managers. The best example I can think of is Casey Stengel. I like Casey, and I suppose he was good for baseball, but he was a clown and a loser with the Mets. It was fantastic to me to see the way the press protected an old man whose greatest contribution to the new Brooklyn team was sleeping on the bench during most of the game.

Baseball had better wake up. You can't keep taking all and giving practically nothing back. I'm not speaking in personal terms. I figure baseball and I are even. I got a lot. I gave a lot. I am talking about a big business which makes fortunes for a few people and which fails to concern itself with more than the size of a stadium and the price of a ticket.

I'm happy that Roy Campanella and I survived the attempts at the old business of "divide and conquer" that some people tried to use to make us enemies. It didn't work. There's no use in my pretending that we didn't have serious differences of opinion, but I think we always had mutual respect for each other. A coolness did exist between us for a number of years while I was in baseball and after I left. However, as time went by, my respect for Campy deepened, and I was convinced that his attitudes had changed. We all have to grow and learn. Not everyone is man enough, as Campy was, to admit that he might have been wrong in his thinking about the right of a black man in sports to express himself.

In 1964 Campy and I were in the office of his Harlem liquor store. He sat in his wheelchair, an intrepid athlete rendered helpless. We were reminiscing and I remember him saying, "It's a horrible thing to sit here and realize what a situation like this means to an individual—to be born an American and have to go to court to find out how much of an American he is. It's a horrible thing to be born in this country and go along with all the rules and laws and regulations and have to battle in court for the right to go to the movies—to wonder which store my children can go to in the South to try on a pair of shoes or where to sleep in a hotel. I am a Negro and I am part of this. I don't care what anyone says about me. . . . I feel it as deep as anyone and so do my children."

Campy had broadened and deepened his view and I respected his manhood in expressing his maturity.

The year 1968 was the year that Mallie Robinson passed away.

It was mid-May when I received the message that my mother was dying in Pasadena. I got on the first plane to go to her, but when I reached her she was gone. After my first feeling of disbelief, I felt I couldn't go into the room where she lay. I didn't think I could bear to look upon her face. Somehow I managed to and I shall always be glad that I did. There was a look, an expression on her face, that calmed me. It didn't do anything about her hurt, but it made me realize that she had died at peace with herself. She had been out in the garden working when she was struck down. Mallie

Robinson. She had been one of those strong black women you always hear about, women who have been the very salvation of the black people.

I had fulfilled my boyhood dream of providing her with a decent home, a nest egg in the bank and a garden for her to work in and watch green and glorious colored things grow. After we had been able to give her all this, we constantly discovered that she was still sacrificing her own pleasures and security to help others—friends, members of the family, even strangers. Many times I felt that my mother was being foolish, letting people take advantage of her. I was wrong. She did kindnesses for people whom I considered parasites because she wanted to help them. It was her way of thinking, her way of life. She had not been a fool for others. She had given with her eyes as open as her heart. In death she was still teaching me how to live.

Chapter XXIV

Epilogue

Life, in spite of all the ups and downs, has been very good to me individually. Personally, I have been very fortunate. Why then, do I insist that "I Never Had It Made"?

It is because I refuse to kid myself about the value of having a comfortable home, about having a little money in the bank, about having received awards and trophies and honors and having had the opportunity to talk and work with some of the most influential people in the world in all phases of activity.

A life is not important except in the impact it has on other lives.

Everything I ever got I fought hard for—and Rachel fought by my side—but I know that I haven't got the right to say truthfully that I have it made. I cannot possibly believe I have it made while so many of my black brothers and sisters are hungry, inadequately housed, insufficiently clothed, denied their dignity as they live in slums or barely exist on welfare. I cannot say I have it made while our country drives full speed ahead to deeper rifts between men and women of varying colors, speeds along a course toward more and more racism.

Life owes me nothing. Baseball owes me nothing. But I

cannot, as an individual, rejoice in the good things I have been permitted to work for and learn while the humblest of my brothers is down in a deep hole hollering for help and not being heard.

That is why I have devoted and dedicated my life to service. I don't like to be in debt. And I owe. Some of my friends tell me I've paid the note a thousandfold. But I still feel I owe—till every man can rent and lease and buy according to his money and his desires; until every child can have an equal opportunity in youth and manhood; until hunger is not only immoral but illegal; until hatred is recognized as a disease, a scourge, an epidemic, and treated as such; until racism and sexism and narcotics are conquered and until every man can vote and any man can be elected if he qualifies—until that day Jackie Robinson and no one else can say he has it made.

I have so many memories.

Rachel and I are not given to sloppy sentimentalism. But we can honestly say that each of us has stood at the center of the other's existence; that we have honored and loved each other; that we have never broken our marriage contract and that we wouldn't trade a day of it—not the sorrows or joys—for all the gold in the world.

Memories.

Of my mother who was a simple, understanding, loving, and courageous woman who gave me both tools and weapons to help in living my life.

Memories of people who have impressed me as vital to the cause of black leadership.

Remembering first observing and getting to know Reverend Jesse Jackson, the country preacher. When he was head of Operation Breadbasket, I accepted his invitation to go to Chicago and be guest speaker at one of his remarkable Saturday morning meetings. Remembering my time as a guest at Jesse's and Jacqueline's home in Chicago, observing this dedicated young leader's almost around-the-clock devotion to his job.

I was proud to become first vice-president when Jesse organized the fast-growing PUSH (People United to Save Humanity) at the beginning of 1972 after he resigned from the Southern Christian Leadership Conference. The organization, which some predicted would exist for a brief while and then fail, has made incredible strides. This has been a result of the outstanding leadership of the thirty-one-year-old who is a protégé of the late Dr. King. Bitterness and rivalry with SCLC has apparently dissolved into some semblance of understanding and cooperation. Powerful alliances have been formed with the other civil rights agencies. With Jesse's gift for major fund-raising and inspiring fellowship, the organization has been able to promote something like a million dollars, mostly from blacks themselves, and has been able to buy its own national headquarters in Chicago. Activity on the national scene has included confrontations with large corporations which are not giving blacks their fair share of jobs, agency business, newspaper advertising, public relations work, and philanthropic support. PUSH was one of the major moving forces in the historic Black Political Convention in Gary, and Reverend Jackson rates the great credit for his role in unseating the Richard J. Daley delegation at Miami although the press has chosen to give most of the praise for this to whites.

I have hopes for Jesse Jackson. I think he offers the most viable leadership for blacks and oppressed minorities in America and also for the salvation of our national decency. I think Jesse's leadership is potentially one of majestic proportions. He is totally dedicated and if we are to arise out of this deepening pit of polarization between us as a people, it will be by supporting the kind of leadership Jesse Jackson offers.

Memories of Adam Clayton Powell. During Adam's latter years I did not agree with him on many subjects, but in his early career he was one of my idols. I thought he could become a commanding force in the nation. He did for a while and he accomplished a great deal, but it was such a bitter disappointment to see him come to the place where he apparently no longer cared. Racism drove him from the Congress, but Adam, I feel, helped to write his own ticket to disaster.

Memories of leaders! The dean of them all, A. Philip Randolph. Courtly, eloquent. A man of integrity. The late Whitney M. Young, Jr., a family friend and a man much misunderstood because he acted out his role as a racial diplomat in the board rooms and the drawing rooms of the mighty.

Leaders. Some, I think, failed us. With all his gifts, Bayard Rustin, in his latter years, has come across to me as one of those who wants to please white people even if the favors and spotlight he gets cost black people a heavy price as in the race-baiting activities of Albert Shanker.

Angry memories.

The people who write or call or tell me in person that they are about to punish me for expressing my views with which they disagree.

As though they're talking to some school kid! Then they go on to threaten to withdraw their approval of me. One day, twenty years ago, they liked the way I stole home or admired my capacity to be insulted or injured and turn and walk away. For that admiration they have given me, I am supposed henceforth and forevermore to surrender my soul. I am not allowed an opinion. If I become naturally, normally indignant, they describe my mood as one of rage. Look what we did for this guy by admiring him and here's how he repays us—by thinking he has the right to say something we don't agree with. I don't owe any living person my soul, my integrity, my freedom of thought and speech. People who believe they have the right to restrain and repress these freedoms are mentally sick.

Ironic memories!

Thinking about how inept many people of my generation are in judging youth. When I requested a meeting with Black

Panthers in Brooklyn, I wanted to talk to them, man to man. I had read about their programs and platforms and found them, in the main, admirable. I believe that most people who have attacked them have not studied their programs. I wanted to hear their response to the main charge that concerned me—that they were initiators of violence. I had a meeting with them in their headquarters in the heart of the black community. I was deeply impressed with them although not sold on every point raised. But as I came out of the meeting, I saw on the surrounding streets a dramatic example of one of the most serious grievances they had expressed. Groups of white policemen were clustered in the area.

I remember my own dangerous confrontation with a white policeman in the lobby of the Apollo Theater recently. It was a day soon after a couple of police officers had been killed in Harlem. I came from my office at Freedom National Bank a few doors down 125th Street to the Apollo. On my way into the lobby, an officer, a plainclothesman, accosted me. He asked me roughly where I was going, and I asked what the hell business it was of his. He grabbed me and spectators passing by told me later that he had pulled out his gun. I was so angry at his grabbing me and so busy telling him he'd better get his hands off me that I didn't remember seeing the gun. By this time people had started crowding around, excitedly telling him my name, and he backed off. Thinking over that incident, it horrifies me to realize what might have happened if I had been just another citizen of Harlem. It shouldn't be necessary to be named Jackie Robinson to keep from getting brutalized in John Lindsay's Fun City or Dick Daley's Chicago.

Another memory about young people and how we condemn them just on the basis of rumor. When the kids at Cornell University were photographed in 1969 confronting faculty and administration people with rifles, the media and black and white leaders condemned them. I wrote them a letter, asking for their point of view. I received an answer which seemed to indicate that the whole story had not been told. I got some papers to publish their side—but only after that first damning impression against them had been spread. We'd better stop using generation gap as an alibi for alienation. Young and old are guilty of that. We'd better build a bridge over that gap. Just because young people are quieter today, we've no right to assume that the problems are solved.

I hope that some day the pendulum will swing back to the time when America seemed ready to make an effort to be a united state. When and if this happens it will be because many people of various races and religions have decided it has to be.

I honor the young blacks of sports who have chosen to be deeply involved. Arthur Ashe who, in his cool way, has chosen to storm the barriers; Floyd Patterson, a gentleman who shared a trip to Mississippi with Curt Flood and me. Floyd, I recall, showed a rare, publicly mischievous side. In plain sight of the press and some very uptight Southern rednecks, Floyd sampled water at two fountains—one marked "for colored" and one "for white," and observed loudly, "Don't taste no different to me." When Floyd and I went to Birmingham, at Dr. King's request, we encountered some local types who acted as though they wanted to do something violent about our visit. But there were brothers—both nonviolent and the other kind—who assured us that everything would be under control and it was.

I honor Archie Moore for his awareness and Kareem Abdul Jabbar, who, after he became a success, never forgot the ghetto from which he came.

There are so many others, and they aren't all black. I'm not buying anti-white attitudes. Too many people who are not black have proven to me that being real isn't qualified by skin color but by character.

Whimsical memories!

The one and only time Rae and I were invited to the White House. It was during LBJ's Administration, and my lady was radiant in her beautiful gown. I knew she was awfully pretty and LBJ seemed to think so also. He danced one dance with his former schoolteacher and one with Rachel and then disappeared upstairs to his quarters. There was a certain look in his eyes that made me know how much he appreciated Rachel.

Remembering how a riot nearly broke out with several hundred young black kids up in Harlem. I saw a white man punched and knocked down and left on the street, and a friend and I picked him up, found a policeman, and helped him into a cab. I returned to where the kids were, to be challenged as to whose side I was on. I didn't back down or show any fear (maybe because I didn't really feel any then) and I told them exactly how I felt about violence. I used some of the language of the street to communicate with them. And I heard one of them, evidently a cooler head than some, saying that you don't attack a brother. After the danger point was over, I began to realize that I had done something which could have jeopardized my life. When I described it to David, he gravely *ordered* me not to ever do anything like that again.

Memories! Of David, after Jackie's death, going through with his plan to take out a year from school and travel, virtually hitchhiking around the world. Knowing he didn't want to leave us at that time but realizing that he knew, and we knew, that he had to go. His letters, so full of the excitement and growth he was experiencing.

Of Sharon being capped as a nurse at Howard University in 1971. And hearing Rachel say I acted as if it were a coronation of a queen. Realizing that Sharon had kept her family identity to herself at school. Believing that happiness will be hers because she feels her achievements are proof that she is worthy and can do something on her own.

Of Mother Isum, Rachel's mother, whose love and devotion have helped us all.

A memory of recent date, when *Sport* magazine honored me as most "significant athlete" of the past quarter century, and the way the tears rose to my eyes when Bill Russell, whom I hold in great esteem, said that paying tribute to Jackie

Robinson was his only reason for being at the kind of affair he didn't usually attend.

"I never saw him play ball," he said. "But I would go halfway around the world to honor him because he was and is a man."

I had a speech to make that day, but I had to just talk instead. What Bill had said threw me completely off-balance. I could not have appreciated those words more from anyone.

Finally, as the time draws close to publication date of this book, one of my personal problems has become intensified. I have been having some very serious problems with my eyes, apparently a direct result of my diabetic condition. As has been reported in the press, there was fear among family and friends—and, of course, my own apprehension—that I was on the way to total loss of my sight. Although I have lost one eye and have impaired sight in the other, there has been a remarkable improvement recently.

I've always been a fighter, but this is one fight I could never have won alone. I am amazed and grateful for the skill of the doctors helping me at this time. But it is something more than just skill; each doctor has taken a personal interest in me, supported me and given me hope. There has been my family— Rachel, Sharon, David, and Mother Isum—surrounding me with love, care, concern and encouragement. And there are the people. People in every walk of life who have written, telephoned, sent telegrams, and spared no effort to let me know that I was not a forgotten sports hero, but I am a man whose personal struggle has reached many, black and white, and given them the courage to go on with their struggles. It seems like they have been trying to share some of the strength they feel they got from me by responding now to me in my time of need. A telegram sent to the editor of the New York *Times* from a black woman in Detroit left me speechless.

I AM TRYING TO GET IN TOUCH WITH JACKIE ROBINSON

THAT ONCE PLAYED WITH THE BROOKLYN DODGERS. WILL YOU PLEASE PRINT THIS AND WHATEVER IT COSTS SEND ME THE BILL AND ILL PAY YOU. "JACKIE I READ IN THE FREE PRESS THIS MORNING THAT YOU'VE LOST SIGHT IN YOUR RIGHT EYE AND IS VERY BAD IN THE LEFT. DO YOU THINK A TRANSPLANT WILL HELP. I WILL BE GLAD TO GIVE YOU ONE OF MINE. YOU CAN CALL ME AT WORK BETWEEN 8:15 AND 5:30 PM."

Fortunately, a recent operation has given me hope and I could decline this beautiful offer.

There have been some meaningful public demonstrations recently that have made me realize people see that I have attempted to make a contribution beyond the world of sports. I have always fought for my principles and spoken out for my ideals. Recognition coming at this time has given me the determination to live as many more productive years as I can.

Three such events are outstanding.

First, there was my trip to Los Angeles early in the summer of 1972 to participate in the ritual of the retirement of my uniform number—Number 42—by the now Los Angeles Dodgers. Being elected to the Hall of Fame is a heartwarming thing. The retirement of your number—which is to say that it becomes uniquely yours from then on and can never be used by another player—well, that sort of caps the Hall of Fame honor.

Second, there was the Jackie Robinson Day—called a "Tribute to Black Excellence"—which was observed in Chicago under the sponsorship of Reverend Jesse Jackson and his organization, PUSH. Reverend Jackson's organization brought our family out to Chicago as their guests for three days and extended us every conceivable comfort and courtesy. There was a special showing of the old picture— *The Jackie Robinson Story*—at one of the community's black-owned theaters. It was a free showing and there was a fabulous reception of some three hundred and fifty professional, business, civic, and sports people in the home of Dr. T. R. M.

Howard, a noted surgeon and huntsman. We made an appearance at a luncheon of youngsters at the Martin Luther King Boys Club on the West Side. The major event was held on Saturday morning at the regular weekly meeting of PUSH. This meeting, devoted entirely to a salute to my family and me, was one of the warmest, most moving occasions I have known. A parade of personalities took part in the Friday reception and the Saturday meeting. To my amazement, the entire Pittsburgh Pirates team turned out, from the top management down to the whole player roster. Some of the kind things they said made me terribly proud. There were recorded messages from many people who couldn't be present.

One of the things which made me feel so wonderful was the recognition which was given to Rae. We've been part of so many affairs where people have uttered the old and well-meaning cliché about Rae being "the woman behind an important man." But this time, Rae was honored as the woman who walked *beside* her man and shared his good and bad moments. Rae not only received flowers, but she received a beautiful plaque. It was given to her by Dr. Howard and the staff of his new Friendship Medical Center. Dr. Ellis Johnson, a leading psychiatrist, presented it, and paid tribute to Rachel's work in nursing psychiatry. The inscription said that she had given her life to healing "her man, her family, and her people."

When Rae accepted the plaque she said, "We came to Chicago, proud of Jack's achievements and your wish to honor him. But we came here, sad also because, just a year ago, we lost our son Jackie. The warmth and love which you have given us today are helping to fill up that big hole in our hearts."

Her words brought tears to many eyes.

The third event took place in New York recently. The Virgin Islands' government honored me in a wonderful affair at Mama Leone's famous restaurant on July 19, which just happened to be Rae's birthday. A surprise (to me) guest was

Dick Young, the sportswriter for the New York *Daily News,* with whom I've had so many run-ins. Clyde Sukeforth, the Dodger scout sent out by Mr. Branch Rickey to bring me in to the Dodger club, was there to reminisce. My old friend telecaster Mal Goode was on hand and Roger Kahn, another old friend and author of the best-selling *Boys of Summer.* There were members of my family from California. I was particularly thrilled to see my old teammate, Sandy Amoros, who made that sensational catch in the final game of the '55 world series giving the Dodgers their first world series victory. It was a wonderful night full of rich memories.

I have many memories. I remember standing alone at first base—the only black man on the field. I had to fight hard against loneliness, abuse, and the knowledge that any mistake I made would be magnified because I was the only black man out there. I had to fight hard to become "just another guy." I had to deny my true fighting spirit so that the "noble experiment" could succeed. When it finally did I could become my own man, many people resented my impatience and honesty. But I never cared about acceptance as much as I cared about respect. In the business world I always strove to learn as much as I could so I would not be just a figurehead. I always believed in the utmost integrity. In politics I believed in following principle even if the man didn't seem to offer outstanding possibilities. I never believed in backing out just because things weren't the best they could be. In civil rights I worked hard to do as much as I could for my people. In everything I have experienced I have been blessed with the love of my family—my wife, Rachel, my children, Sharon, David, and Jackie, my wonderful mother, and my brothers and sister. I have always fought for what I believed in. I have had a great deal of support and I have tried to return that support with my best effort. However there is one irrefutable fact of my life which has determined much of what happened to me: I was a black man in a white world. *I never had it made.*

275